BETRAYING THE OMAHA NATION, 1790–1916

BETRAYING THE OMAHA NATION, 1790–1916

Judith A. Boughter

University of Oklahoma Press
Norman

This book is published with the generous assistance of Edith Gaylord Harper.

Library of Congress Cataloging-in-Publication Data

Boughter, Judith A., 1940–
    Betraying the Omaha Nation, 1790–1916 / by Judith A. Boughter.
        p.   cm.
    Based on the author's thesis (master's)—University of Nebraska.
    Includes bibliographical references and index.
    ISBN 0-8061-3091-1
        1. Omaha Indians—Government relations.   2. Omaha Indians—
    History.   I. Title.
    E99.04B68   1998
    978.2004'9752—dc21   98-4456
                                                                    CIP

The paper in this book meets the guidelines for permanence and durability of the Committee on Production Guidelines for Book Longevity of the Council on Library Resources, Inc. ∞

1 2 3 4 5 6 7 8 9 10

Contents

Illustrations

Preface

Not being a native of Nebraska, I have only recently come to appreciate the colorful and complex pioneer and Indian history of my adoptive state. Both the Oregon and the Mormon Trails led through Nebraska's Platte River valley, and we are constantly reminded of this state's Indian heritage when we glance at a map and see the many towns, counties, and waterways bearing Indian names. Some Nebraska Indian tribes are well known: the Sioux fought a losing campaign against the U.S. Army; and the eloquence and grace of Chief Standing Bear forced the entire nation to recognize the plight of the Poncas in the late nineteenth century. But the Omahas are unfamiliar to many people outside the scholarly community, even though Nebraska's largest city bears the tribal name.

This small Nebraska tribe has been the subject of a number of studies by ethnographers and sociologists. Early ethnographers James Owen Dorsey and W. J. McGee observed the Omahas and reported their findings to the Smithsonian Institution in the late nineteenth century. And the groundbreaking *The Omaha Tribe*, by Alice C. Fletcher and Francis La Flesche, faithfully recorded all aspects of Omaha culture. James Owen Dorsey, Margaret Mead, Reo Fortune, and R. H. Barnes have all investigated Omaha sociology, whereas Omaha allotment, competency commissions, and taxation have been studied by, among others, Joan Mark, Janet McDonnell, and Richmond R. Clow. The Omahas also play a prominent role in historical geographer David Wishart's recent study of land losses by Nebraska Indian tribes.

But until now, no one has written a comprehensive history of the Omahas from their legendary origins to their near-destitution by the early twentieth century. At first armed with little more than desire and Michael Tate's *The Upstream People*, an annotated bibliography of materials on the Omahas, I began to research Omaha history. I followed a paper trail leading from the National Archives in Washington, D.C., to the Federal Records Center in Kansas City, on to the Nebraska State Historical Society, and as far afield as a small monastery library in North Dakota. Occasionally, the trail led to a dead end, but at other times I would unearth treasures—correspondence explaining events that I was terribly curious about, or informative documents such as petitions from the Omaha people asking for goods, cash, or assistance that the government had promised them.

Many people left records that became part of the Omaha story. Early French and Spanish traders, Meriwether Lewis and William Clark, and other Missouri River travelers wrote accounts of this small but important Indian tribe. Later, Mormon diarists dutifully recorded the story of their relationship with the Omahas at "Winter Quarters" along the Missouri. Required by the Bureau of Indian Affairs (BIA) to file annual reports, articulate and often deeply caring Indian agents sent accounts of Sioux attacks, failed crops, and unsuccessful hunts, along with reports of Omaha "progress." These agents' and superintendents' annual reports, along with hundreds of handwritten BIA letters preserved on microfilm by the National Archives, are the foundation of my story.

The La Flesche Family Papers, on microfilm at the Nebraska State Historical Society, and newspapers from towns near the Omaha Reservation provided a running commentary (and not a little gossip) regarding the leasing of Indian lands. Locating news stories in the *Pender (Nebraska) Times*, for example, was simple. Events at the Omaha Reservation made the front page nearly every day. I unearthed most of the tragic story of alcohol use among the Omahas from the hastily filed, fire- and water-damaged records of the Omaha and Winnebago Agencies, records now housed at the Federal Records Center in Kansas City, Missouri.

The James McLaughlin Papers at the Assumption Abbey Archives in Richardton, North Dakota (papers fortunately on microfilm and available through interlibrary loan) shed light on the Omaha competency commission, and research notes gathered by Dr. Richmond Clow and his associates proved how skewed the results of the competency "interviews" really were.

With all of these materials plus scores of congressional documents in hand, I searched for the best way to approach the Omahas' story. Regardless of the source and subject, these primary documents revealed a century-long effort on the part of traders, real estate speculators, well-intentioned reformers and missionaries, and the federal government either to deprive the Omahas of their lands or to dilute their rich culture. Each of the following chapters addresses at least one aspect of the gradual economic and cultural "dispossession" of the Omaha nation.

Originally, this work was to be the initial section of a three-part history of the Omaha people. To date, only the first and the last parts have been completed. To accompany this study, my friend and colleague Mark R. Scherer, of the University of Nebraska at Omaha, has written an account of the recent legal battles fought by the Omahas to try to regain lost lands. Our hope is that in the near future, a historian will follow the Omaha story through the 1920s, the Great Depression years, and World War II, thus completing the trilogy. It is a story that deserves to be told in its entirety.

With a few revisions and additions, this book is basically my master's thesis, written for the History Department at the University of Nebraska at Omaha at the request of my thesis adviser, Dr. Michael L. Tate. When I began this project, I had no idea how complex it would become or how far it would lead. I would like to thank those individuals who helped me create what I hope is a coherent story from the numerous and varied materials on the Omaha Indians and on these Indians' relations with whites from the 1790s to 1916.

The staff of the Federal Records Center in Kansas City kindly supplied me with finding lists and were most helpful when I visited their facility to do research. I would like to thank Nebraska State Historical Society personnel for promptly filling my interlibrary loan requests for microfilm of Nebraska newspapers and for assisting me in the use of their archival materials. My sincere thanks go to my colleague Jo Behrens for sharing her rare volumes of *Council Fire* and to Dr. Richmond Clow for making his research notes on Omaha taxation available to me. I owe a special thank-you to Mary Mick and Catherine Walker, of the Interlibrary Loan Department at the University of Nebraska at Omaha, who kept their good humor despite my almost daily requests for microfilm, rare books, and articles from obscure journals.

Dr. Michael Tate deserves many thanks for his good advice, for his careful and thoughtful editing, and especially for his invaluable bibliography on the Omaha Indians, a work that led me to many important sources. My thanks go also to Dr. Charles Gildersleeve, and to Dr. Harl Dalstrom for sharing his extensive knowledge of Nebraska history. I am grateful to the University of Nebraska Foundation for the Presidential Graduate Fellowship, which allowed me to devote eighteen months to research and writing. And as always, I appreciate my husband's support and encouragement.

The staff at the University of Oklahoma Press was most helpful in guiding me through the publication process. I would especially like to thank Randolph Lewis and Alice Stanton. My thanks go also to Teddy Diggs, my skillful editor, who improved my work but never changed its meaning or its intent.

Finally, I am grateful to the Omaha Indians who left their own accounts—in testimony, in petitions, and especially in wonderful letters that revealed their private thoughts on the events that shaped their lives. Unfortunately, only a few of the people left written records; thus the overwhelming majority of Omahas from those earlier generations must remain forever silent. It is my hope that this study will provide a glimpse into their lives, thoughts, and actions during this crucial period in their tribal history.

BETRAYING THE OMAHA NATION,
1790–1916

Introduction

Then another [Omaha] man advanced in front of the
[sacred] pipes, leading his four-year-old son. The man
and boy were both in the dress of the white man. He
had long been living and working on his farm, in every
way committed to our mode of life, which added to the
pathos of his act. "The pipes," he said, "were the care
of my fathers. My son is born into their rights. Now we
do not often see them." Tears filled his eyes, and with
breaking voice he added, "I want my boy to touch the
pipes of my fathers."

Alice C. Fletcher, "Personal Studies of
Indian Life," 1892–93

Centuries ago, a nation of people who would become known as the
Omahas followed the buffalo from as far east as the West Virginia
mountains and eventually settled among the fertile, rolling hills along
the Missouri River in what is now Nebraska.[1] Today, the Omahas are
one of only a few plains and prairie tribes who continue to live on a
portion of their ancestral homeland. Unlike their unfortunate neighbors
and kinspeople the Poncas, they were not removed to Indian Territory
(present-day Oklahoma), and unlike the Sioux bands, they never
waged a disastrous war against the U.S. Army. Instead, they befriended
and emulated whites, even intermarrying with traders. Having been
attacked time and again by the Sioux, the Omahas hesitated to leave
the relative safety of the Bellevue Agency when they ceded their lands
to the government in 1854. But with a promise of military protection,
they reluctantly returned north along the Missouri River to their
beloved Black Bird Hills, where their ancestors lay buried and where
they had seen their happiest days.

But the Black Bird Hills had changed. The Omahas would pay a
terrible price for their choice of these lands and for some of their
leaders' affinity for white ways. White settlers and land speculators

resented Indian ownership of fertile northeastern Nebraska lands and, beginning in the early 1850s, used every means at their disposal to separate the Omahas from their real estate. Unfortunately, Nebraska senators and congressmen worked closely with land speculators to promote special legislation that—little by little, law by unfair law— encouraged Indians to lease, and eventually sell, most of their land.

Because a few tribal leaders appeared ready to be assimilated into white society, the Omahas became sociological "guinea pigs." Totally ignoring that the majority of Omahas knew little English, understood nothing of capitalism, and had no desire to be farmers, government officials and reformers included them among the Indian tribes who became prototypes for several disastrous Indian programs of the late nineteenth and early twentieth centuries. Omaha lands were allotted five years before passage of the 1887 Dawes Act. Along with such tribes as the Kiowas, Comanches, Cheyennes, and Arapahoes, the Omahas were allowed to informally lease grazing lands long before Congress enacted a leasing act for all Indians. Time and again, Congress and the Bureau of Indian Affairs (also referred to as the Indian Office) ignored the warnings of economic collapse on the Omaha Reservation. Despite obvious problems with Omaha allot- ments, the Dawes Act extended the process to nearly all Indians throughout the United States, and leasing irregularities on the Omaha and Winnebago Reservations did not prevent the government from legalizing the practice of leasing nationwide.

When Robert G. Valentine became commissioner of Indian affairs in 1909, he wanted to see more Indians become independent by giving them complete control over their lands. Convinced that local Indian agents were too busy and not objective enough to recommend indi- vidual Indians for landownership, Valentine established special com- missions that would visit the Indians to determine whether they were prepared to be landowners.[2] The very first of these "competency com- missions" operated on the Omaha Reservation in 1909–10.

The Omahas had not always been victimized by whites. Their first European contacts were French traders, and during the late eighteenth century, as the most powerful Indian nation on the middle Missouri River, they defined the terms of their own trade, as well as the trade of tribes farther upstream. But a smallpox epidemic in 1800 claimed the lives of hundreds of Omahas, including their brilliant, autocratic chief, Black Bird. The tribe's influence and population quickly waned.

For many years, enemy tribes had been held in check by the mighty Black Bird, but with the powerful Omaha chief gone, the Sioux now preyed on his people. Mounted and well-armed Sioux bands moved rapidly south and west along the Missouri River. Buffalo had become scarce in the Sioux hunting grounds east of the Missouri, and lured westward by the large buffalo herds on the Great Plains, the Sioux raided Omaha villages to capture horses and to drive the Omahas from their rich hunting grounds.[3]

Because of the incessant Sioux attacks, many observers predicted the Omahas' demise. Yet the Omahas survived, even though their traditional leadership and tribal customs were subsequently undermined by government officials and fur traders who created "paper chiefs" and introduced the Indians to whiskey and greed. Tribal autonomy also began to slip away as the Omahas recognized the supremacy of the U.S. government in "peace treaties" signed in 1815 and during the 1820s.[4] In two subsequent agreements, at Prairie du Chien, Michigan Territory, in 1830 and at Bellevue six years later, the government robbed the Omahas of much of their hunting grounds and left the people with neither their full payment of annuities nor adequate protection from their Sioux adversaries.[5]

During the 1840s, the Omahas came face-to-face with Manifest Destiny as waves of white emigrants crossed Indian country, killing off small game, polluting streams, and decimating the buffalo herds. Most emigrants continued west along the Platte River Trail, but the Mormons remained at Winter Quarters, on Omaha lands, for two full years, creating problems for the Indians and a political dilemma for the government. During their controversial stay, the Mormons did provide the Omahas some degree of protection against the Sioux, but when the Mormons departed for Salt Lake, the Dakota bands escalated their raids against the unprotected and badly outnumbered Omahas.

Fur traders and westbound emigrants had shown no interest in owning Omaha lands, but in the late 1840s the government, to clear a path for further westward expansion and for a railway to the Pacific Ocean, devised a plan to move all Indians either north or south of the main emigration corridor along the Platte River. Railroad advocates, expansionist lawmakers, and Nebraska "boomers" all agitated for the creation and settlement of a Nebraska Territory. At virtually the same time as the passage of the Kansas-Nebraska Act in 1854, a new treaty forced the Omahas to relinquish their remaining Nebraska lands and to relocate on a tiny fraction of their former domain.

The original reservation provided for the Omahas in their 1854 treaty proved completely unsatisfactory to the tribe.[6] In efforts to relocate them away from white populations, the treaty framers planned to settle the Omahas on a reserve near their historic enemies, the Sioux. Frightened and confused, the Omahas retreated southward to the Platte River and refused to go farther north until they were guaranteed protection in a home of their own choosing. Once the Bureau of Indian Affairs coaxed the Omahas onto their present reservation in Thurston County, the government broke nearly every promise it had made to the Indians when they had relinquished their lands.

Politics, greed, and corruption combined to create controversy during the Omahas' early reservation period. Agents seldom remained for long; many were inept or dictatorial, and at least one proved to be dishonest.[7] Rivalries among "progressive" and "traditional" tribal leaders split the Omahas politically and culturally, leaving the reservation in chaos. Ethnocentric Presbyterian missionaries further undermined tribal unity by favoring progressive Omahas, and thus ignoring the majority of the tribe, and by attempting to rob Omaha children of their "Indianness." In 1869, President Ulysses S. Grant's "Peace Policy" brought Quaker agents and more dissension to the reservation as the Friends and the Presbyterians fought bitterly for control of the mission school and of Omaha souls.

In 1865 and again in 1873, the already small Omaha reserve was further reduced when the government coerced tribal leaders into selling part of their lands to the Winnebagoes, who had fled their desolate reservation in South Dakota and had sought shelter with the Omahas. The 1865 Winnebago Treaty also provided for the first Omaha land allotments, which were completed in 1871.[8] But six years later, when Omaha allottees questioned their land titles in the wake of the Poncas' forced removal to Indian Territory, they found that they held nothing but worthless paper.

When pioneering anthropologist Alice C. Fletcher visited the Omahas in 1881, concerned tribal leaders asked for her help in confirming their rights to the land. As a result of Fletcher's lobbying, Congress passed an allotment act in 1882, granting the Omahas land in severalty, complete with tax-free status for twenty-five years.[9] A year later Fletcher, with the aid of the Omaha Francis La Flesche, allotted nearly 79,000 acres of reservation land to 954 Indians. But allotment left the tribe in a precarious legal position and created more problems than it solved. Subject to Nebraska laws, but denied services because of their tax-exempt status, the Omahas made an unsuccessful attempt to govern themselves and run their own mills and shops.

In Thurston County, Nebraska, which contained most of the Omaha Reservation, a local land syndicate based in the tiny town of Pender and informally headed by aspiring Indian agent William E. Peebles took advantage of the confused Omahas. While the tribe floundered in legal and political limbo, these local "land sharks" pounced on Omaha lands, renting them from Indians for a pittance and re-leasing them at huge profits. Those who resisted the "Pender Ring," as the land syndicate was called, found themselves embroiled in ugly and expensive court battles.[10]

The perceived success or failure of Omaha allotment left lawmakers and reformers divided over the subject of a general allotment act. Although many in policy-making positions supported land in severalty, many more, including members of the House Indian Affairs Committee, saw it as a potential disaster.[11] Ignoring negative reports on the Omaha "experiment," Congress followed the advice of Alice Fletcher and other proponents and compounded its earlier error by passing the 1887 General Allotment (Dawes) Act, which applied to Indians throughout the United States.[12] In 1893, all but about five thousand acres of the remaining Omaha lands were allotted, and in 1909, proceeds from the sale of these few remaining acres were scheduled to be divided among 520 landless Omaha children born after 1893.[13]

In the 1890s, leasing made the Omahas idle landlords, but beginning in 1902, laws legalizing and even encouraging land sales made them paupers. A 1902 law allowing heirs of deceased Indians to sell their lands was closely followed by a disastrous clause in the Burke Act of

1906, which authorized the interior secretary, at his discretion, to declare an Indian "competent" to receive land, with no sale or tax restrictions.[14] This short paragraph in a bill otherwise designed primarily to protect Indians paved the way for the first competency commission, whose irresponsible and arbitrary actions left many Omahas landless and destitute. Still, "progressive" bureaucrats later expanded the commissions to a majority of reservations, with the same tragic results.

By late 1916, after decades of exposure to reformers' good intentions, the Omahas were left with mortgages, tax bills, and a generation of children with no land to call their own. The irony and tragedy of the Omaha story is that this small peace-loving Indian tribe, whose "progressive" leaders truly wanted to "walk the white man's road," were led partway down that road and then were expected to continue on their own, without the necessary skills or resources to survive in the world that had been created for them. This study attempts to explain the many events and forces that shaped the Omahas' world during those unfortunate times and to introduce the characters—good and evil, Indian and white—who influenced this crucial period in Omaha tribal history.

Chapter 1

From Rulers of the River to an Embattled Culture, 1790s–1830

> The white people speak of the country . . . as "a wilderness" . . . without human interest or history. To us Indians it was as clearly defined then as it is today; we knew the boundaries of tribal lands, those of our friends and those of our foes; we were familiar with every stream, the contour of every hill. . . . It was our home, the scene of our history, and we loved it as our country.
>
> Francis La Flesche, *The Middle Five*, 1900

In 1854, the Omaha Indians signed a treaty with the U.S. government in which they relinquished what remained of their ancestral lands and agreed to settle on a three-hundred-thousand-acre reservation in the northeastern corner of present-day Nebraska. The 1854 treaty was the most damaging of a series of acts, agreements, and dealings that would drastically reduce the Omaha land base and nearly destroy the tribe's ancient and intricate culture. To appreciate the Omahas' loss, we need to understand their past—their tribal legends, their reverence for the land, their almost total dependence on the buffalo, their rise to power, and the beginning of their tragic decline by the early nineteenth century. The Omahas were never a large tribe, but in the late eighteenth century their strategic location and a powerful leader gave them an importance out of proportion to their numbers. For years, they dictated trading terms on their stretch of the Missouri River and reduced the threat from upstream tribes by denying them access to white traders and guns. But by the early 1800s, weakened by disease and with their leader dead, they began to lose control of their lands and their destiny.

The Omahas, relative latecomers to the plains, left few clues to their eastern woodlands past. Because they quickly adopted Plains Indian culture and European trade goods, there is no distinct archaeological record of the tribe before the late 1700s, and their early migrations are preserved only in legends, which are difficult to prove or disprove.[1] Fortunately, these oral traditions were recorded by frontier explorers as well as professional ethnographers, and recent archaeological findings have given further credence to some of these interpretations. A few sources claim that the Omahas and their cognate tribes came from somewhere north of the Great Lakes, moved south, crossed the Mississippi River, and then settled, at a place where Europeans first contacted them.[2] But most legends agree that the Omahas' ancestors emigrated from the east, probably following the buffalo herds, and migrated in a northwestern direction to the present Iowa-Nebraska region, where they made their initial contact with whites.[3]

The most often repeated version of the Omaha Sacred Legend says that long ago, the Omahas lived with the Poncas, Osages, Kansas, and Quapaws "near a great body of water" east of the Mississippi River, where the Illinois tribes referred to them collectively as the "Arkansas." As they moved west, the tribes separated at the mouth of the Ohio River, with the Quapaws going downstream and the rest of the Arkansas continuing up the Mississippi, taking the descriptive name U-ma^n'-ha^n', "those going against the wind or current."[4] The two groups must have gone their separate ways before A.D. 1540, since the Spanish explorer Hernando de Soto encountered the Quapaws on either the Mississippi or the Arkansas River at about that time and made no mention of an affiliated people.[5] This date is reinforced by a Siouan time concept that refers to a period of about seventy years as an "old man." In 1880, the Omahas claimed to be under their fifth old man, thus dating their existence as a separate tribe to the early 1500s.[6] At the Osage River, the remaining four tribes parted company. The Omahas and Poncas crossed the Missouri River and, after wandering for many years, arrived near the Red Pipestone Quarry in current-day Minnesota.[7]

Omaha ethnographers and tribal spokespeople disagree as to the location of the people when they cut their Sacred Pole and organized their government. According to legend, the Omahas received the Sacred Pole and the two Sacred Pipes and assigned customs and taboos to specific clans while living near Lake Andes in Dakota Territory, but tribal historians disagree. Wherever the Sacred Pole appeared, apparently a government had already formed, since the purpose of the Sacred Pole was to conserve the new tribal order.

Legends also say that the Omahas lived in the upper Mississippi region when they selected as their leaders a council of seven "wise, generous, and kind" men.[8]

The migrations by the Poncas and the Omahas continued; they traveled in present-day Minnesota, Iowa, South Dakota, and Nebraska, moving from river to river and establishing villages as they went (see Map 1). The Omahas first appeared on European maps in the 1670s, on lands in present-day southwestern Minnesota and northwestern Iowa, where tradition says they arrived by following the Des Moines River. By 1702, they had moved westward, to the Big Sioux River, where they built at least one village. The bitter animosity between the Omahas and the Sioux probably began here, where the Omahas met defeat at the hands of either the Yanktons or the Brulé Tetons. The vanquished Omahas fled farther west, toward the Missouri River, and in 1714 they were in South Dakota near the mouth of the White River, in Arikara country. The Omahas borrowed aspects of Arikara culture during a troubled stay that produced constant warfare and a series of poor harvests.[9]

After a tribal split that resulted in the defection of the Poncas, the Omahas moved southeast along the Missouri River to a site on Bow Creek, Nebraska, where they built an earth lodge community that became known as "Bad Village" as a result of a murder and intratribal warfare that divided the tribe. But according to legends, the tribe reunited in about 1750 near what is now Ponca, Nebraska. By 1758, there were 3,200 Omahas living in forty villages. Warfare with the Sioux and a desire to position themselves closer to Spanish trade routes drew the Omahas away from Ponca, and they moved even farther south into present-day Dakota County, to the banks of what is now known as Omaha Creek. Here they built their "Big Village."[10]

The new Omaha village became a familiar sight to Spanish and French traders plying the Missouri River, and two representatives of the Missouri Company described it in their reports. In 1796, Jean-Baptiste Truteau placed the Omaha village "two leagues distant from the banks of the Missouri." A year later James Mackay, in his "Table of Distances," wrote, "The village is situated in a beautiful Prairie near to the foot of the hills a league from the Missouri." More observant than Truteau, he also mentioned Omaha Creek.[11]

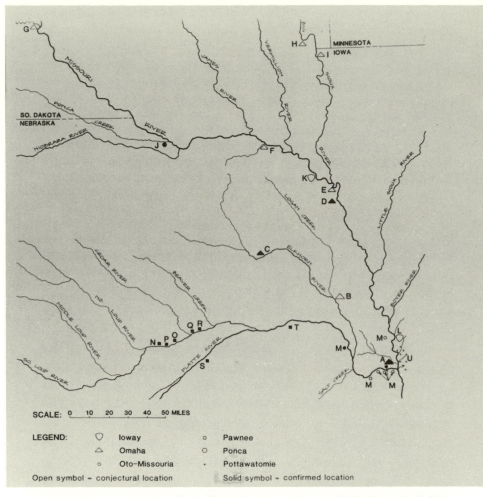

Map 1. Omaha and other tribal village sites in northeastern Nebraska and adjoining areas. Reprinted from *Archaeology and Ethnohistory of the Omaha Indians: The Big Village Site*, by John M. O'Shea and John Ludwickson, by permission of the University of Nebraska Press. © 1992 by the University of Nebraska Press.

But the Omahas would not remain in their idyllic home. During the winter of 1800–1801, smallpox struck the village, and in their confusion and despair the people abandoned their infected towns on the Missouri River and embarked on a "mourning war" against other Plains tribes. In 1804, finding no sign of Omaha occupancy where their village had stood, Meriwether Lewis wrote: "[They] have become a wandering nation. . . . They rove principally on the waters of the . . . Rapid River" (the Niobrara).[12] Eventually, the tattered remains of the tribe returned to Big Village, only to face renewed Sioux raids. Afraid to stay on Omaha Creek, the Omahas turned southwest, to an unnamed village on the Elkhorn River. Still, the people continued to travel to Big Village to bury their dead.[13] In 1841, Little Village, at the mouth of Logan Creek, in what is now Dodge County, became the Omahas' temporary home. The people returned once more, briefly, to Omaha Creek, but when the Sioux burned Big Village in the summer of 1845, they fled to the relative safety of the Indian agency at Bellevue, Nebraska, where they remained until they traveled north to their reservation in 1855.[14]

As the Omahas wandered along the Missouri River in search of a permanent home, they were not isolated from whites. Their first white contact may have been with Hudson's Bay traders, but the tribe was known to the French before 1724, when traders built a post on the Missouri River to halt Spanish influence.[15] In 1763, as a result of its defeat in the Seven Years' War, France ceded the region west of the Mississippi River to Spain to keep it out of British hands. Therefore, the Omahas' first regular white contacts were French-speaking Spanish subjects.[16] These early meetings appear to have been amicable; in fact, in 1795 the trader James Mackay spent the winter in a cabin he built among the Omahas. In a grandiose gesture, Mackay dubbed his crude sanctuary "Fort Charles."[17] Thus the records show that whites contacted the Omahas early and often; by 1854, when the Omahas signed the treaty creating their reservation, they had been exposed to white influence, with all its political, social, and economic effects, for over 150 years.

In the years between the arrival of the first French traders and the devastating 1854 treaty, two Omaha constants remained—corn and buffalo. For as long as tribal tradition had existed, buffalo and maize were the chief Omaha foods, the buffalo representing the hunter and maize the horticulturist.[18] In one of the earliest documentations of Omaha food sources, Lieutenant Governor Francisco Cruzat of Spanish Illinois implied that horticulture had some importance to the tribe but was secondary to the hunt. According to Cruzat, the Omahas had always survived by "hunting beaver, deer, buffalo, and stags," and "their . . . cultivation of the soil extended only to the planting of maize and pumpkins for their necessary support."[19] At one time, corn was probably more sacred than the buffalo, since the former sprang from Mother Earth, and the Omahas conducted elaborate ceremonies dedicated to corn cultivation. But by 1700, guns and horses had changed Omaha culture from a traditionally horticultural one to a society that depended heavily on the buffalo, whose religious symbolism became increasingly significant. Yet Omaha tradition saw corn and buffalo as inseparable; the corn would not grow without the buffalo, and if planting rituals were ignored, the buffalo would not come.[20]

Although the Omahas continued to plant gardens in small tracts along the rivers, over half of their food came from hunting, and in their search for game, they may have ranged far and wide, from the Des Moines River in the east to the Nebraska Sandhills in the west.[21] One western traveler claimed that the Omahas "owned" the country north of the mouth of the "Great Platte," but "owned" was too strong a word. The trader Auguste Chouteau explained that different tribes often claimed the same lands, making it difficult to determine tribal limits. He admitted that the Omahas claimed a large area bounded roughly by the Missouri and Platte Rivers, but he could not pinpoint a western boundary.[22] An 1816 map drawn from Chouteau's notes and indicating the territorial limits of Indian tribes clearly shows the "Mahas" located between the Platte and the Missouri (see Map 2).

Like other Nebraska tribes, the Omahas acquired and held territorial hunting rights by use and warfare, and these claims terminated only when a band no longer wanted to hunt in a given area. Of course, hunting grounds were sometimes disputed, and rivalries caused contention among the tribes. Compromise was possible, however. For example, after fighting for years over territory near the Republican and Elkhorn Rivers, the Omahas and the Pawnees decided to hold the land in common: above the Platte, the Omahas directed the hunt; south of this river, the Pawnees took charge.[23]

Omaha culture was elaborate and beautiful. The people revered all living things and treasured the land. Behind the complicated tribal organization lay a system of duality: the sky was father, the earth was mother, and their union was essential to life. The tribal divisions, or moieties, consisted of the Earth People, responsible for all rites and

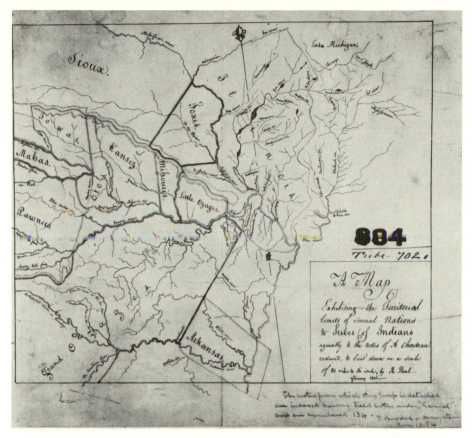

Map 2. Auguste Chouteau's map of Indian territories, 1816. Central Map Files, No. 884, Record Group 75, National Archives, Washington, D.D.

duties related to the tribe's physical well-being, and the Sky People, in charge of all things supernatural. This duality also demanded two principal chiefs and two Sacred Pipes that could never be separated.[24]

The Omahas spent little time in their permanent villages but followed the buffalo for months at a time. In adhering to a traditional Plains "annual round," they spent only about three months of the year in their fixed villages. When the summer crops were well established, the tribe conducted its annual buffalo hunt, returning in September for the important corn harvest. With the corn safely stored, the tribe once more deserted its villages to trap along the rivers. A winter bison hunt completed the round.[25] Preceded by elaborate, lengthy rituals, the annual hunt was orchestrated so that individual hunters did not alarm the herds and cause the entire tribe to go hungry. Consequently, the highly social Omahas acted as a unit, with the benefit of the tribe taking precedence over individual hunting prowess.[26]

As their tribal government evolved, the Omahas recognized the need for something to symbolize tribal unity, something visible and accessible to the people. The two tribal pipes, with their complex rituals, did not fill this need, but the Sacred Pole did.[27] The revered pole was cut from a magical tree that burned in the night and was home to the Thunder Birds. The Omahas cut down this tree, decorated it, and called it a man. The chiefs said of this "mystery tree": "Whenever we meet with troubles we shall bring all our troubles to Him. We shall make offerings and requests. All our prayers must be accompanied by gifts."[28] The Sacred Pole is cottonwood, but to the Omahas it was and is a person—a man who would provide for and protect his people through all their travails. He migrated with the tribe to their home on the Missouri River and stood for tribal identity when they controlled a portion of the river. Through conflict and sickness, he never deserted them. As a symbol of the chiefs' power, the pole had special significance during the annual buffalo hunts, when it was carried quite visibly on its "keeper's" back. On the hunt, the presence of the Sacred Pole was vital, for it held the tribe members together at a time when they might scatter.[29]

At the root of the Omahas' belief system lay Wako^n'da, a "mysterious life power" that permeated all of nature and every phase of the Omahas' lives. To these Indians, Wako^n'da was the "source of all things." It caused "day to follow night" and controlled the changing of the seasons. The concept of Wako^n'da was fundamental to the Omaha people. One member of the tribe noted, "No matter how far an Omaha may wander in his superstitious beliefs . . . he invariably returns to Wako^n'da." The belief that all life experiences were guided by Wako^n'da made the Omahas fatalistic; often, tragedies that befell the tribe would be attributed to this powerful, unseen force, and the people would make no attempts to overcome their problems.[30]

Sources disagree as to when the modern Omaha sociopolitical organization began, but legend speaks of seven old men who visited the tribe and set its government in motion. Two old men of the tribe carried out the mythical visitors' plan and were given responsibility for the two Sacred Pipes, which became their "badges of honor."[31] Perhaps in deference to the legendary seven, early tribal government was controlled by a council of seven chiefs whose functions were to "maintain order, keep the peace, and . . . preserve decorum within the tribe." But above all, the seven chiefs answered to Wako^n'da for the tribe's welfare. The council reigned supreme; its members could not be unseated except by resignation or death, and their decisions, coming directly from the all-powerful Wako^n'da, could never be questioned.[32]

The traditional Omaha hierarchy included two chiefly orders, one unlimited in membership and the other much more exclusive. The lower order, "brown chiefs," referred to the color of the earth. Until a brown chief achieved greatness, he was indistinguishable from all others, like the color of the ground. "Dark chiefs," on the other hand, represented elevated objects visible from a distance. A chief who performed great and generous deeds rose above the others and appeared as a dark figure against the horizon.[33] Contrary to the popular image of Indian chiefs, Omaha leaders did not advance primarily because of their courage or military skills. Among Omahas, generosity, gift-giving, and wisdom were revered, and of the seven dark chiefs, the two who had distributed the greatest number of gifts became the principal leaders, each representing one-half of the tribe. Dark chiefs could not be removed from office, but when a principal chieftainship did become available, it was filled by the remaining chief who could "count" the most gifts.[34]

Chiefs were elected, and a man with a spotty reputation could become a tribal leader in the hope that his new responsibilities would make him a better person. Character, however, was the main criterion. Usually, a candidate for chiefdom had to demonstrate leadership qualities and be tenacious. Omaha ethnographer Alice Fletcher wrote, "The path to honor is open to every man in the tribe who has the courage, ability, and persistency to reach distinction." But above all, "a chief must be a man who can govern himself."[35]

However, this idealistic, bootstrap approach to chiefdom was only part of the picture. Clever horse stealers, savvy traders, and men who had been told the secrets of the gift-giving process could use their wealth and inside information to enter the chiefly ranks. Trade goods often opened the door to chiefdom; seen as magical, these goods were associated with the Indian elite, who "used them to legitimize their sanctity as leaders."[36] In addition, if a member of the Omaha oligarchy resigned when he became old or ill, he kept his title and could designate his successor, a process that sometimes became quite political, since the retiring chief's favorites had an advantage[37] Anthropologist Reo Fortune, who disputes Fletcher's "achievement by ability" explanation, stated: "The social theory [was] aggressively democratic. The social practice [was] prevailingly aristocratic."[38] Even Alice Fletcher and Francis La Flesche admitted that nepotism was alive and well among the Omahas: "The order and value of these . . . acts were not generally known to the people. . . . Those who became possessed of this knowledge were apt to keep it for the benefit of their aspiring kinsmen."[39] It appears, then, that the path to Omaha chieftainship was strewn with contradictions. In theory, generosity made chiefs, yet if the secrets of the gift-giving requirements were limited to certain individuals, did this not make chiefdom in a way hereditary?[40]

The Omahas' early ethnographers differed on interpretations of chieftainship traditions and never reached a consensus about whether leadership was achieved through elaborate gift-giving or by inheritance. In short, they disagreed about methods of acquiring chieftainship and also about when, why, or even if methods of power transfer changed. However, recent scholarship has shed new light on Omaha leadership in the 1800s. Using treaty signatures and James Owen Dorsey's tribal genealogies, two researchers have shown that principal Omaha chiefs definitely inherited their offices and that there was traditionally a third "quorum" leader, chosen from the "weaker" Earth moiety. Between 1815 and 1870, Omaha chiefs' signatures on at least seventeen government documents reveal a recurring hierarchical order; signing first on nearly all the documents were the two principal chiefs, followed by the quorum chief and the four remaining members of the seven-man council. The "Elk" gens, the "On the Left Side" clan, and the clan of the "Earthlodge Maker" were heavily represented among the first three signers of many treaties, indicating that principal chieftainship was largely confined to these three groups. With the aid of Dorsey's genealogies, the researchers demonstrated that within these clans, chiefdom was hereditary, based on primogeniture, and "concentrated among a limited number of families within specific lineages." But despite their strong argument in favor of heredity, the authors of this new study cannot completely rule out competition as a factor in chieftainship, and Indian agents' reports refer to "paper chiefs" as a constant threat to traditional leaders.[41]

Oddly, the first chiefs in Omaha recorded history were usurpers who gained their influence not through normal channels but by being courted and declared "chiefs" by whites. In the late 1700s, an Omaha of uncertain identity visited St. Louis and on his return announced that he had been made a chief. This unknown chief then appointed "soldiers," one of whom was young Black Bird. A handsome Indian, Black Bird impressed the St. Louis traders, who awarded him a chieftainship. As early as 1777, traders dealt with "principal chiefs," showing that individuals held power and negotiated for the tribe. In his report on favored Indian tribes, Francisco Cruzat listed the ambitious El Pajara Negro ("Black Bird") as leader of the Omahas.[42]

After the Louisiana Purchase, Americans continued the award-giving policy begun by the Spanish and the British; in 1806, two Omahas—Hard Walker and a different Black Bird—received "commissions," accompanied by medals.[43] Obviously, government meddling in Omaha politics continued; five years later, on May 13, 1811, Big Elk and White Cow, rivals for Omaha leadership, entered the camp of an American exploring party and asked the party's leader to decide which of them should be the tribe's principal chief.[44] The Omahas had come a long way from the leadership of seven wise men.

In their glory days, the Omahas saw themselves as "the most powerful and perfect of human beings."[45] For a quarter of a century, they controlled a significant section of the Missouri River, influencing neighboring tribes and dictating to colonial governments. The Omahas were at their most powerful between 1775 and 1800. Under their despotic chief Black Bird, they ruled the river, pitting English, Spanish, and eventually American traders against each other. And because they had guns, they had no rivals among Missouri River tribes.[46] By 1775, Spanish documents listing Missouri Valley trading partners assigned two traders and five thousand pounds of trade goods to the "Mahas."[47]

On May 5, 1794, members of the Board of Trade of the western district of Illinois met in St. Louis to organize "an exclusive Company for trading with all the tribes that [were] found farther up [the Missouri River] than the Poncas." At this organizational meeting, twenty-eight merchants drew up articles of incorporation for the new Missouri Company, which was originally chartered for a ten-year period. According to the articles, each member would help capitalize the new venture and would then share in the company's profits or losses. When making arrangements for their first trip up the Missouri in early June 1794, the traders assigned the mighty Omahas three traders and 12 percent of their trade goods.[48] Personal bribes, in the form of medals, flags, and gifts, also flowed up the Missouri River. Jean-Baptiste Truteau, leader of the first Missouri Company trading mission, considered the Omaha village a perfect spot to establish a post from which to supply the upper Missouri trade, but he knew his scheme would require Black Bird's permission. To gain and keep the great chief's goodwill, Truteau suggested giving him a medal, a large flag, and annual presents.[49] Continuing the gift-giving process begun by the colonial powers, Meriwether Lewis and William Clark ascended the Missouri River well supplied. Before leaving in the spring of 1804, they packed fourteen bales of Indian presents, including a large Jefferson peace medal for the current chief of the Omahas.[50]

Despite the gifts that came their way, the Omahas traded on their own terms. Because of commercial agreements with the Sauks, Foxes, and Grand Pawnees, they had no real need for Spanish trade goods, and they made traders' lives miserable. From the bluffs overlooking the Missouri, Black Bird and his warriors would watch vessels approach, then stop the boats and demand that the traders unload the wares and carry them to the village, where the chief would bargain. The traders complained of "insults and violences" at the hands of Omaha and Ponca chiefs, and apparently several traders were killed by Black Bird.[51] Truteau emphatically stated that the most dangerous spot for a trader ascending the Missouri was passing the Omahas and Poncas. To overcome this obstacle, the Spanish protected their store-houses with palisades armed with swivel guns.[52]

Heading upriver with a load of firearms in August 1794, the hapless Truteau tried to think of ways to keep his guns from falling into Omaha hands. Because it was late summer, the trader knew the tribe would soon be returning from their buffalo hunt, and he doubted that he could get beyond their village undetected.[53] Truteau had reason to worry. When Spanish traders did meet the Omahas, the Indians usually profited. Both Big Rabbit, a second-ranking chief, and the clever Black Bird forced the long-suffering merchant to grant them "credit," a thinly disguised form of theft.[54] The Missouri Company sent three expeditions upriver after 1796. The first safely passed the Omahas, the second did not, and the third was allowed through only after paying tribute to Black Bird, his minor chiefs, and the entire Omaha tribe.[55]

The Omahas were justified in halting Spanish traffic on the Missouri River. They realized that their position as middlemen would end if the Missouri Company managed to reach tribes farther upriver, but even more important, they wanted to keep their enemies unarmed and under their control. Being politically astute, the Omahas knew they could continue their hegemony only if traders were kept downstream.[56] But by attacking Spanish trade missions and commandeering merchandise, much of which was earmarked for them anyway, Black Bird and his people may have hurt their own cause. So serious was the Omaha problem that in 1801, the Missouri Company decided to reroute its trade to the tribes of the upper Missouri via the Platte River, bypassing the troublesome Omahas and Poncas.[57]

No one man is more closely associated with the rise and fall of the Omaha tribe and the Missouri River fur trade than the enigmatic Chief Black Bird. Known to the French as Oisseau Noir and called El Pajaro Negro by the Spanish, he was described alternately as a "paper chief" and a "pliant tool" of traders and as a beloved, gentle leader.[58] Similarly, some accounts of Black Bird's autocratic rule stress his cruelty and vindictiveness, although others note that his power was spiritual.[59] According to ethnographers, explorers, and traders, Black Bird was an Indian Borgia, controlling his people with poisons supplied by traders who wanted to see him remain in control. Arsenic gave the chief seemingly supernatural powers; it was easy for him to play on his people's beliefs by foretelling a rival's death, then poisoning the rival to ensure that the prediction would come true.[60] One especially ethnocentric observer saw fear and awe as major sources of Black Bird's power, but he condoned the chief's methods, since "ignorant and savage man," he said, was best ruled that way.[61]

As a trader, Black Bird managed to ingratiate himself to whites while he cheated them. He worked both sides of the street, managing to enrich both himself and the traders. When a merchant unloaded goods, Black Bird confiscated the lion's share for himself, then allowed his trading partner to so severely overcharge the rest of the Omahas that the partner still made a huge profit.[62] On one occasion, after choosing his share of a trader's goods, the wily chief comforted the trader: "Now, my son, the goods which I have chosen are mine, and those in your possession are your own. Don't cry, my son; my people shall trade with you at your *own* price."[63]

Black Bird liked to be called "the Prince of the Nations," since he wielded complete power over neighboring tribes, especially the Poncas, who considered "this great rascal of the Omahas" their protector. In 1796, Jacques Clamorgan, director of the Missouri Company, ordered medals for the Poncas but refused to distribute them without Black Bird's concurrence.[64] Realizing the Omaha chief's importance to his trading company's financial success, James Mackay argued that although Black Bird was "more despotic than any European prince," it was absolutely essential to keep him "elevated above every other chief." When suggesting an expensive annual gift to the prestigious Omaha, Mackay explained, "It is better to fatten one who rules as a despot over various tribes, than to fatten many at less expense."[65]

In 1800, the mighty Black Bird finally met an enemy he could not subdue when he contracted smallpox after visiting a neighboring village. Always larger than life, he remained so even after death. According to romantic tales of his burial, the chief asked to be buried astride his favorite horse on a hill overlooking the Missouri River so that he could forever watch the traders come and go.[66] So lasting was the late Black Bird's reputation as a power on the Missouri that in 1804, when Lewis and Clark set out on their journey, among their bags of gifts was a special one for the current Omaha chief. The bag contained red leggings, an army jacket, and an American flag.[67] Regardless of his methods or motives, Black Bird was a powerful presence on the Missouri in the late 1700s, and under his leadership, the Omahas had few equals.

Along with Black Bird, Big Elk, who died in 1853, was among the best-known of the powerful Omaha chiefs. A diplomat rather than a despot, he held whites in high regard and at one point expressed a desire to someday "be a white man himself."[68] A signer of treaties in 1815, 1825, 1830, and 1836, Big Elk tried to lead his people into the future. He was also a prophet. After returning from a visit to Washington, D.C., shortly before his death, he told his people: "There is a coming flood which will soon reach us, and I advise you to prepare for it. Soon the animals which Wako^n'da has given us for sustenance will disappear beneath this flood to return no more, and it will be very hard for you. Speak kindly to one another; do what you can to help each other, even in the trouble with the coming tide."[69]

Troubles did come, in the forms of disease, warfare, and the cumulative social, economic, and cultural problems associated with overdependence on the fur trade. Although Sioux and Sauk attacks were an unfortunate fact of life for the Omahas and although the fur trade slowly robbed the tribe of its culture, it was smallpox that caused almost overnight devastation, turning the rulers of the Missouri into a forlorn band of prairie nomads. Shortly after 1800, the Skidi Pawnees conquered the mighty Omahas without a fight. Chief Black Bird, engineer of many Omaha successes, probably caused the tribe's downfall by carrying smallpox back from a Pawnee village. Within a few days after his return to camp, Black Bird was dead, and many of his people also died before the epidemic ran its course.[70] Having lost their chief and possibly as many as four hundred warriors, the Omahas could no longer control the trade or prevent assaults by neighboring tribes, and they were forced to loosen their stranglehold on the middle Missouri.[71]

Understandably, the death of an autocrat such as Black Bird created a leadership vacuum, and the late chief's successor, Big Rabbit, was soon challenged by the traditional chiefs Big Elk and White Cow. The Sioux wasted no time; taking advantage of the power struggle and the Omahas' weakened condition, they resumed their attacks. In addition, the smallpox-ravaged Omahas soon lost control of their hunting grounds along the middle Platte. With so much of their spiritual and cultural life revolving around the buffalo, their shrinking hunting grounds were a "psychological blow."[72]

Sources do not always agree on the dates of the Omaha smallpox outbreak, but a letter from the Louisiana governor-general to all traders—ordering them to avoid the Omaha camps because the tribe had "suffered last winter from smallpox"—dates the epidemic to the winter of 1800–1801.[73] Likewise, informants dispute the severity of the outbreak; the reported number of dead varies from 400 to two-thirds of the tribe to all but 300 Omahas. William Clark referred ambiguously to the deaths of "400 men & Women & children in perpoposion [*sic*]."[74] Some whites thought the Omahas would become extinct. In 1810, Washington Irving predicted that the Omahas before long would "be numbered among those extinguished nations of the west that exist but in tradition."[75] Some today believe that casualty reports among the Omahas were exaggerated, since their social organization remained intact and since a French trader who may have visited the tribe in 1802 reported 600 men and a huge cache of furs.[76] Regardless of the numbers, smallpox devastated the Omahas socially. The people did not understand the disease, and believing that their unborn children would also be disfigured, the survivors reportedly entered into a tribal suicide pact that they hoped would take them all to "some better countrey [*sic*]."[77]

In the aftermath of the epidemic, the Omahas once again fell prey to their longtime enemies, the Sioux. For over one hundred years, with only a respite under Black Bird, the Dakota bands had raided Omaha villages and forced the people to relocate along the Missouri River. In the late seventeenth century, the Omahas had neither horses nor guns, making them easy marks for armed enemies. Omaha traditions say that their people who lived near the Red Pipestone Quarry were "attacked and slaughtered" by the Yankton Sioux after about 1680. The people fled to near present-day Sioux Falls but were once again raided. The Omahas' next home, near the mouth of the Big Sioux River, proved to be an unfortunate choice, since the Dakotas' war parties regularly traveled along that river. Attacked several times between 1700 and 1740, the practically unarmed Omahas had no choice but to flee.[78]

After 1723, the Omahas, once again pressured by the Sioux, moved up the Missouri River, leaving good agricultural soil for marginal lands. French records show that attacks were planned against the Missouri River tribes in 1727 and 1729.[79] In 1729, two French emissaries explained to their minister that a band of Sioux failed to appear for a scheduled parlay because a "number of the prairie Sioux" had enlisted their help in a war with the Omahas.[80] In about 1750, the

Omahas, Iowas, and Poncas relocated in northern Nebraska, but the Sioux followed. Keeping ahead of their enemies, the Omahas moved farther south to Omaha Creek.[81]

The Sioux threat intensified during the early 1800s, in part because the Sioux, unlike almost all the other Plains tribes, actually grew in number, since many who were in the path of smallpox had been vaccinated.[82] Members of the Lewis and Clark expedition recorded a major battle in late August or early September 1804, in which the Brulés destroyed forty Omaha lodges, killed sixty-five to seventy-five men, plus some boys and children, and took forty-eight prisoners, including twenty-five women. A soldier with the exploring party described in horror the grisly spectacle of Sioux women dancing while holding poles decorated with Omaha scalps.[83] This deadly battle may have been the result of a tragic error. The Sioux had no central government, and bands acted independently. According to reports, one band of Brulés had agreed to a truce with the Omahas and Poncas, but another had not and continued to attack. When the Poncas took revenge on the wrong Sioux village, the truce fell apart, resulting in the Omaha slaughter.[84]

Threatened by the Sauks as well as the Sioux, the Omahas fled to the Elkhorn River in about 1820 and remained there, not wanting to face the Yankton Sioux who had taken over their lands in northeastern Nebraska.[85] The Omahas nearly starved during the war-torn 1820s, when they were reduced to eating only corn because they were "too busy fighting the Yankton and Brulés to hunt."[86] The depredations continued; in 1821, the Sioux attacked the Omahas near Fort Atkinson, killing two of Big Elk's brothers.[87] In a report accompanying the 1825 Fort Atkinson Treaty, General Henry Atkinson and Major Benjamin O'Fallon informed the secretary of war that the Omahas were "at peace with their immediate neighbors, but at war with the Sioux."[88]

The Sioux continued to control northeastern Nebraska throughout the late 1820s, but the well-armed Sauks, who had moved across the Missouri River, now posed a problem. It may have been the Sauks, not the Sioux, who drove Big Elk and his tribal faction from Big Village in 1829.[89] Commissioner of Indian Affairs William Clark, desperate to restore order among the Nebraska Indians, invited the Missouri River tribes to an 1830 peace parlay at Prairie du Chien. Frightened of the

Sauks, the Otoes refused to attend. The Omahas decided to go, but their negotiator Big Elk, certain that the Sauks would murder him en route, left his precious peace medal behind for his son.[90] Just thirty years earlier, an Omaha chief had ruled the Missouri River; now an Omaha leader risked his life to make peace.

Smallpox left many Omahas dead, and the hostile Sioux and Sauks kept the tribe on the run, but fur traders who injected themselves into Omaha lives undermined traditional leadership, disrupted the tribal economy, and nearly destroyed the people's culture. Ever since its inception, the cornerstone of Omaha government had been traditional chiefs whose legitimacy came directly from Wako^n'da. Traders were a divisive influence, and as a result of their interference, two kinds of chiefs came to be recognized: (1) "paper chiefs," so-named because whites gave them documents supporting their leadership claims, and (2) traditional chiefs, established by tribal right and custom.[91] Meddling by traders and governments diluted traditional chiefs' influence; superior hunters favored by traders became important, as did newly appointed paper chiefs, many of whom had no right to the title. Because they claimed to have U.S. government support, paper chiefs could become influential, but their strength was practical rather than spiritual.[92]

Traders understood the vulnerability of traditional chiefs and knew which tribal members could be "bought." In a letter to the governor-general of Louisiana, Spanish Illinois Lieutenant Governor Zenon Trudeau claimed there were men among the Omahas who would be willing to undermine the authority of unfriendly chiefs in exchange for medals and blank commissions.[93] Acting on this knowledge, traders showered pro-trade chiefs and headmen with gifts: "Medals were hung about their necks. . . . And efforts were made to keep them loyal to the trading companies."[94] Clever "trade chiefs" sometimes went to great lengths to ingratiate themselves to whites. In competing for trade and its potential profit, some Indian entrepreneurs married their daughters to traders, arrangements that gave the brides financial security and that led traders to believe they were assured of their fathers-in-law's business.[95]

Contrary to romantic accounts that picture Indians as commercial "babes-in-the-woods," the Missouri River tribes were quite familiar with barter; for centuries they had traded their surplus among fellow Indians. Well aware of the value of goods, these people were "horse traders" in both senses of the word.[96] But practical, established trade customs changed with the coming of European goods, which were mostly items that could be accumulated—durable goods such as tools, guns, and cloth. No longer were only necessities received in trade; now possession of "things" gave their owners new riches and enhanced their status.[97] Indians began to crave luxuries, which eventually became necessities. They no longer hunted only for food but for what pelts could buy, and after the War of 1812, the Omahas found themselves scrambling to supply traders with pelts so that they could procure the goods they had come to need.[98]

"Pelts for profit" became a major factor in the decline of Omaha culture. Previously, the tribe had hunted buffalo without reducing the herds, but to traders, game was money, and to meet commercial demands, the Omahas began to kill the animals indiscriminately.[99] In what may be the first letter from a member of the Omaha tribe, Chief Big Elk in 1828 petitioned the government to help his people, whose method of subsistence had changed so drastically. In his wisdom, Big Elk saw the economic problems caused by fur traders: "The white people who have been in the habit of coming into my village have had great influence with us and have consiquently [*sic*] kept us scouring the country in search of skins untill [*sic*] the animals themselves have left us."[100]

As traders' demands increased, the Omahas began to ignore religious rites associated with the hunt, and tribal bonds unraveled. Before, hunting had been accompanied by religious ceremonies paying homage to Wako^{n}'da, the great benefactor. But since commercial hunting was inconsistent with religious customs, these observances fell out of favor, weakening traditions and splintering the community.[101] Historically, Omahas were not self-centered or individualistic, and during annual hunts, the good of the tribe had always prevailed over individual rights. Now, solitary hunters armed with modern weapons could kill at will and keep their prizes. Hunting in this manner had no religious significance, but the pelts piled up for aggressive hunters.[102]

The pursuit of game had, of necessity, always occupied much of the Omahas' time and energy, but with dwindling buffalo herds and the raised expectations of white traders, the Omahas now extended their hunts, to the detriment of village life and egalitarianism. With no one at home, villages suffered neglect, and new standards for wealth inflated the status of hunters. No group paid a higher price for tribal greed than women; always hard workers, wives found themselves overwhelmed by the huge numbers of hides to be processed for traders. The result of this wifely labor shortage was an increase in polygyny, especially among wealthy and influential men.[103]

Although goods acquired in trade introduced Indians to more efficient tools and some new handicrafts, they also destroyed young Indians' incentives to learn traditional skills. For instance, metal pots led to the disappearance of pottery-making, glass beads ended quill-work, and by 1920, Francis La Flesche could locate only two aged Omahas who recalled the highly skilled, ancient art of bow-making.[104]

In what has become a modern tragedy, rival fur companies competing for pelts introduced the Omahas to liquor. Ignoring the pleas of old chiefs and leading men and a law forbidding liquor sales to Indians, traders continued to ply the Omahas with illegal whiskey, since alcohol was cheap and the fur profits were huge.[105] Liquor destroyed lives and clouded judgment; even talented Big Elk fell under the influence of traders after he discovered whiskey.[106] Seeing liquor's debilitating effects on native buffalo hunters, some traders suffered momentary attacks of conscience, but the race for Indian pelts was on, and the liquor continued to flow.[107]

An important agent for cultural change, the fur trade altered both inter- and intratribal relations. With the exception of a few environmentalists, such as Edwin James of Stephen Long's 1820 expedition, neither trading partner considered the future consequences. The fur trade returned large profits, and its investors had no incentive to limit the number of furs brought out of the Missouri River region.[108] At the whites' insistence, Indians slaughtered huge numbers of buffalo, and as the herds shrank, so did the hunting grounds. Intertribal wars became commonplace, and with the buffalo gone, the Plains Indians could no longer feed themselves.[109] The fur trade had more impact on Indians than on whites. Indians lived where the trading occurred, and many along the Missouri River spent their whole lives influenced by traders. Ultimately, the Indians paid the price when the buffalo disappeared from this region and the fur trade ended.[110] In order to trade, Indians had abandoned their traditional subsistence patterns and now found themselves politically as well as economically dependent on the U.S. government.[111]

The activities of white fur traders harmed the Omahas in many ways, but traders had no interest in real estate, and after many years of white contact, the Omahas still held their territory in common, not realizing that the land they treasured was coveted by whites.[112] "The only title to land recognized among the Nebraska Indians was continuous occupancy and use,"[113] and Omaha land tenure tradition extended even to garden plots, where occupancy was everything. A tract being cultivated was never intruded upon; however, if it was left vacant, anyone could use it.[114] In addition, the procedure by which land could be bought and sold meant nothing to Indians. In their thinking, land could not change hands, but the right to occupy and use it was protected, and trespassers could be punished under certain conditions.[115]

Disregarding "occupancy and use," the conquering nations of Europe never truly recognized Indian title to American lands and based their own claims on discovery and exploration. When the lands that later became Nebraska passed to the new United States after the 1803 Louisiana Purchase, the U.S. Supreme Court, in a series of decisions, ruled that the government had the right to "extinguish the [Indian] title, either by purchase or conquest."[116] But neither the Supreme Court, the land claims of white pioneers, nor army occupation convinced some experts that the United States had established a "basis for ownership of Indian lands." On the other hand, some have tried to rationalize U.S. ownership and the dispossession of the American Indian.[117] In an oration delivered at the 1802 anniversary of the Sons of the Pilgrims, John Quincy Adams expressed this latter group's thoughts:

> The Indian right of possession itself stands . . . upon a questionable foundation. Their cultivated fields, their constructed habitations, a space of ample sufficiency for their subsistence, and whatever they have annexed to themselves by personal labor, was undoubtedly by the laws of nature theirs. But what is the right of a huntsman to the forest of a thousand miles over which he has accidentally ranged in quest of prey? . . . Shall the lordly

savage not only disdain the virtues and enjoyments of civilization for himself, but shall he control the civilization of the whole world?[118]

To Adams and like-thinking Americans, the answer was an emphatic "no."

None of the three colonial powers operating in the Nebraska region attempted to claim Omaha lands—probably because such an attempt was unnecessary. Omaha land cessions did not begin until long after the Louisiana Purchase. Some of the earliest Indian treaties, including those with the Omahas, were touted as treaties of "peace and friendship" but were preliminary to later agreements that would involve Indian land titles.[119]

On July 20, 1815, at Portage des Sioux, near St. Louis, Black Bird's grandson Waanowrabai, Big Elk, and six other Omaha chiefs and warriors affixed their "x" marks to the initial treaty between the Omaha Indian tribe and the U.S. government.[120] Short and to the point, this original treaty of peace and friendship returned relations between the Omahas and the government to pre–War of 1812 status and forgave hostilities committed by either party. Peace was promised forever, and most important for the future, the Omahas put themselves under the exclusive protection of the United States.[121]

The Omahas were one of a number of tribes influenced by British traders before the War of 1812. By returning Omaha-white relations to "the same footing upon which they stood before the late war," the United States intended to replace Great Britain as the Omahas' trading partner. As planned, shortly after the treaty signing, Americans did establish trade with the Nebraska tribe.[122] With its promise of Omaha dependency, the innocuous-sounding Portage des Sioux Treaty was a first step toward the fateful land cession of 1854.

The Omahas' first actual land cession was temporary. To increase its presence in the west, the U.S. Army needed land along the Missouri River to build Cantonment Council Bluff (later Fort Atkinson), and it instructed Brigadier General Henry Atkinson to procure the necessary territory. On September 23, 1820, Atkinson and the Omahas signed a treaty by which the tribe would cede to the government a fifteen-square-mile parcel of land, with the flagpole of the new fort placed at the center. If ratified by Congress, the treaty provided that in return for their lands, the Omahas would receive supplies, weapons, and ammunition by June 1821. In addition, the Omahas retained the right to hunt on portions of the cession not needed by the army.[123] Congress failed to ratify the treaty, but both the Omahas and the army continued as if it had. The government, to its credit, kept its promise to deliver goods to the Indians, and content with the trade, the Omahas never questioned the legality of their land cession. The unratified treaty became obsolete in 1829 when the army abandoned Fort Atkinson in favor of Fort Leavenworth, and the Omahas reoccupied the land.[124]

In 1825, the government began to assert its control over the Omahas. Billed as another "peace and friendship" agreement, the October 6 Fort Atkinson Treaty, signed by General Atkinson, Indian agent Benjamin O'Fallon, and fourteen prominent Omahas, was condescending, restrictive, and one-sided.[125] Now the Omahas acknowledged American supremacy as well as protection and agreed that the United States should regulate their trade. The government offered the Omahas "crumbs": Article Two arrogantly extended to the Indians "from time to time, such benefits and other acts of kindness as may be convenient." Article Three further restricted trade, limiting Omaha commerce to American traders and stating that the U.S. government would determine trade sites. According to the fourth article, the government agreed to provide traders to the Omahas, with the understanding that the Indians would protect them.[126]

Article Five dealt with possible future crimes committed by either whites or Indians. Though ethnocentric, it began fairly enough, allowing for equal punishment for criminals of either race. But the article contained a disturbing proviso. The treaty provided for the unconditional recovery and return of any property stolen by an Indian; yet the proviso required proof if a white man was accused of stealing Indian property.[127]

Not one acre of land changed hands in the 1825 Fort Atkinson Treaty, but it marked a surrender of Indian rights and sovereignty and set a precedent by which the U.S. government took from the Indians and gave little in return. The Omahas had already lost so much. The buffalo were disappearing, many lives had been lost to enemy raids and disease, and thanks to the fur trade, Omaha values had changed and their culture was in disarray. All they had left was the land, and it too was now threatened. Little by little, treaty by treaty, the Omahas would see their land base erode until, in 1855, they would make a final move to their reservation. But in 1819, Big Elk, still trusting the whites, saw no future threat. At a fall tribal council, he had assured Agent O'Fallon that he and his nation loved the whites, and in response to American troop movements along the Missouri River, the chief had told his agent: "Some think, my father, that you have brought these warriors here to take our land from us, but I do not believe it. For though I am but a poor, simple Indian, yet I know that this land will not suit your farmers."[128] How very wrong he was.

Chapter Two
Making Way for Whites
Treaties and Troubles, 1830–1853

> I am like a large prairie wolf, running about over these
> barren prairies, in search of something to eat, with his
> head up, anxiously listening to hear some of his fellows
> howl, that he may dart off towards them, hoping to find
> a friend who has a bone to divide.
>
> Omaha Chief Big Elk, 1835

In 1819, shortly before the Omahas signed their first treaty with the
U.S. government, Omaha leader Big Elk appeared confident that the
presence of the U.S. Army and a few whites who had ventured west of
the Missouri River posed no real threat to the Omahas' lands or to their
way of life. But over the next three decades, as he nervously watched
white settlers coming west in increasing numbers, as he witnessed
white fur traders undermining the authority of Omaha leaders, and as
he experienced firsthand the damaging effects of alcohol, he was
forced to face reality. In his 1853 "farewell address" to the Omahas,
Big Elk warned his people that their lives were about to change.

Big Elk's predicted "flood" soon began to engulf his people as the
government moved eastern Indians onto traditional Omaha hunting
grounds and as whites discovered that the "Great American Desert"
could be farmed profitably. Between 1830 and 1853, the Omahas
signed two official treaties and several agreements that were never
ratified, received cash for land for the first time, and joined the ranks
of annuity Indians. The tribe also witnessed the further destruction of
the great buffalo herds as white hunting parties slaughtered the
precious animals by the thousands. The Sioux conducted relentless
raids, time and again forcing the Omahas from their homes. Alcohol,
supplied by unscrupulous whites, continued to be a serious problem,
and traders pounced on Omaha annuities and attempted to manipulate
treaties to their benefit. The Omahas were no match for the government's new ideology of Manifest Destiny. Like the Otoes, Missourias,

Pawnees, Kansas, and Osages, they had the misfortune to be "border tribes" blocking western migration, and as such, they became victims of political infighting over territories and lucrative railway routes to the Pacific. Despite the humanitarian efforts of some agents and a few officials in the Bureau of Indian Affairs, the Omahas continued to suffer and in late 1853 were poised to sign a historic treaty that would drastically reduce their land base and confine them to a reservation much too close to the Sioux.

On July 15, 1830, at Prairie du Chien in Michigan Territory, the Omahas made their first permanent cession of land to the U.S. government when, along with the Sauks and Foxes, Sioux bands, and the Iowa, Otoe, and Missouria tribes, they ceded hunting grounds east of the Missouri River, in present-day Iowa.[1] The government's primary motive for arranging a treaty at this particular time was to prevent bloodshed among the Indians. Misunderstandings over boundaries and land cessions in the 1825 Fort Atkinson Treaty had caused a great deal of dissension among the Iowa and Nebraska tribes. The Sauks and Foxes asserted that the terms of the treaty awarded them lands east of the Missouri River, lands already claimed by the Omahas and Otoes. On the other hand, the Omahas and other destitute bands accused the Sauks and Foxes of selling their hunting grounds and using their annuities to finance a war to take control of the disputed lands. Because there was little game left in their own territory, access to these lands remained crucial to Omaha survival. The Sauks, weary of waiting to be told where their tribal boundaries lay, stepped up the pressure, and a major Indian war seemed imminent.[2]

On February 1, 1830, Omaha agent John Dougherty informed the secretary of war that the Yanktons, Omahas, Otoes, and Iowas desired a treaty to guarantee peace with the Sauks and Foxes. The tribes proposed that the government buy the disputed land and reserve it as a common hunting ground. Accordingly, President Andrew Jackson ordered a conference at Prairie du Chien, and as an incentive to the Indians, made $3,000 in goods available if and when they reached an agreement.[3]

The job of securing delegations from all involved tribes fell to Indian Superintendent William Clark and Colonel Willoughby Morgan, commander at Fort Crawford. Even after the value of the gifts was raised to $5,000, it took over two months to assemble the tribal representatives.

Clark threatened the Sauk and Fox chief Keokuk with bodily harm if he refused to attend the council, and the Omahas' fear of the fierce Iowa tribes forced Agent Dougherty to consider sending his charges to Michigan Territory by a more circuitous route.[4] On July 10, after their safe arrival, the tribal representatives signed an informal treaty of peace, and five days later, the delegates, including the Omahas Big Elk, White Horse, and White Cow, put their names to a formal document ceding their western Iowa lands.[5] This treaty marked the Omahas' first payment for lands and began their troubled history as annuity recipients.

The opening lines of the Prairie du Chien Treaty clearly state its two purposes: to remove the bases for friction among the tribes; and in light of the disappearing buffalo herds, to encourage means of subsisting other than the hunt.[6] By the provisions of Article One, the Omahas relinquished all rights to land east of the Missouri River (see Map 3), a government admission that they had previously held title to the land by virtue of its being their long-used hunting grounds. The first article included an ambiguous and later troublesome passage stating that the ceded land was to be assigned and allotted to the tribes "now living thereon, *or* to such other Tribes as the President may locate thereon, for hunting and other purposes" (emphasis added).[7]

In return for their lands, the Omahas were to receive $2,500 "annually for ten successive years . . . either in money, merchandise, or domestic animals, at their option." In addition, the government pledged the services of a blacksmith for ten years and $500 worth of agricultural implements. Articles Five and Eight offered further incentives; for each of the next ten years, the Omahas would receive a $3,000 annuity for their children's education, and at Prairie du Chien, they shared in $5,132 worth of merchandise.[8] At the Indians' request, the treaty also established a reservation between the Grand and Little Nemaha Rivers in present-day southeastern Nebraska for Omaha, Iowa, Otoe, and Yankton and Santee Sioux mixed-bloods. Since these "Half-Breed Tract" lands had originally belonged to the Otoes, the other tribes agreed to pay them, from the collective annuities, $3,000 over ten years.[9]

Obviously, the Omahas were confused by the strange wording of the first article, since they continued to hunt on the ceded land.[10] In 1837, without prior notice, the government moved the Prairie Bands of

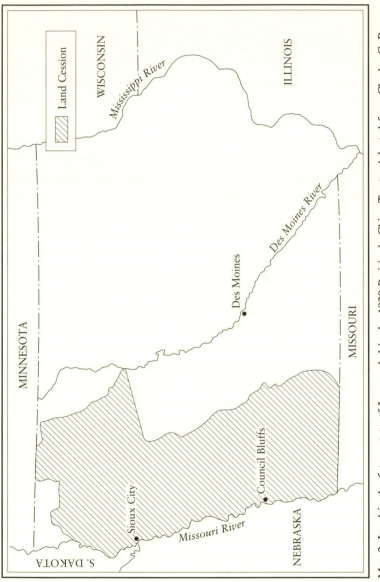

Map 3. Land in the future state of Iowa ceded in the 1830 Prairie du Chien Treaty. Adapted from Charles C. Royce, comp., *Indian Land Cessions in the United States*, Eighteenth Annual Report of the Bureau of American Ethnology, part 2 (Washington, D.C.: Government Printing Office, 1899), plate 131.

Pottawatamies, plus small bands of Chippewas and Ottawas, onto a reservation in what is now southwestern Iowa. Nearly three thousand "eastern" Indians were now located almost directly across the Missouri River from the Bellevue Agency, cutting the Omahas off from their western Iowa hunting grounds, which they understood were still theirs to use.[11]

Both Dougherty and Pottawatami Agent Edwin James recognized the unfairness of the government's actions, and Dougherty presented the Omahas' case in Washington that fall. When Indian Commissioner Carey A. Harris requested information on the Iowa lands, Dougherty responded with an angry letter protesting the government's move and citing problems with the 1830 treaty. Dougherty understood that the sole reasons for the treaty were to promote peace and to more clearly define the blurred tribal boundaries that had been a frequent source of dissension. The agent argued that neither he nor the Indians believed they were surrendering all rights and title to those lands for "the paltry consideration of Five Thousand dollars annually for Ten Years!!" Dougherty, who had been the Omahas' interpreter as well as their agent at Prairie du Chien, stated that the Pottawatamies were merely *joint* owners of the western Iowa lands and that both the treaty commissioners and the Omahas believed that hunting rights would remain forever. The irate agent's argument hinged on a single word in Article One. As stated, the treaty allowed the president to locate certain tribes on the ceded land, to the exclusion of the Omahas. Dougherty pointed out that the inadvertent substitution of the word "or" for "and" completely changed both the meaning and the intent of the treaty and that the president was never meant to have the powers falsely granted him by Article One. Warning that the Omahas would be in a desperate condition without either access to the hunting grounds or liberal compensation, Dougherty urged Harris to send enough provisions to tide them over until they could learn agriculture.[12]

Early in 1838, in response to Dougherty's plea for help, Commissioner Harris sent the agent a draft copy of a treaty by which the Omahas would relinquish any remaining interest in the Iowa lands in return for a cash payment of $15,000. The Omahas signed the treaty on April 22, but the Senate refused to ratify it, leaving the unfortunate tribe with no Iowa hunting grounds and little money to buy much-needed food.[13]

The land ceded by the Indians in 1830 included a parcel west of the original Missouri state boundary running north from the juncture of the Kansas and Missouri Rivers. The ink was barely dry on the Prairie du Chien Treaty when it came under fire from citizens of western Missouri who objected to Indian hunting grounds blocking their access to the Missouri River and preventing white settlement in the area. Missourians' desire for this land was understandable; the area in question, known as the Little Platte region, is that part of present north-western Missouri "watered by the Little Platte and Nodaway rivers, one of the world's richest bodies of brown loess soil . . . and according to Indian legend, the 'beginning of the road to Paradise.'" Originally omitted from Missouri because of a desire for neat boundary lines and the lack of initial white demand for these lands, the Little Platte region was now coveted by settlers along the Missouri border.[14] Land-hungry Missourians claimed that the state line had been incorrectly marked, and they gave several reasons why the Little Platte region should be incorporated into the state of Missouri: (1) doing so would create the natural boundary of the Missouri River as a more likely way to separate the races; (2) Indians held no land title; (3) the country was unsuitable for Indians because the area was too small for any tribe and, no doubt more important to Missourians, because Indians in the Little Platte region would be "troublesome neighbors"; (4) the land would bring a good price; and (5) the boundary changes would help protect settlements from Indian attacks. A memorial to Congress, signed by over 150 concerned citizens, asked, "Shall so beautiful and fertile a country remain a wilderness?"[15]

The Missouri state legislature quickly joined private citizens in pleading the case for annexation of this desirable area. Lawmakers warned of future "calamities" due to the "restless hordes of native savages" and pictured the area as one that would be valuable to a "cultured population." Taking a sarcastic tone, the legislature reminded Congress that the government must have been aware of the "wretched condition" of the border tribes, since Indian agents constantly called this situation to the public's attention, and noted that if the tribes really were that destitute, this did not bode well for white Missourians. Claiming that starving Indians would steal to eat, the memorialists continued: "If the Indian tribes alone were to suffer . . . we should leave them in their misery to the wisdom and humanity of Congress. But we, too, are involved in the evils of their lot."[16]

In 1835 and 1836, Missouri Senator L. F. Linn conducted an extensive correspondence with Indian commissioners and agents to drum up support for his state's annexation campaign. His correspondents all seemed to agree, especially on two points: the land was an inappropriate spot for Indians; and Missouri needed access to the river. In a May 1835 letter to Secretary of War Lewis Cass, Linn stated his feelings on the matter: "The humane policy pursued by the Government . . . has accumulated horde upon horde upon our borders, ready and willing at a favorable moment to rush upon our frontier settlements; the inconvenience of their presence is sufficiently great without throwing them between us and our great navigable waters."[17]

Linn and his fellow legislators knew the Indians who signed the 1830 treaty were willing to sell their lands, and in their eagerness to acquire treaties, the Missouri congressmen offered to conduct the negotiations themselves, at no charge. But standing in the way of a Missouri border extension was the 1834 Indian Trade and Intercourse Act, which stated, "All that part of the United States west of the Mississippi and not within the states of *Missouri* and Louisiana, or the territory of Arkansas . . . [was] deemed to be the Indian country" (emphasis added). The Trade and Intercourse Act required traders to be licensed, prohibited white settlement in the designated areas, and provided that anyone introducing alcohol into Indian country would have the liquor confiscated and would be subject to a large fine.[18]

The Little Platte region was clearly part of Indian country and, as such, was subject to all the provisions of the recently enacted law. When confronted with the terms of the new Indian Trade and Intercourse Act, Senator Linn and his colleagues assured Secretary Cass that they understood the government's promise not to disturb the Indians and that they were in favor of the policy—except in the case of the Missouri border. Their concern seemed to be that unless the state owned the land, they would have no guarantee that the Little Platte region would not be permanently turned over to Indians.[19]

Missouri had its way. In its report to the Senate on March 16, 1836, the Committee on Indian Affairs agreed that Indian title to the Little

Platte lands should be extinguished as soon as possible but did not think it necessary to appoint a treaty commission. Instead, the committee members believed it would be cheaper and more efficient to have Indian agents who were already in the field conduct the negotiations.[20] But Congress was impatient; in June 1836, months before the treaty negotiations took place, it approved a bill to extend the Missouri border.[21]

On October 15, 1836, at Bellevue, upper Missouri, Indian agent John Dougherty, subagent Joshua Pilcher, and tribal leaders of the Omahas, Otoes, Missourias, and Yankton and Santee Sioux consummated the treaty often referred to as the "Platte Purchase." According to Article One, the Indians agreed to relinquish all claims between the state of Missouri and the Missouri River (see Map 4), thus creating "a natural boundary between the whites and Indians." In addition, as compensation for abandoning their fall hunts to attend the treaty negotiations, each tribe shared in $4,520 worth of "presents." Article Three of the brief treaty immediately affected the Omahas. Since they were forced to relocate near Bellevue because of the Sioux threat, the government promised to break and fence one hundred acres of farmland near the new Omaha village "as soon as it can be done after the ratification of this convention."[22]

The Platte Purchase was a bargain for the government. The Indians received no cash, and no future annuities were promised. In return for this "beautiful . . . valuable" tract, the tribes received nothing but the trade goods distributed at the treaty signing. In his diary, Rev. Moses Merrill, missionary to the Otoes, thanked the Lord for making agents Pilcher and Dougherty so generous.[23] Obviously, Merrill knew nothing about potential land values. Traders, often lurking at the fringes of Indian policy, meddled with the treaty; among original provisions excluded from the ratified document was one to repay Omaha debts to traders Joseph Robidoux Sr. and Lucien Fontenelle.[24] And late in 1845, the government still had not plowed and fenced the one hundred acres near Bellevue that had been promised to the Omahas nine years earlier.[25]

Not since the smallpox epidemic at the turn of the century had the Omahas been as dispirited and destitute as they became in the years following the Bellevue Treaty. During the late 1830s and throughout the next decade, the Omaha people were raided by Sioux, victimized

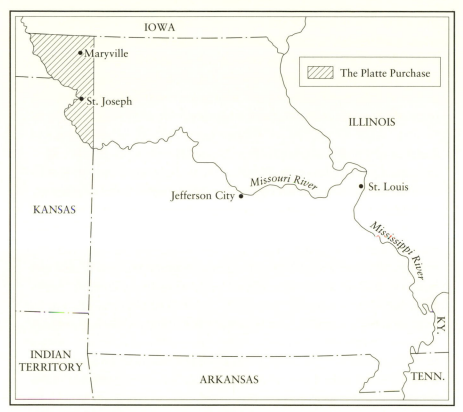

Map 4. The Platte Purchase. Adapted from Royce, *Indian Land Cessions*, plate 144.

by traders, and ignored by the U.S. government. White emigrants cut a destructive swath through Omaha lands, and for two years, Latter-Day Saints illegally squatted in Indian country, defying the government and destroying Omaha resources. After 1840, left without annuities and often too frightened of the Sioux to venture onto the prairie in search of game, the little band of Omahas barely managed to survive. Their numbers dwindled: in 1838, there were approximately 1,400 Omahas; five years later, Agent Daniel Miller's census counted 1,301; by 1847, this once "considerable tribe" numbered just over 1,000, many of them children.[26] Concerned Indian agents, superintendents, commissioners, and even Mormon sympathizers begged the government to help the struggling tribe, but the "Great Father" either did not hear or chose not to listen.

It was evident as early as 1830 that the Omahas were in trouble. Liquor kept them in poverty, the Sioux threat made a permanent home impossible, and any halfhearted government attempts to turn them into farmers failed miserably. The supply of game had run so low that the Omahas "starve[d] almost half the year—and [were] very badly clad."[27] In 1831, Agent John Dougherty, who perhaps did not appreciate their dedication to the hunt, saw the Omahas' future as one of limited choices: they must either "cultivate the Soil or perish by hunger."[28] Despite these problems, Omaha leaders appeared willing to cooperate with the government. In 1833, just a few weeks before presiding over an informal treaty of peace among the border tribes, Special Commissioner Henry L. Ellsworth forwarded a plea for help from the Omaha tribe. While expressing their desire to till the soil and educate their children, they reminded the president that they were starving and needed assistance. Describing their band as once "numerous and happy," Big Elk and the other leaders begged, "Will not our great father help us . . . that we may once more have enough to eat, and our women and children not starve and die when the cold weather comes?"[29]

When the Prairie du Chien Treaty annuities expired in 1841, the Omahas were once more forced to depend on hunting profits, but they were "so reduced in number, and so poor in horses, that their hunting trips [were] attended with but little success."[30] With small hunting profits and no annuity extension, the Omahas were soon destitute.[31]

During the winter of 1843–44, they needed food so badly that they crossed the river and stole corn, cattle, and pigs from the Pottawatamies. Big Elk promised to make restitution, but Pottawatami Agent Richard Elliott had little sympathy for the starving Omahas, calling them "too lazy to work and too cowardly to hunt."[32]

In 1845, Agent J. L. Bean described the Omahas as a people with "no resting place," situated as they were between the Sioux and the Pawnees. That summer the Sioux had burned the Omaha village at Black Bird Hills, forcing the tribe to flee downriver to the Bellevue Agency. After their arrival, they lived on "roots, the wild pea, with now and then a stray raccoon or muskrat." Almost completely unarmed, they were terrified to leave the agency to look for larger game. The Pottawatamies shared their own provisions but finally had to tell the Omahas not to come back because their supplies were running low. Bean was convinced that had it not been for the hoes and axes made by their blacksmith to help them dig roots, many Omahas would have died. He feared for the Indians: "How they are going to get through the Spring months the Lord only knows."[33] In response to Bean's urgent request for help, Superintendent Thomas Harvey asked Indian Commissioner William Medill to authorize the purchase of $600–$800 worth of corn to see the band through its crisis.[34]

The corn arrived, but the Omahas remained "a poor dispirited people."[35] By 1846, the band had shrunk to "a pitiable handful of scarcely more than a hundred families," and at least one observer believed they would shortly disappear.[36] Mormon advocate Thomas Kane accused the government of not sending the Omahas "a single sheep or a single soldier to stand in the way of their death by murderers or starvation."[37] In 1849, Father Pierre-Jean De Smet, Jesuit missionary and keen observer of American Indians, painted a grim portrait of the Omahas. According to De Smet, the tribe was in "a state of nearly absolute destitution," hunting birds, digging roots, and remaining wary of more powerful enemies who often killed the old, the women, and the children.[38] But perhaps Presbyterian missionary Edward McKinney best summed up the 1840s when he reported that the Omahas' "entire destitution . . . [left] them almost always both naked and hungry."[39]

Many of the Omahas' problems in the 1830s and 1840s were either the direct or the indirect results of white contact, and in most cases, "whites" meant traders. Whether bartering for furs or annuity money, traders adversely affected Indian economy, society, and government. John Dougherty was especially vocal regarding traders' influence, which he believed counteracted government efforts to improve the Indians' condition. The conscientious agent became frustrated because he saw himself and the traders constantly pitted against each other: "While the agent is advising the Indians to give up the chase and settle themselves . . . the traders are urging them on in search of skins."[40] In 1838, he became so angry that he recommended a change in the intercourse law to allow a government officer to clear an Indian village of white men, including licensed traders.[41]

In the 1840s, traders who formerly had gone to the Indians to barter for furs now traded goods for annuity money. Indians derived little benefit from annuities, since many Indians owed traders money, and their creditors hovered about the posts ready to snap up the cash when it arrived. Indian Commissioner T. Hartley Crawford knew exactly what was happening, and he argued, "The recipients of money are rarely more than conduit pipes to convey it into the pockets of their traders."[42] Also, annuity payments made to chiefs and headmen created a powerful temptation for them to misuse tribal funds by purchasing items on credit. As a result, individual debts became tribal ones, and in some cases, the government had to make annuity payments directly to traders.[43] Even former traders took a lively interest in Omaha annuities; for example, before the payments ended in 1841, Joshua Pilcher, ex-trader and now superintendent of Indian affairs, suggested that the government buy some Omaha land, the profits from which would help the tribe. From past experience, Pilcher knew that a continuation of annuities from land sales would be a boon to traders. Pilcher's successor, David D. Mitchell, also a former trader, repeated the land purchase recommendation the following year.[44]

Many traders had friends in high places and did not hesitate to use their political influence to remove "over-zealous" agents from their posts. In 1847, Indian Commissioner Medill received a tip that the "most active representatives of the Indian Traders" threatened to pull political strings to prevent crusading St. Louis Superintendent Thomas Harvey from prosecuting fur companies for "fraud and liquor smuggling." The biggest problems were the large trading companies, such as Pierre Chouteau Jr. and Company and W. G. and G. W. Ewing, who took advantage of Indians to acquire their annuities. These companies were nearly impossible to prosecute, since they bribed agents, traded through "front men," and had U.S. congressmen in their pockets.[45] The American Fur Company had powerful representation in Congress in the person of Missouri Senator Thomas Hart Benton, who helped install former traders Pilcher and Mitchell as Missouri River Indian Service employees.[46]

Indian agents did sometimes attempt to police traders. In 1850, Omaha Subagent John E. Barrow, on hearing that the Bureau of Indian Affairs planned to grant additional trading licenses, asked Commissioner Luke Lea to refer applicants to him, since he knew the types of people who were waiting across the river to come into Indian country. Calling western Iowa a den of "thieves, counterfeiters, robbers, and liquor dealers to Indians," he assured the commissioner, "No place in America is inhabited by a more unmitigated set of villains than in the country immediate[ly] opposite called Council Bluffs."[47] But screening applicants did not work in practice. Nearly anyone could obtain a license, and those who could not simply traded illegally. With no enforcement arm, the Bureau of Indian Affairs could do little to prevent such abuses.[48]

Of all the white man's vices carried into Indian country by traders, alcohol was by far the most pervasive and destructive. Unscrupulous traders may have cheated the Omahas of their annuity payments, but liquor robbed them of their dignity and destroyed the vitality of their traditional culture. The easy availability of illegal whiskey curtailed hunts, turned formerly honest Omahas into thieves, and forced the people deeper into poverty. Competing traders plied hunters and chiefs with liquor; soon no transaction between Indians and traders took place without alcohol, and many tribesmen became so addicted to whiskey that anyone attempting to trade without it went away empty-handed.[49]

In November 1831, St. Louis Indian Superintendent William Clark fired off an angry letter to Secretary of War Cass condemning traders for abusing a special regulation that allowed them to bring whiskey into Indian country "for the use of boatmen." Before transporting this whiskey across borders into Indian country, traders had to promise that it would not be "sold, bartered, exchanged, or given to Indians." Clark had learned from reliable sources that whiskey designated for boatmen was being watered down and sold to the Indians "by the gallon keg." The traders' lack of good faith prompted Clark to recommend that no liquor whatsoever be allowed in Indian country.[50] But by the early 1830s, alcohol abuse had become so widespread that "not an Indian could be found among a thousand who would not (after a first drink) sell his horse, his gun, or his last blanket, for another."[51]

Despite the 1834 intercourse laws, whites continued to contact Indians, and in the 1830s and 1840s, the Bureau of Indian Affairs received numerous complaints about the importation of liquor onto Indian lands along the Missouri River. In 1841, Superintendent Mitchell reported that three hundred barrels of whiskey had been smuggled in and that well over one hundred Indians had died in drunken brawls. Besides the loss of life, alcohol abuse led to civil wars resulting in tribal breakups and caused hunters to stay home, leaving their families to starve.[52] In an 1831 letter to John Dougherty, Upper Missouri Subagent J. L. Bean lamented: "Liquor flows as freely as the Missouri. . . . If it was possible to imagine half the human misery I have witnessed . . . you would use utmost influence in having it stopped."[53]

But the liquor continued to flow, and the government had little success in stemming the tide as both large and small trading companies smuggled alcohol into Indian country. When the government put a stop to upriver liquor shipments by the American Fur Company, the company, fearing a loss of business, smuggled in a still and made its own whiskey, some of which entered the Omaha camp. In late 1831, Joshua Pilcher reported having seen Big Elk leave an American Fur Company post with an eight-gallon keg.[54] Of the small traders, the most difficult to control were the liquor sellers who persuaded Indians to cross state lines to trade, where they were not subject to the intercourse laws. Agent John Miller argued that whiskey purchased from these Iowa and Missouri dealers impeded the Omahas' prosperity and turned them into horse thieves. When the Indians traded their own ponies for liquor, they then stole at least an equal number from whites.[55] In just one year, the Omahas traded thirty horses for liquor and were cheated in the deal, a pony bringing only two to four gallons of watered whiskey. During winter, Miller's charges crossed the frozen Missouri River to barter with Pottawatami mixed-bloods who got their trading whiskey from whites living near the Missouri line. When lectured about the evils of drinking, the Omahas replied simply, "The white man makes it and sells it to us."[56]

Medal-giving continued well into the nineteenth century, perpetuating trader influence and eroding the power of traditional chiefs. Throughout his long career, the usually pro-white Big Elk complained of trader interference with his leadership. When Major Thomas Biddle visited the Omaha camp in 1819, the chief told him that it was difficult to govern his people when traders gave medals and made "chiefs of every man who [could] obtain a party to trap beaver." Biddle regretted that traders' meddling and alcohol had cost the government the services of a "valuable and sensible Indian" possessing "some traits that do honor to human nature."[57]

Big Elk continued his campaign against trader influence. Twenty-five years after his conversation with Biddle, in the winter of 1844, the aging chief complained to his agent that trader A. L. Papin had given medals to several of his young men, who now considered themselves his superiors. Big Elk confided that one of these young competitors had even threatened his life, and he predicted that "before the grass was an inch long" he would be a dead man unless the medal-giving stopped. Although he also had a medal, the chief swore that when he had received his, he had been told to be kind to everyone. Feeling like "an old scabby Buffalo Bull who had got separated from his band on the Prairies," the old man covered his head with his robe and lay down, thinking "his Great Father had thrown him away." When confronted by Miller, Papin told the agent that thousands of medals had been given to Indians and that in a young man's mind, a fifty-cent pewter medal was as valuable as a horse.[58]

Big Elk probably had reason to fear for his life. On December 6, 1847, American Hat, an Omaha chief friendly to whites, was murdered by three young tribesmen. Earlier on the night he was killed, the chief told Agent John Miller about death threats he had received because he cooperated with the government. Realizing that the older chiefs were a strong civilizing influence on the tribe, Miller urged the government to protect them.[59]

The Omahas had their first brush with Manifest Destiny in the 1840s as emigrants began to surge west in search of Oregon, California, and Great Basin lands. While traveling through Indian country, future settlers showed little respect for the land or for natural resources as they "fouled the water, used up the wood, ruined pastures, and drove off game animals."[60] White hunters accompanying emigrant trains "wantonly killed the buffalo," sometimes keeping only the tongues. Though admitting that Indians also killed large numbers of buffalo, Superintendent Harvey warned: "All experience proves that game rapidly disappears before the fire-arms of the white. . . . He kills for the sake of killing."[61] The destruction of game became an economic and demographic disaster for the Omahas, whose lands included a section of the heavily traveled Oregon and Mormon Trails. The Omahas' increasingly far-ranging hunts in the early 1840s often took them into Sioux territory, where their lives were constantly at risk.[62]

Reporting that emigrant traffic had "excited the anxiety of several of the western tribes," who regarded passage through their lands as a violation of their treaties, Harvey feared that settlers and their livestock would become targets of hungry Indians who blamed whites for their troubles.[63] With this in mind, officials in the Bureau of Indian Affairs offered their own solutions to the problem. Harvey suggested locating the hunting tribes on acreage south of the Missouri River, on land that could be purchased from the Omahas at a low price.[64] Mitchell, Harvey's successor, offered an alternative to farming: supplying the Indians with cattle and sheep and turning them into herdsmen—"the Tartars of America."[65] But by 1853, Indian Commissioner George W. Manypenny thought it in the best interests of both races that the border tribes be "placed out of the paths of emigrants."[66]

The Otoes, Pawnees, and Omahas "suffer[ed] and [felt] the effects of this vast emigration more than all the other tribes together"; in his 1850 report, Council Bluffs Subagent John E. Barrow warned Superintendent Mitchell that unless westbound emigrants stopped trampling the Omahas' fields, villages, and hunting grounds, some Omahas would commit acts of atrocity.[67] Barrow had correctly sensed the Omahas' mood, for in the spring of 1851, tribal leaders visited F. J. Wheeling of Council Bluffs, a friend of the Indians, to complain about emigrant problems. The Omahas intimated to Wheeling that along with the other border tribes, they intended to stop the cross-country travel that was "starving them and their children." Wheeling urged the Omahas not to add to their problems by going to war and suggested instead that they visit the president. Early in 1852, he and J. E. Johnson, also of Council Bluffs, escorted an Omaha delegation to Washington, D.C. Years later, the two Good Samaritans still had not been reimbursed for their expenses.[68]

Most of the westbound emigrants simply passed through Omaha lands, but one group stayed. In midsummer 1846, several thousand Latter-Day Saints (Mormons), fleeing persecution in Nauvoo, Illinois, and bound for Salt Lake City, descended on western Iowa. When a military emissary from President James K. Polk contacted the group, requesting five hundred volunteers for the Mexican War, Mormon leader Brigham Young made a private agreement with the army to provide a battalion in exchange for the right to winter on Indian lands. Neither Young nor his army contact had the authority to make such a deal, but later, in council with Big Elk and his band, Young gave the Omahas the impression that the Mormons had government permission to stay.[69] Knowing they were illegally on Indian lands,[70] the Mormon leaders appealed to Superintendent Harvey to let them stay until all the Saints had safely gone west. Harvey refused, stating that they had no government permission to remain. The Mormons presented a problem for the Indian Office: removing them could cause a bloody conflict; allowing them to stay would harm the Omahas.[71]

Although they had obtained permission to remain for a time in Iowa, most of the Mormons crossed the river to Winter Quarters, on land claimed jointly by the Omahas and the Otoes (see Map 5). Both tribes wanted to negotiate with the emigrants, who were well-armed and could hopefully protect them from the Sioux, but it was the Omahas who signed a patently illegal treaty with Brigham Young's people in August 1846.[72] Early on the morning of August 28, the Mormon High Council met with an Omaha delegation, including the aging Big Elk, his son Standing Elk, interpreter Logan Fontenelle, and seventy other chiefs and warriors. It was clear from the outset that each party knew exactly what it wanted of the other. Besides asking permission to remain for two years and to use timber and grass, the Mormons hoped the Omahas would welcome them. For their part, the

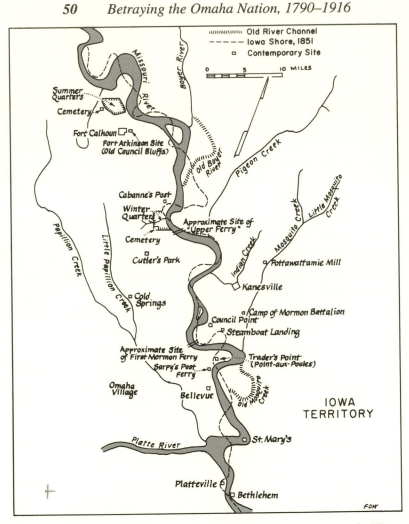

Map 5. Area of Council Bluffs, 1846–1850. Reprinted from *Mormons at the Missouri, 1846–1852: "And Should We Die . . . ,"* by Richard E. Bennett, by permission of the University of Oklahoma Press. © 1987 by the University of Oklahoma Press.

Omahas wanted protection from the Sioux and were prepared to demand much in return for their cooperation.[73]

As the council progressed, Young explained that his people needed a place to spend the winter until the Mormon Battalion returned, and in exchange for Omaha hospitality, he offered the services of gunsmiths and announced plans to set up a trading post, which also would be illegally placed on Indian land.[74] After advising Young not to negotiate with the Otoes, Big Elk declared himself agreeable if his "Grandfather the President" approved. The chief offered warriors to help guard Mormon cattle and asked the emigrants to please not kill all the game. To outmaneuver the Otoes, the wily old chief suggested that the Mormons settle on Omaha lands, so that he and his people could use their improvements after they left.[75] Big Elk agreed to sign "a writing," and on September 3, at the Omaha camp, the two parties signed an agreement allowing the Mormons to stay.[76]

The Omahas and the Mormons had a treaty, but they had no peace. Unsuccessful in recent hunts and unskilled as farmers, the desperate Omahas "either stole or starved."[77] The Mormons' cattle were handy, and rustling became an Omaha way of life, making a mockery of Big Elk's pledge to provide Indian cowhands. To protect their cattle, the Mormons camped in square formations and used dogs as early-warning systems, but the thefts continued, and Young sent a delegation to the Omaha village to discuss the tense situation. When confronted, the chiefs freely admitted they knew about the rustling, and they agreed to stop the depredations in return for $200 worth of corn. However, the Omahas did not see themselves as stealing from the Mormons. The Indians viewed their relationship with the Saints as a reciprocal one, with food as payment for use of the land, and they further justified killing the Mormons' cattle by arguing that the Saints frightened the game and destroyed their precious timber supply.[78]

It was inevitable that the approximately four thousand Mormons at Winter Quarters would deplete the natural resources of the area. They may have destroyed only small amounts of timber, but trees were so scarce that the extra lumbering proved disastrous for the Indians. In addition, the Mormons' expert marksmen killed much of the small game that the Omahas now depended on.[79] By 1847, the Mormons had become "troublesome neighbors to the Indians," who were left with the choice of freezing to death or invading enemy territory to obtain wood.[80] Thomas Kane, the Mormons' gentile "lobbyist," presented their case in Washington, using as his argument the August 1846 "treaty" and pointing out that the Mormons protected the Omahas. In Kane's opinion, that protection was a fair exchange for timber and game. The Mormon apologist portrayed the Saints as the temporary "saviors" of the "pauper Omahas," even sharing their meager food supplies with the starving Indians.[81] But Kane failed to mention the mutual distrust and the Mormons' broken promises. Big Elk remembered it all: "You can take our wood and it won't grow up tomorrow . . . must not kill your Cattle but our game all scared away—You were here to protect us, but down comes the Sioux and murderers [*sic*] us. . . . You can't raise up our timber and can't raise up our dead men."[82]

Just as the Mormons had Thomas Kane, the Omahas had Agent John Miller. A true friend of the Indians, Miller never failed to defend their interests, and in the two years of the "Mormon occupation," he and Brigham Young grew to despise each other. Miller was convinced that despite the Mormons' insistence that they were moving on, they planned Winter Quarters as a continuous halfway house.[83] From his reply to a letter from Brigham Young, it appears that the Mormons had asked Miller to move the Omahas south to join the Otoes. After refusing, the agent advised his adversary: "I will respectfully suggest . . . to you and your people, that the best services you can render the Omahas . . . will be . . . to leave."[84] In May 1848, the Mormons did leave, but not before Young cursed Miller, saying "his bones should rot and his soul be damned."[85]

The Omaha-Mormon controversy did not end when the Saints moved on to Utah. In May 1851, the prospector, Nebraska booster, and self-proclaimed general Thomas Jefferson Sutherland wrote a letter to Indian Commissioner Luke Lea in which he accused Orson Hyde, editor of the Mormon newspaper *The Frontier Guardian*, of encouraging Mormons and other emigrants to mistreat Indians. In an editorial, Hyde had cautioned travelers not to "feed them [or] suffer them to come about their camps" and also urged Kanesville residents to whip any Omahas who crossed the Missouri River. These were strange and hypocritical words coming from a prominent member of a sect that only five years before had "crossed the river" and contributed mightily to the Omahas' destitution.[86]

The 1840s were especially deadly years along the Missouri River. Omahas starved, froze to death, and were killed by the Sioux. Indian agents' reports were filled with accounts of Sioux depredations as the Dakota bands continued their merciless assault. Because they were never truly safe, the Omahas failed to become the farmers that the government hoped for. The one hundred acres near Bellevue remained unbroken in 1843, but the Omaha agent believed it would be senseless to encourage the tribe to farm as long as the Sioux were on the attack.[87] The chiefs requested troops who never came, and not even the fire-power of the Mormons could protect the band when the Sioux attacks intensified in 1847.[88]

The testimony of traders, agents, and the Sioux themselves all point to a war of extermination against the Omahas. In 1844, a trader at Fort Vermilion informed the Council Bluffs subagent that he never heard the Sioux discuss attacking any tribe except the Omahas. At a parlay with the Mormons after his people had killed thirty of the emigrants' cattle, Chief Eagle of the Sioux flatly stated that his tribe intended to kill Omahas, not whites. Like the Mormons, the Sioux placed the government in an awkward position; on the one hand, it was fairly obvious that they intended to wipe out the Omahas; but on the other hand, an army campaign against them could lead to plains warfare and further danger to white emigrants.[89]

For years, agents and superintendents campaigned for military garrisons to protect the Omahas, who had no guns or ammunition to protect themselves. Superintendent Mitchell believed forts were justified, and in 1844, Superintendent Harvey called for "an adequate military force." In response to Harvey's and Agent John Miller's requests for protection of the border tribes, in June 1848 the army established Fort Kearny, south of the Platte River. The Indians argued that a fort should not be located below the Platte because the river was hard to ford and crossing it would embarrass the soldiers. This location also seemed ridiculous to John Miller, who desired a fort above the Platte, where the Sioux and the weaker tribes lived. He questioned the purpose of Fort Kearny: "Protection for what? Not for the Indians." In April 1847, Harvey suggested establishing a garrison north of the Missouri River in Sioux country, and the following year, Miller proposed forts at Grand Island, at Pawnee Village, and at the Mormon camp on the Missouri River, which would be available when the Latter-Day Saints continued on to Utah.[90]

Perhaps the most ferocious Sioux attack of the 1840s occurred while the Omahas were being "protected" by the Mormons. On December 12, 1846, a large Yankton war party completely destroyed an Omaha village, killing seventy-three women and children while their husbands and fathers were hunting.[91] According to a Mormon account, most of the victims had been shot while asleep, after which the attackers cut off their noses in a gesture of contempt.[92] Agent Miller sent Logan Fontenelle to investigate; on the way, the interpreter met the sixteen terrified survivors, nine of whom were badly hurt. Miller was distraught. He asked Superintendent Harvey: "Major, what will these poor Omahas do—will the government do nothing for them? If they go South, the Ioways are on them—if they go up the river, the Sioux are killing them off."[93] The government did nothing, and the Omahas continued to be victimized by their enemies both at home and on hunts until the mid-1860s.[94]

While the Omahas struggled to survive, American Indian policy changed. Concentrating large numbers of Indians west of Missouri between the Red and Platte Rivers interfered with white emigration, blocked a central railroad route, and did nothing to improve the Indians' condition. To clear a path for westward expansion, the Bureau of Indian Affairs formulated a policy to group Indians north and south of a corridor through which people and rails could pass.[95] The activities of Indian commissioners and superintendents in the 1840s actually preceded congressional agitation for an organized Nebraska Territory. Although the plan may have been considered for some time, the first published statement of the new policy to divide Indians into two colonies appeared in Commissioner T. Hartley Crawford's 1841 annual report. In presenting his plan, Crawford foresaw "a dense white population . . . interposed between the two settlements," and he declared the scheme "an important point of national policy" that would benefit everyone.[96] Although the colony concept was still not concrete, treaties during the 1840s roughly followed north-south boundaries.[97]

In the fall of 1848, realizing that the Indians would not survive as they were, Superintendent Harvey presented his design to settle those Indians with no farmland on a tract south of the Missouri River, to be purchased from the Omahas and Poncas.[98] However, Harvey's idea was never explored, since almost simultaneously, bowing to pressure from territorial organizers, Indian Commissioner William Medill unveiled a plan to clear a large western corridor. For the border tribes to survive, Medill urged moving smaller groups, including the Omahas, away from the main migration routes. Considering it "a measure of great humanity," the commissioner originally planned to relocate the Omahas among the Osages and Kansas to the south. The Omahas were "much attached to the whites," and considering their mild manner, Medill hoped to teach them white ways as an example to other tribes. The commissioner was confident that the destitute Omahas would sell their land cheaply and would cost little to "civilize."[99]

Medill's report naturally emphasized his plan's advantages to the Indians, arguing that separation from whites and confinement on small reservations would ensure their survival. But his plan was not strictly humanitarian, for the economy also had to be considered; grouping tribes would require fewer agents, meaning lower salary budgets. In addition, removing Indians played into the hands of expansionists such as Thomas Hart Benton of Missouri and Illinois Congressman Stephen A. Douglas, who promoted a central rail route to the Pacific and who knew that Congress would not back a railway through Indian country.[100]

In 1849, the new Indian commissioner, Orlando Brown, repeated Medill's suggestion that the Omahas be moved south, and his successor, Luke Lea, advocated the two-colony policy in language almost identical to Medill's. In 1851, Lea linked Indian policy to the Nebraska question: "The necessity for an appropriation to carry these measures speedily into effect is the more apparent . . . in view of the . . . demonstrations of the public feeling in favor of the early organization of a territorial government over the territory in which these Indians reside."[101]

St. Louis Superintendent D. D. Mitchell did not believe that separating the border Indians into northern and southern colonies would work. As an alternative, he suggested an early form of severalty that would not involve relocating the Indians. He proposed giving each family a plot of land without right of transfer for fifty years, reasoning that by the end of that time, the Indians would have been influenced by whites and could protect their land. At that point he would make them citizens. Any surplus land would be purchased by the government for "something like a fair price" and would be opened to white settlement. In Mitchell's opinion, the lands were worthless to the border tribes since the game was gone, and in discussion with the tribes, he reported that the "more intelligent" among them favored his proposal.[102]

In the late 1840s, pioneers crowded the Indian country's eastern border, anxiously awaiting the natives' removal so that they could take possession of the lands. But not everyone stayed east of the Missouri River. Nebraska "boomer" T. J. Sutherland, who attempted to mount an exploring party to search for Nebraska gold in 1852, sang the praises of the Indian country, calling it "the most splendid country in America, and insisted that "the Indians had no right to keep such fine lands."[103] A year later, a group of Council Bluffs businessmen, including Dr. Enos Lowe and future congressman Bernhart Henn, formed a town company to encourage settlement in the proposed Nebraska Territory. As early as June 1853, each of the company's partners had crossed the river to investigate sites for a future town.[104] Reports sent back by these first whites to infiltrate Indian country described Nebraska as a "delightful country glowing in beauty" and encouraged others to follow. Sadly, the government's "solemn guarantee" that this country would be Indian land "forever" meant nothing.[105]

Soon lawmakers joined the clamor for white occupation of Indian lands, and no other congressional voice was louder or clearer than that of Stephen A. Douglas, promoter of a Pacific railroad through Chicago. As a member of the House of Representatives in 1844, Douglas acted on the recommendation of Secretary of War William Wilkins and introduced a bill to organize the Territory of Nebraska.[106] In 1848, Senator Douglas, declaring that an Indian barrier had become "ludicrous," presented a second Nebraska bill. In his proposal, the territory would stretch from forty to forty-three degrees north latitude and from the Missouri River to the Rocky Mountains. Though Douglas' bill was tabled, interest in Nebraska grew.[107]

The Nebraska question came to the fore in December 1852, when Missouri Representative Willard Hall introduced a bill to organize Nebraska and suggested that the lands west of the Missouri River be called the "Territory of the Platte."[108] The bill was referred to the House Committee on Territories, where it became known as the Richardson Bill, named for the committee chairman, William A. Richardson of Illinois. In the ensuing debate, Volney E. Howard of Texas attacked the Hall-Richardson proposal, claiming that it was unfair to the Indians. Howard was not known for his pro-Indian views, and Hall suspected that he may have had an ulterior motive. If Nebraska remained Indian country and Texans could drive their Indians north, Nebraska would become so dangerous that emigrants, traders, and especially the proposed railroad would be forced to travel through Texas.[109] In reply to this and other criticisms, Richardson sprang to the defense of his bill: "Five thousand settlers would do more to protect the lines of travel to Oregon, California, and New Mexico . . . than all the troops in your regular Army." An exasperated Congressman Hall added: "Everybody is talking about a Railroad to the Pacific Ocean. In the name of God, how is the railroad to be made if you will never let people live on the land through which the road passes?"[110]

Expansionist lawmakers had help in their effort to organize the Indian country. In December 1849, the Missouri state legislature asked Congress to make the Nebraska issue a reality, and in the summer of 1852, citizens of Parkville, Missouri, composed a memorial to Congress. They asked for "the immediate organization of the Territory of Nebraska" and demanded that Indians residing there be moved to assigned parcels of land so that the country could be quickly settled by whites. The Parkville petition was forwarded to Missouri Senator David Atchison, who presented it to Congress without comment. According to Stephen Douglas, the petition from the Missouri town was just one of "piles" of memorials from westerners; "scarcely a day passes in which we do not receive more of them."[111] In western Iowa, Senators Augustus C. Dodge and George W. Jones held meetings on the Nebraska issue, and in October 1853, a Council Bluffs group supporting a provisional government for "Nebraska" met at Bellevue and elected Hadley D. Johnson as their delegate to Congress. A month earlier, Rev. Thomas Johnson of the Shawnee mission had been chosen to represent the southern part of "Nebraska" country—the Kansas area. The two Johnsons sat in the House for a short time but were later removed.[112]

Because the country west of Missouri and Iowa had been permanently reserved for Indians and guaranteed to them in treaties, some congressmen objected to opening Nebraska to settlement. To placate these dissenters, the Richardson Bill was amended to provide that no whites could settle on Indian land as long as the Indians held title to it. Despite the amendment, the bill failed to pass in the Senate, but the 1853 Indian Appropriation Act included a rider authorizing $50,000 to negotiate with the Indians west of Missouri for their lands and for their consent to a territorial government.[113] President Franklin Pierce wasted no time complying with the provisions of the Indian Appropriation Act. During the winter of 1853–54, newly appointed Indian Commissioner George W. Manypenny made a fact-finding visit to Indian country to explore the area, to gather information to be used in treaty negotiations, and to prepare the way for the extinguishment of Indian land titles.[114]

None of the border tribes welcomed Manypenny. Alarmed and angry over illegal white incursions onto their lands, they had made plans to convene a great council in which the tribes would band together to drive out the white intruders. They had good reason to be angry. For several months before the commissioner's arrival, Thomas Hart Benton had been stumping the border country, and in a series of speeches, he had argued that Nebraska was now open to white settlement. Claiming that he had new information from the office of the commissioner of Indian affairs, he proclaimed:

> In all the debates on the Nebraska Bill last winter . . . it was generally conceded by every body [*sic*] that the Nebraska Territory belonged to the Indians. . . . But it appears that this is all a mistake. The fact seems to be that this whole country from the Missouri to the Rocky Mountains, with the exception of a few Indian reservations—covering only about one fourth of the ground—is now open to settlements! It already belongs to the United States, and there is no law to prevent the immediate occupation and settlement of the country![115]

To encourage potential settlers, the former Missouri senator even had an "official map of Nebraska" printed, showing which Nebraska lands were not occupied by Indians. Benton had sent a map of Indian country to the Bureau of Indian Affairs in Washington and had asked that the areas ceded by the Pawnees, Kansas, and Osages and the lands recently settled by eastern tribes be outlined. Commissioner Manypenny's assistants had complied with Benton's request and sent him back the altered map. Benton grandiosely titled his map "Official Map of the Indian Reservations in Nebraska Territory drawn by the Commissioner of Indian Affairs at the request of Col. Benton, and published to show the public lands in the Territory subject to settlement."

He had hundreds of copies printed and distributed.[116] Manypenny was in Indian country when the maps began to circulate; after finding a copy in the possession of "exploring parties," he angrily issued a press release denying any involvement in publication of the map and reiterated the official position that no land in the proposed Nebraska Territory could be settled.[117]

But even after disassociating himself from Benton's scheme, Manypenny had difficulty calming the anxious Indians, most of whom initially resisted selling their lands. By the time the commissioner returned east, many of the tribes had reluctantly agreed to sell but only on the condition that they remain on reservations on their former lands. Since this was not what the Bureau of Indian Affairs had in mind and would, in Manypenny's opinion, retard Indian advancement, the government deferred actual treaty negotiations, hoping the Indians would see the benefits of relocating. Before departing, the commissioner made arrangements for Indian delegations to visit Washington the following spring to sell their lands.[118]

Manypenny's trip west was an eye-opener. He was disturbed to find that the border tribes' general condition had been misrepresented in agents' and superintendents' reports. The Indians were not as prosperous and "civilized" as he had been led to believe. Instead, he found most of them "indolent and intemperate, degraded and debased," leaving him convinced that despite the best efforts of missionaries and the government, the plan to relocate Indians in a country of their own had been a failure. He believed that allowing small bands to wander through large tracts at will had led to Indian degradation, and he had little confidence in the Indians' ability to reform without "a change of residence."[119] In his annual report in December 1853, Commissioner Manypenny asked for additional funds to negotiate with the Indians west of the Missouri and strongly recommended the organization of Nebraska Territory.[120]

Although Indian country had been steadily eroding since the 1830s, the passage of the Kansas-Nebraska Act in 1854 effectively ended the "permanent Indian frontier."[121] Father De Smet observed, "The aborigines [were] forced to sell and cede their lands, with the ashes of their ancestors . . . to make room for strangers."[122] During 1853 and 1854, the Bureau of Indian Affairs engineered a series of treaties by which the border tribes ceded approximately thirteen million acres of land, and by 1854, what remained of the Missouri River tribes had been either relocated or assigned to "small portions of their former lands."[123] In March 1854, the Omahas would surrender their Nebraska lands and find themselves bound for a reservation they were too frightened to accept. Once again, they became a wandering nation in search of a safe, permanent home. Their suffering at the hands of the government had only just begun.

Chapter 3
Politics and Broken Promises
The Early Reservation Years, 1854–1881

We have much trouble in this land, but we have no one
to help us.

Two Crows, circa 1879

Returning to Washington, D.C., in the fall of 1853, Indian Commissioner
George Manypenny had quickly put the treaty-making process in
motion. On October 19, he instructed Agent Thomas Gatewood to
accompany an Omaha delegation to the capital to negotiate a land
cession.[1] With their leaders' fateful trip to Washington, the Omahas
entered a new era in which they were buffeted from all sides—by the
government, by hostile white settlers, by missionaries, and by oppor-
tunists who were hoping to make a quick dollar at the Indians' expense.
The early reservation years also saw tribal dissension, patterns of forced
and voluntary acculturation, the demise of the annual buffalo hunt, and a
new concept of chieftainship. Despite broken promises and neglect, the
Omahas remained loyal to the government and attempted to become the
agriculturalists that the Bureau of Indian Affairs wanted them to be. It
was in part this loyalty and cooperative spirit that captured the fancy of
white reformers and prompted the government to allot Omaha lands in
1882. Omaha history from 1854 to 1881 has traditionally been viewed
through the eyes and words of whites and acculturated or politically
active Indians, many of whom vied for power and profit. Unfortunately,
the average Omahas were allowed little voice in these events precisely
because they did not want to walk the "white man's road."

Agent Gatewood finally received Manypenny's orders two months
after they were issued, and when he informed the Omahas that the
government wanted them to send representatives to Washington, the
people refused to allow a delegation to negotiate a treaty at any place
without the presence of all the men of the tribe. In other words, the
treaty was an undertaking too important to trust to a few men, even if
they were chiefs. Knowing that the government was anxious for a

treaty, Gatewood negotiated on his own.[2] On January 27, 1854, at the Council Bluffs Agency, the Omahas and their agent signed an agreement known simply as the "Gatewood Treaty."[3]

Although this treaty was never ratified, the document and the events surrounding it reveal the Omahas' state of mind immediately before their official treaty was consummated. By negotiating a treaty without proper authority, Gatewood displayed poor judgment, but he may have been trying to make the best of a difficult situation. His charges were willing to negotiate but not to delegate—an ambiguous position that revealed much about changes in tribal politics. At an earlier time, one or more chiefs would have had complete control. But at least sixty Omahas attended the January 1854 council, where six men were appointed to travel to Washington with Gatewood to finalize the treaty.[4]

The first of the five articles of the treaty described in detail the boundaries of the lands to be ceded by the Omahas. Article Two stated that as soon as the government provided a means for fulfilling the treaty stipulations, the Omahas would settle on lands beyond Ayoway Creek, north of present-day Ponca, Nebraska. In addition, they relinquished all former treaty claims except the remainder of the $25,000 that had been provided for agricultural purposes in 1851. It was agreed that the president would distribute these funds at his discretion.[5]

The heart of the treaty was Article Three, which promised the Omahas $40,000 per year for thirty years and provided arms, ammunition, a blacksmith, and a blacksmith shop. Perhaps underestimating the Omahas' historic fear of their mortal enemies, Gatewood also pledged protection from the Sioux and promised a future peace treaty to halt all hostilities. In return, the Omahas vowed not to make war and to submit all disputes to government arbitration. In a clause that seemed unfair to the tribe, the Indians agreed that if an individual Omaha stole from whites or other Indians, restitution would be made from tribal annuities. Finally, the Omahas agreed to pay debts to traders out of their first-year annuity: $6,300 to Peter Sarpy and $500 each to Logan Fontenelle and Lewis Saunsoci. Article Four provided that all payments to the Omahas would be in cash, and the treaty concluded by giving six men—Logan Fontenelle, Joseph La Flesche, Village Maker, Standing Hawk, Little Chief, and Yellow Smoke—

authority to represent the tribe and to "*slightly* modify, alter, or amend" the current treaty (emphasis added).[6]

On February 20, 1854, Superintendent Alfred Cumming notified Commissioner Manypenny by telegram and by letter that Agent Gatewood and the Omaha delegation were en route to Washington armed with the signed draft of a treaty, and he warned the commissioner that the tribal representatives' power to negotiate could be restricted by the word "slightly" in Article Five.[7] On his arrival, Gatewood explained to his superior that he had been unable to persuade the Omahas to allow a delegation to act freely on their behalf and that he had thought it proper to make a treaty and give the delegation amending power. Manypenny disagreed. The irate commissioner was convinced that had Gatewood acted properly, the Omahas would have allowed their representatives to negotiate for them in Washington. He disapproved of the premature treaty, especially its provisions for long-term cash annuities and the payments to Sarpy, Saunsoci, and Fontenelle: "The treaties, if they can be so called, are made in violation of law and are in my judgment such as might not be approved or sanctioned. Their provisions are in direct conflict with the reforms desired, and would have no other effect than to degrade the Indians and enrich the traders."[8]

It was important to Manypenny that these early treaties with Indians west of Iowa and Missouri be drawn up correctly, so as not to compromise the ones to follow. He wanted the "influences adverse to the moral as well as the temporal interests of these people [met] at the threshold," and he would rather see no treaty than an improper one. Like Superintendent Cumming, Manypenny worried that the wording of the fifth article of the treaty would allow neither the government nor the Indians enough latitude to negotiate the type of agreement he wanted.[9] But the commissioner fretted needlessly; in spite of the Omaha delegation's limited powers, the government hammered out a treaty quite different from and less advantageous to the Omahas than Gatewood's document.

Agent Gatewood told Commissioner Manypenny that his treaty was the result of Omaha intransigence, but events in January 1854 made the agent's motives suspect. An article in the *St. Mary's (Iowa) Gazette* on January 25, 1854, stated that on the previous day, Agent Gatewood had visited the Iowa side of the Missouri River, returning to the

Omaha village the same day. On January 25, two days *before* the treaty signing, Peter Sarpy informed the *Gazette* editor that a treaty with the Omahas had been "consummated."[10] Perhaps not coincidentally, Article Three of the Gatewood Treaty included the provision to pay Sarpy money owed him by the tribe. Gatewood's handling of the treaty situation was definitely unwise, and his actions may have been dishonorable, but to local white settlers, the agent was a hero. The *St. Louis Republican* declared: "Maj. Gatewood has . . . overcome all obstacles, and accomplished in two weeks . . . what his chief failed to do . . . in a whole season. Half of all the Indian country is now ceded, and were the negotiations intrusted to the gallant Gatewood it would not be many `moons' until the WHOLE OF IT were thrown open to the Anglo-Saxon plough! A thousand guns for Nebraska and the go-ahead James M. Gatewood!"[11]

But Gatewood's career as Omaha agent would be short-lived. He had already angered both Cumming and Manypenny by reporting late to his post, then compounded his error by being absent without leave shortly after he arrived in Nebraska.[12] The abortive treaty was simply the last in his series of miscues. Congress never approved his appointment to the Omahas, and he was relieved as agent in the summer of 1854.

With Gatewood's impromptu document discredited, the Omaha leaders agreed to a complicated treaty that would have enormous impact on their people's present and future. Composed of fifteen articles, this agreement reflected the government's new approach to American Indian policy. There were some similarities to the Gatewood Treaty, but for the most part, this was an entirely different document. In 1842, Agent Daniel Miller stated that the Omahas claimed "the country bounded by the Missouri river on the east, by Shell creek on the west, by the river Platte on the south, and on the north by the Poncas country." Although the "Poncas country" constituted a rather indefinite northern border, these boundaries were closely followed in the actual land cession (see Map 6).[13]

Article One provided that if the lands north of Ayoway Creek, designated as the Omahas' future home, proved unsatisfactory, the Indians could select another site either "within or outside of the ceded country." To make this determination, a delegation from the tribe was

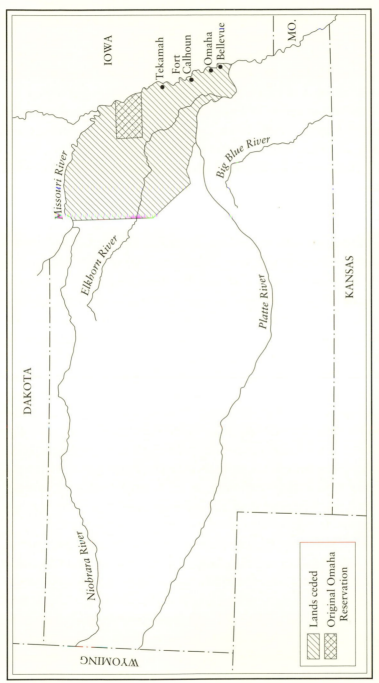

Map 6. Land ceded by the Omahas in the Treaty of 1854. Adapted from Royce, *Indian Land Cessions*, plate 148.

to accompany their agent on an exploratory trip to the assigned region. If the site to the north suited the tribe, it was automatically their home; if not, the president was authorized to provide a new reservation of not more than three hundred thousand acres. As soon as possible, and not later than April 1855, the Omahas were to vacate their homes near Bellevue and move to their reservation of choice.[14]

As they would have in the Gatewood Treaty, the Omahas relinquished all claims under earlier treaties except for the balance due from the 1851 appropriation. Article Four addressed one of Manypenny's major problems with the provisional treaty. Instead of $40,000 per year for thirty years, or a total of $1,200,000 in cash, the Omahas would now receive $84,000 in decreasing annuities spread over forty years, with the president deciding whether payments would be in cash or in clothing, provisions, and other items for their "improvement." Annuities were subject to deduction, however; use of liquor could result in lost payments, and annuity funds would pay for any depredations committed by Omahas. In a proviso no doubt disappointing to traders, no individual debts would be paid from annuity funds, but the government did agree to pay the Omahas' $1,000 debt to Lewis Saunsoci for "services."[15]

In Articles Seven and Eight, the government made promises that it would later break. Regardless of where the Omahas decided to settle, the United States promised protection from the Sioux and other hostile tribes as long as the president considered it necessary. And to nudge the Omahas toward "civilization," the tribe would be provided with a sawmill, a gristmill, a blacksmith shop, and the services of a miller, a blacksmith, and a farmer for ten years. Looking to future western growth, Article Fourteen provided rights-of-way for roads and railroads through the reservation.[16]

No other provision of the 1854 treaty was as important to the Omahas' future as Article Six, which provided land in severalty to the Indians. In the future, the president could have the Omahas' reservation surveyed and divided into lots to be assigned to individuals or families who would make the land their permanent homes. The following allotment schedule would apply: single Indians over age twenty-one would receive 80 acres; a family of two rated 160 acres; families of three to five, 320 acres; families of six to ten, 640 acres;

and families of more than ten, 640 acres plus 160 acres for each five additional members. Rules of inheritance would be determined by the president, who could also issue patents with the stipulation that the land could not be leased for a term longer than two years. In an attempt to curtail hunting, the article stated that if a person granted a patent should refuse to farm it or should "rove from place to place," the patent could be canceled and annuity shares withheld. In the event that a patent holder failed to return, the land could be reassigned or sold as excess. Any lands remaining after all the Omahas had been assigned permanent homes would be sold for their benefit, under rules "to be determined later." Finally, these lands could not be sold, taxed, or forfeited until Nebraska had a constitution and its legislature removed the above-mentioned land title restrictions, with congressional approval.[17]

As had been the case in previous Omaha treaties, Commissioner Manypenny's 1854 negotiations were hampered by outside parties "seeking to mold the treat[y] to suit their views and interests," which usually meant giving Indians as much cash as possible.[18] Shortly before negotiations began, the Iowa congressional delegation asked Manypenny to include in the forthcoming treaty provisions to pay for depredations allegedly committed by Omahas against Iowa citizens.[19] And as usual, traders were also suspect. In January 1854, Presbyterian missionary William Hamilton expressed concern that traders would play a large role in the treaty, since they controlled many agents and headmen. He warned that unless Manypenny was very careful, traders—instead of Indians—would negotiate the treaty.[20] Father Pierre-Jean De Smet considered the entire treaty process unfair. In his opinion, the sure destitution of the Omahas and other border tribes was "found in the disparity of the parties who make the treaty. On one side stands a shrewd and perhaps, unscrupulous Government officer; on the other, a few ignorant chiefs, accompanied by their half-breed interpreters, whose integrity is far from being proverbial."[21] But Manypenny ignored the Iowa legislators, and except for the payment to Saunsoci, outsiders had little impact on the treaty, which was signed on March 16, 1854, and was quickly ratified by the Senate on April 17.[22]

Shortly after the treaty was ratified, questions arose regarding Fontenelle's role in the negotiations. After being told that Fontenelle was not a chief, Commissioner Manypenny wrote to George Hepner, the new Omaha agent, and asked him to investigate the matter.[23] When questioned, the Omahas told Hepner that all the delegates sent to Washington in March 1854 were "chiefs on a par" and that a man could become a chief by inheritance, by transfer, by charitable acts, by bravery, or by an ancient method rarely used at that time—smoking a pipe and interpreting the curl and ascent of the smoke. Hepner surmised that since Fontenelle met none of the other criteria, he was recognized as a chief because of his charitable acts: frequent feasts for the headmen and "some other influence which the department well understands."[24] Hepner assumed Manypenny knew that Fontenelle had been a favorite of Thomas Gatewood and that the former agent had passed him off as a chief in Washington.[25] Oddly, the makeup of the Omaha treaty delegation and the names appearing on the treaty disagree. According to his contemporaries, Two Grizzly Bears was a member of the delegation that went to "sell land," yet his signature is absent. One account says that when Commissioner Manypenny questioned Fontenelle's presence in Washington, Two Grizzly Bears identified the man as his interpreter.[26] Judging by the names on the treaty, Fontenelle may have signed for Two Grizzly Bears, thus leaving his name on an important document he was perhaps not qualified to sign.[27]

Fontenelle's true status within the Omaha tribe has never been resolved. Most whites who knew him considered him a chief, but many of Fontenelle's contemporaries insisted he was never a leader according to Omaha traditions. To many Omahas, he remained merely a "half-breed" interpreter. In an 1854 narrative, Two Crows discussed the impending departure of the treaty delegation, which would be accompanied by *interpreters* Saunsoci and Fontenelle, and the Indian narrator of an account of the battle in which Fontenelle was later killed referred to him as "the white interpreter who was with us."[28] Yet Henry Fontenelle insisted that his brother was named the principal chief at a tribal council held during Commissioner Manypenny's visit in 1853, and it is possible that because of Logan's facility with English, he was made a chief "for the express purpose of helping the Indians to make the treaty with the United States."[29] Because his father was a French trader and he was never adopted into the tribe, Logan Fontenelle probably did not qualify for chieftainship, yet despite his questionable credentials, when he died in 1855, both Agent George Hepner and Omaha leader Joseph La Flesche referred to him as a principal chief.[30]

Properly signed or not, the 1854 treaty became effective, and Commissioner Manypenny instructed Agent Hepner to take a party of Omahas north to inspect their reservation so that they could be moved early in the spring of 1855.[31] Of the Omahas, only Logan Fontenelle agreed to accompany Hepner so far north. Along with Thomas Griffy, a white man whose status is unclear, Fontenelle and the agent made their way north to Ayoway Creek. On their return, Hepner filed a report totally rejecting the proposed reservation. It was, he said, too cold, too hilly for farming, and much too close to the Sioux and the Poncas. The agent did not believe the Omahas could survive there: "Should they be compelled to locate on this reservation, I doubt whether one would be left to tell their fate in twelve months." The area the Omahas wanted, and needed in order to survive, ran from the middle of the main channel of the Missouri River east of the lower end of Black Bird Hills, then eighteen miles up the main channel of the river. This area, approximately three hundred thousand acres, was eighty miles north of Bellevue; it possessed trees, arable land, and probably ample water for mills. Hepner urged the government to provide protection and to move the Omahas there as soon as possible. Based on Hepner's unfavorable view of the Ayoway Creek region, St. Louis Indian Office clerk John Haverty recommended that the Black Bird Hills site be substituted.[32]

This was the story told in the official correspondence on the Ayoway Creek rejection. But in a deposition before Nebraska Territorial Secretary Thomas Cuming on behalf of Dr. B. Y. Shelley, whose land became part of the Omaha Reservation, Thomas Griffy told a different story. In Griffy's version, Fontenelle and Hepner admitted they were simply "going through the motions" and had no intention of even looking at the land to the north. Fontenelle claimed to be familiar with the area, and as "the principal chief and business agent of the Omahas," he refused to accept it, insisting instead on Black Bird Hills. In reply, Hepner intimated that the Indians could get that desirable land only if he agreed and that he would agree, for the right price.[33] If accurate, Griffy's testimony showed Hepner to be an opportunist out to line his own pockets. The agent's offer to accept a bribe gave credence to Joseph La Flesche's accusation that he was involved in a partnership with Peter Sarpy and Logan Fontenelle and perhaps explained why Iowa Senator A. C. Dodge wanted to know if Sarpy accompanied Hepner on his inspection tour.[34]

As early as January 1854, before the treaty negotiations and long before the Omahas made their wishes known, two Iowa congressmen forwarded to Interior Secretary Robert McClelland a letter from Council Bluffs businessman Hadley Johnson strongly objecting to locating the Omahas at Black Bird Hills. To Johnson's protest, the legislators added their own, not for political reasons, they said, but for the sake of peace, prosperity, and the welfare of the Indians. They argued that a reservation at Black Bird Hills would place the Omahas close to sources of liquor and too close to white citizens already seething over numerous alleged Omaha depredations.[35] As if to underscore the Iowa delegation's objections, petitions and claims from Harrison County, Iowa, arrived in Commissioner Manypenny's office, along with the request for a treaty provision to pay for depredations by Indians.[36]

Word that the Omahas had definitely chosen to settle at Black Bird Hills generated a flood of letters to the Bureau of Indian Affairs from Iowa lawmakers and their constituents and from speculators who had designs on these fertile lands. Writing to his congressman on behalf of "many citizens" of Woodbury and Monona Counties in Iowa, Addison Cochran, himself a large landowner, pointed out that some families had already settled at Black Bird Hills to take advantage of the good soil and abundant timber and water and that they wanted "other neighbors than Indians who [had] been in the habit of killing or driving off their stock." Cochran asked the congressman to please use his influence to locate the Omahas elsewhere.[37] Enos Lowe of Council Bluffs wrote that an Omaha reservation would interfere with "the great Railway Route North of the Platte," and he pointed out that an election district had already been marked off at Black Bird Hills.[38] Iowa's congressmen agreed wholeheartedly with Lowe and urged Manypenny not to approve the Omahas' move, since it would mean "eventual injury both to the Whites and the Indians."[39] Hadley Johnson expressed surprise that the Omahas were going to Black Bird Hills, since Senator

Dodge had told him that such a move would not happen. Johnson considered the locating of Omahas there to be "bad policy" because he was sure the Indians were plotting another, more lucrative treaty and they would be moved again in the near future.[40]

In view of all the protest letters, Secretary McClelland began to have second thoughts regarding the Omahas' reservation choice. Perhaps to buy time, he instructed Manypenny to have Agent Hepner conduct a second exploration of the ceded land to find a less controversial home for the tribe.[41] When he received McClelland's orders, Hepner fired off a blistering letter explaining why a reinvestigation was unnecessary and also disclosing underhanded dealings by white settlers and speculators. He refused to look for another reservation site because (1) it was midwinter, (2) the selection was to be made only with the Omahas' consent, (3) he knew they would not accept any other location, (4) the Omahas had once lived at Black Bird Hills but had been driven away by the Sioux, and (5) he had trouble getting the Omahas to go north of Fort Calhoun, only a short distance above the Bellevue Agency.[42]

The angry agent then shredded white objections, point by point. Discussing the mythical white village at Black Bird Hills, Hepner reported that when he was there in November 1854, no one lived there and no settlement preparations had been made. The only structure was a $2.00 "claim house" built by a Council Bluffs company in which Hadley Johnson was a partner. Under the circumstances, Hepner said the president need not worry about "driving off white settlers to accommodate the speculating Indians" because "none [were] there to chase." He admitted that an election district called Tecama (now the Tekamah area) had been established, with polling places at Tecama and Black Bird Hills, but added that this was a front to make it appear that people lived there. Apparently, families from Council Bluffs and other communities each sent a representative north to be counted. At election time, Hepner claimed that a group started for Tecama, "got within twenty miles of the place, halted in the prairie, held the election and returned." As a result, "some fifty [voters] were [listed] in the district, when in fact not a family lived in it." Hepner could not understand why a reservation at Black Bird Hills would pose a problem for a railroad, since the proposed reservation site extended only eighteen miles along the Missouri River and since whites would settle only near the river, where there was timber. As for drunken Indians committing depredations, the agent said the Omahas drank less than any equal number of whites.[43]

Hepner knew the government wanted to locate the Omahas as far north as possible, but he reminded his superiors that because of fear of the Sioux, no one but Logan Fontenelle had offered to investigate the Ayoway Creek site with him. In Hepner's opinion, forcing or even persuading the Omahas to locate north of Ayoway Creek would be an "act of inhumanity," since he even anticipated problems moving the Indians to Black Bird Hills without protection.[44]

Realizing that the Omahas had the right to choose their reservation but not wanting to deprive white settlers of the rich Black Bird Hills land, Manypenny proposed a compromise, suggesting that the Omahas make their home on the Big Blue River, near the Otoe Reservation. Secretary McClelland agreed, but only if the Omahas consented to the move. If they refused to go south, he wanted them located at Black Bird Hills.[45] In compliance with telegraphed instructions, Agent Hepner presented Manypenny's plan to the Omahas, who flatly rejected the offer, arguing correctly that their treaty gave them permission to go where they chose. They vowed to plant their corn near Bellevue and not to leave the vicinity of the agency until they had received their annuities in cash. Calling his determined charges "saucy and contrary," Hepner suggested a "show of force" to make them leave immediately.[46] But the government had a treaty to honor, and on May 11, 1855, McClelland gave Manypenny permission to move the Indians to Black Bird Hills and to place the area off-limits to whites.[47] Later that month, the Omahas arrived at their new home. In early June, Hepner reported that the trek north from Bellevue had gone well except that the Indians, as predicted, had balked at going north of Fort Calhoun. Only the assurances of leaders such as Joseph La Flesche and Lewis Saunsoci, and the promise of money when they arrived at Black Bird Hills, persuaded them to move on.[48]

Letters of protest continued even after the Omahas arrived at their reservation. In June 1855, a vindictive B. Y. Shelley, who later would successfully petition Congress for reimbursement of money spent in developing his Black Bird Hills land, accused Hepner of duplicity and charged that a few "half-breed" speculators were involved in this "fraud." He said settlers wanted their land back and did not want to be driven from their homes "at the point of the scalping knife."[49] But in a petition to the president, residents of Nebraska Territory and Iowa stated perhaps the true reason that the Omahas were unwelcome at Black Bird Hills. The residents did not want Indians to have "the most highly favored section of the territory."[50]

Just eleven days after Hepner described the uneventful trip to Black Bird Hills, a party of Yankton or Santee Sioux murdered an Omaha just six miles from the tribe's camp. Unnerved but determined, the Omahas left on their summer hunt, but Hepner was sure they would have problems on the plains.[51] Once again the agent was right. He left the Omahas to escort the Otoes and Missourias to their reservation on the Big Blue River and returned to discover that Logan Fontenelle and five others had been killed and scalped by Sioux in a battle on Beaver Creek, in present-day Boone County, Nebraska.[52] Accounts of Fontenelle's death vary slightly, but most agree that he was hunting with a small party eight to ten miles from the main Omaha camp when he was surprised by a Sioux war party. Others hunting nearby, including La Flesche, returned safely to camp. That evening, the Omaha hunters buried the five known victims of the Sioux attack. Because Fontenelle "had a fast horse," his fellow tribesmen assumed he had escaped. But on their way home, the Omaha hunters discovered Fontenelle's bullet-riddled and arrow-pierced body. On a trip that took ten days, the frightened and grief-stricken Omahas carried his body to Bellevue for burial.[53]

Fontenelle's murder was a psychological blow to the troubled Omahas. After they buried him, they refused to return to Black Bird Hills and instead camped along the Platte River, about fifteen miles west of Bellevue. Saying they could do nothing while "so exposed to their enemies the Sioux," the Omahas asked to "borrow a piece of ground from their great father" until they received protection at Black Bird Hills.[54] Agent Hepner suggested that the Omahas join the Otoes on the Blue River, but they refused to live among other tribes. Commissioner Manypenny agreed to let the Omahas spend the winter near Bellevue, with the understanding that they would return to their reservation in the spring. But the people had no corn planted and were afraid to hunt.[55]

The Omahas remained huddled on the Platte, badly frightened, with little food and no real leader. To add to their misery, white settlers near Bellevue threatened to drive them away, but the Omahas stood their ground, preferring to be killed by whites than by the Sioux.[56] Both J. B. Robertson, the agency farmer, and Agent Hepner pleaded with the Omahas to return to Black Bird Hills. Robertson pointed out that the recent disaster would not have happened had they been settled and farming. Some of the headmen agreed, and the farmer thought they might return if given protection. In mid-October, Hepner spent three days in council with the Omahas but reported little progress. The Indians admitted they feared not only the Poncas and the Sioux but also traders from Sergeant Bluff, Iowa, who had threatened to call the Sioux down on the Omaha camps.[57]

Black Bird Hills was very special to the Omahas, but in their fear they would have relinquished the lands of their choice. Speaking in a September 1855 tribal council, Standing Hawk and La Flesche asked to exchange their reservation for one on the Platte River, where their lives and homes would be safe. Pouring out the pain and frustration the entire tribe must have felt, Standing Hawk decried the loss of their land, the delay in annuity payments, their forced removal, and the death of Logan Fontenelle due to lack of protection.[58]

Peter Sarpy delivered the Omaha leaders' speeches to Manypenny in Washington and returned with the commissioner's proposal that the Omahas unite with the Pawnees. According to Sarpy, the Omahas approved the plan and even offered to sell the Pawnees part of their land. To ensure that the Omahas would stay on their reservation when they returned from their fall hunt, Sarpy sent supplies to Black Bird Hills and planned to arrange peace treaties between the Omahas and the Poncas and among the Sioux bands. In late November, the trader informed Manypenny that he believed the Omahas had been persuaded to leave their temporary camp on the Platte.[59] Sarpy's arguments must have been convincing, because the Omahas did return to Black Bird Hills in May 1856. However, the Pawnees did not join them, the proposed peace treaties never materialized, and the Omahas were once again unprotected and on their own.

As it did in so many treaties, the government failed to keep its promises to the Omahas. Annuity payments came late; mills were delayed and often inoperative; the government expected the Indians to farm without capital or machinery; and the Omahas remained victims of Sioux attacks through the mid-1860s. They lived in constant fear, staying as far south and east on the reservation as they could. When their newly arrived Presbyterian minister, William Hamilton, mentioned in 1856 that he might locate the mission school near the northern border of the reserve, the Omahas warned: "Do not go there. The Sioux will kill the children."[60] In 1859 alone, Sioux raiding parties stole fifty-nine horses, and summer hunts remained risky. The 1859 hunt on the plains of central Nebraska ended in tragedy; a party of seventy Omahas, mostly the old and the ill who could not keep up, were attacked by either Cheyennes, Arapahoes, or Sioux. Seventeen Omahas died, but not before the group took four enemy scalps.[61]

In September 1860, an outlaw Santee Sioux band or a party of Brulé Sioux under Little Thunder attacked the Omahas within sight of the mission and threatened to torch the agency buildings. Following this outrage, many Omahas deserted their villages, and some even left the reservation, actions that of course brought complaints from nearby settlers. Agent George Graff worried about the Omahas' livelihood as well as their safety, fearing they would starve if they did not return to plant corn.[62] At a council earlier in the year, La Flesche had reminded the government of its treaty obligation to protect his people, but months later they continued to wait for the protection promised them six years earlier.[63] Omahas and whites on the reservation were quickly losing patience with the government and with the Sioux. The Indians threatened to retaliate, and after eleven Winnebagoes temporarily residing on the Omaha Reservation were murdered, Agent Robert Furnas built an unauthorized two-story log blockhouse as an armory and a place of refuge, arming it with a six-pound cannon he found on the prairie. The agency also established a cavalry unit composed of whites, mixed-bloods, and English-speaking Omahas, who hoped to receive arms and ammunition from Fort Leavenworth, Kansas.[64]

In 1865, Acting Commissioner of Indian Affairs R. B. Van Valkenburgh asked Agent Furnas to send him a report on Sioux depredations so that he could determine how to reimburse the Omahas for their losses. With the aid of testimony from Omaha chiefs and headmen, two former agents, and mission employees, Furnas compiled a detailed list of thirteen Sioux attacks dating from June 1854 to May 1865. In the raids, $1,000 worth of personal property had been stolen; the Omahas had lost 152 horses, and twenty-two of their people had been slain. Furnas calculated the value of the horses at $60 each, and since "there ought to attach some pecuniary consideration for loss of life," he considered the twenty-two Omaha lives to be worth a total of $2,000. Reminding the Indian Office that the Omahas were "a loyal and peaceable tribe," he asked that their claim be seriously considered.[65] But in 1875, the tribe had not yet been compensated for losses at the hands of the Sioux.[66]

In December 1854, Saunsoci had asked Agent Hepner when he would be paid the $1,000 provided him in the March treaty.[67] This is but one of many instances of late payments, underpayments, and arbitrary deductions from money owed the Omahas. For example, the Omaha Agency had no funds for the first nine months of 1861, and Agent O. H. Irish had to use his own money plus credit to keep the mill and farm operating.[68] Annuities often came late and on no particular schedule, requiring agents and superintendents to remind the government that the Omahas were in need.[69]

In some cases, it appears that the government deliberately cheated the tribe. In 1862, La Flesche wanted to know why most of the Omaha annuity was paid in paper money when the more rebellious tribes received theirs in silver and gold. He considered the practice unfair, since it made a $7,000 difference in the Omahas' yearly income and since the government expected its payments in coin. When the Omaha annuity fell short in 1864, Agent Furnas investigated and found that without the tribe's knowledge, funds had been deducted to pay for a trampled field, a stolen horse, and "expenses" to a former agent's widow.[70] In 1866, the chiefs and headmen questioned the payment of part of their annuity in goods when they had previously been paid cash; with the many deductions reducing their payment, they needed the cash.[71] In addition, the Omahas waited more than fifty years to be paid for the additional 483,365 acres of land they had ceded to the government when they had chosen their smaller reservation at Black Bird Hills. It was not until they filed suit with the U.S. Court of Claims in 1910 that they received $94,739.34, or 19.6 cents per acre, for the extra land.[72]

In 1855, Commissioner Manypenny had reported that the Omahas would have a sawmill "next season." Seasons came and went; in October 1856 and again in the fall of 1857, Agent Robertson urged the Indian Office to erect the promised mill, since many Omahas wanted to build homes and live like whites.[73] When encouraged not to go on the hunt, one chief asked, "What can we do if we stay here, we have nothing to do with?"[74] The Omahas finally received their sawmill in the summer of 1858, but after running for three or four months, its boiler exploded, putting the mill out of commission for a year and a half.[75] On the tenth anniversary of the treaty, the chiefs wanted to know if the ten-year life of the mill dated from the treaty signing, from the ratification, or from the actual installation of the equipment. Asked to investigate, Agent Furnas contacted former Omaha farmer Joseph Betz, who corroborated the Omahas' testimony that the mill had successfully operated for only five and one-half of the promised ten years. Consequently, Furnas recommended repairing the mill and continuing its operation for at least one more year so that all the Omahas could build homes. The mill continued to run but eventually had to be rebuilt.[76]

The sawmill was an integral part of the Omahas' efforts to become more like whites, since it enabled them to build frame houses to replace their earth lodges. Once on the reservation, the people clustered in three villages four to five miles apart: farthest south was Ton´-won-ga-hae's village; Ish´-ka-da-be's earth lodge settlement was in the center; farther north, La Flesche and the progressive Omahas of his "young men's party" formed a village patterned after white communities. Built near the proposed Presbyterian mission, La Flesche's cluster of neat frame homes and gardens became known derisively by more traditional Omahas as the "make-believe white man's village." By 1861, La Flesche's little town boasted nineteen homes—more than in the neighboring white village of Decatur, Nebraska. But after 1865, residents gradually abandoned the white man's village as they moved onto allotments. Despite its desertion, the village never became a ghost town, since a shortage of building materials required the homes' owners to tear them down and reassemble them on the new farms. In 1888, all that remained of La Flesche's village was a list of its occupants and a tiny sketch "drawn from memory by one of the Indians who [had] lived there."[77]

Joseph La Flesche, also called E-sta´-ma-za or "Iron Eye," dominated Omaha history during the early reservation years. The son of French trader Joseph La Flesche Sr. and an Indian woman,[78] La Flesche lived among the Omahas and earned the respect of their leaders. Adopted by the revered Big Elk, La Flesche joined the Omaha tribal council sometime between 1845 and 1850 and became a principal chief on Big Elk's death in 1853. A trader, tribal leader, campaigner for acculturation, and Christian, La Flesche has been described as a "man of sagacity, integrity and intelligence" as well as a self-serving, "shrewd . . . Indian Politician."[79] Like his mentor, he admired whites and believed his people could survive only by adopting their ways. Much to the annoyance of the more conservative Omahas, La Flesche supported a white style of education and befriended the missionaries assigned to the Omaha Reservation. Yet he never completely abandoned Omaha traditions; for years he participated in the hunt, and he had several wives.

After witnessing a murder during a drunken brawl, La Flesche had promised himself that if he ever achieved a position of authority, he would prohibit drinking among his people. When he became a chief, he used $1,000 in tribal funds to establish a police force to stop drunkenness. Punishment was severe; regardless of station, anyone caught drinking could be flogged.[80] Of course, La Flesche's authority did not go unopposed. Members of the "chiefs' party," who wanted to retain the tribal hunt and other ancient ways, resisted his attempts at acculturation and at one point threatened his life.[81] But Agent Irish considered the Omahas lucky to have such a chief, and the Presbyterians sang his praises, saying that he was "doing everything in his power to civilize and elevate his people." Charles Sturges, superintendent of the mission school, called La Flesche "an industrious man, [and] a friend of the mission," but qualified the praise, cautioning, "Money is his idol."[82]

It was La Flesche's pursuit of power and of the Omaha trading dollar that led to his conflict with the equally ambitious Agent Robert Furnas in 1865. On the reservation, La Flesche and Henry Fontenelle served in the lucrative and coveted positions of traders for the Omahas, who strenuously resisted having a white trader among them. Shortly before he left the agency in 1864, Agent Irish appointed the two mixed-bloods official traders, but their credentials were delayed so that the new agent, Furnas, could share in the trading decision. Furnas, who would be a decisive factor in La Flesche's career, owed his position as Omaha agent to Samuel G. Daily, congressional delegate for Nebraska Territory, and Daily had his own ideas about who should secure the Omaha trade. Cautioning Furnas not to give the business to "those half-Breeds at the Reserve," Daily told the agent to appoint the best man as trader, making sure to give him as small a portion of the proceeds as possible. Furnas chose Robert Teare of Brownville, Nebraska, for the job. Although the official "trader," Teare was merely an employee; Furnas, Daily, and Indian Commissioner William P. Dole invested in the trade and split the profits.[83] The financial arrangement among Furnas, Daily, and Dole was a good example of an "Indian ring," which usually consisted of a politician, an agent, and a trader. "The politician appointed the agent, who in turn contracted the services of a trader, who in most cases had a monopoly." Teare now had the trading license, but Fontenelle and La Flesche continued to sell goods to both the Omahas and the recently arrived Winnebagoes. When Teare protested, Commissioner Dole, concerned about profits, told Furnas to stop their activity, with troops if necessary.[84]

As a former Civil War military commander, Furnas expected to be obeyed. Along with the trading issue, La Flesche may have annoyed the agent by not submitting to his authority. Whatever the reasons, Furnas never missed an opportunity to accuse the chief of obstructionism, self-aggrandizement, and hypocrisy. In a bitter indictment, Furnas charged La Flesche with "producing discord among the tribe," leaving the reservation without permission, encouraging tribal police to inflict unfair punishment, lending money at usurious rates, and refusing to allow his people to deal with licensed traders. Furnas claimed that it was the "accidental" chief's wealth, not his personal popularity, that kept him in power. Citing his lavish feasts, Furnas quoted La Flesche as saying that he could "fill the Omahas' bellies and then do as he pleas[ed] with them." If true, the agent's most serious charges showed La Flesche to be an enemy of his own people. According to Furnas, the chief advertised his support of tribal advancement but behind the scenes did everything he could to hold the Omahas back. What most incensed Furnas was La Flesche's opposition to an

1865 treaty amendment providing universal Indian education. Accusing the chief of wanting only his own children to have a white education, Furnas charged that La Flesche, that "dreadful incubus upon the tribe," would not, "if he could help it, allow the masses to be educated or benefited, for then they would be *equal with him*."[85]

Furnas argued that as long as La Flesche pulled the tribal strings, the Omahas would not progress. Therefore, the agent recommended that he be permanently deposed as chief and, if necessary, banished from the reservation. Superintendent E. B. Taylor agreed with Furnas' assessment, but newly appointed Indian Commissioner Dennis Cooley was reluctant to take such harsh measures against an influential Omaha who had been of such use to the government in the past. Since La Flesche's actions seemed to be heavily influenced by mission school superintendent Rev. R. J. Burtt, Cooley asked the Presbyterian Church to recall Burtt, in the hope that his removal would change the chief's behavior. According to Furnas, La Flesche had boasted that the missionary would shield him from any charges of misconduct. Burtt was dismissed, and with his alleged protector gone, La Flesche hastily fled the reservation with his entire family on the night of April 17, 1866.[86] A few months later, Furnas reluctantly admitted that he may have judged La Flesche too harshly and agreed to allow the former leader back on the reservation, but only if La Flesche was willing to be "subordinate to the agent."[87] La Flesche did return home, but he never again held a seat on the tribal council and apparently was recognized as a leader only among his band of followers in the young men's party.[88]

Was La Flesche a self-serving politician as Furnas charged, or did he really want to see his people advance? Did he worship money? In the long run, did he help or hinder his people? The questions are legion. Most of the evidence shows a man who correctly gauged the future and wanted his people, and especially his own family, to be prepared for the white world. His campaign to stop alcoholism was truly admirable, though his methods were not. In trying to force his people along the white man's road, perhaps he pushed too hard. In an assessment of his career, it appears odd that the only real criticism of this remarkable man, besides criticism from rival chiefs, came from an Indian agent with a hidden agenda. But La Flesche may have done his people a disservice simply by being who he was—an acculturated, high-profile Christian Indian whose image possibly convinced reformers and the government that all Omahas could become land-owning farmers. Perhaps it is best to let Joseph La Flesche speak for himself. Suffering from complications from an improperly amputated leg and confronting his own mortality, he was quoted as stating that all he lived for was "to see his people on the road of improvement, their money matters all made straight, and the Mission full."[89]

Furnas, with "friends in high places" and an involvement in a profitable Indian ring, wielded more power than most other Omaha agents, and his personal feud with La Flesche certainly set him apart. In his correspondence and his actions, Furnas appeared grasping, domineering, and vindictive, and perhaps he was. But for the most part, he did a good job under trying conditions. Reformers and the government dictated Indian policy, but the agents were the ones who dealt with everyday affairs. The temptation to cheat was strong. Generally far from Washington, agents often became despots and occasionally became thieves. Most agents were overworked; all were underpaid. It took a man of rare character to settle himself, and often his family, in the western wilderness for $1,500 a year. "For the weak and dishonest, it was a wide-open opportunity for quick wealth; for the honest man, it was an impossible job."[90]

Omaha agents were no different from others in these respects. Although the 1860s are considered the most corrupt period in nineteenth-century Indian administration, three Omaha agents in succession had left their posts under questionable circumstances in the 1850s. George Hepner, already suspect for his alleged role in the reservation selection, soon came under fire for neglecting the Omahas and being in league with a group of Indian leaders. According to the missionary Hamilton and citizens of Council Bluffs, Hepner lived in St. Mary's, Iowa, and saw the Indians under his care only when absolutely necessary. In 1856, responding to numerous complaints, Nebraska Territorial Secretary Thomas B. Cuming filed a formal protest with Commissioner Manypenny.[91] But charges that Hepner shorted the Omahas on provisions proved his undoing. When a shipment of flour bound for the Indians arrived in Omaha and was determined to be underweight and of poor quality, *The Nebraskian*, Omaha's territorial newspaper, attacked the agent in print. Noting that Hepner was conspicuously absent when the flour arrived, an editorialist asked, "Was he a party to the attempt to defraud the poor Indians, furnishing them inferior flour at the prices of a better article?"[92] In February 1856, Secretary of War Robert McClelland ordered Hepner to explain his actions or risk removal from office. Hepner defended himself to the satisfaction of investigator Daniel Vanderslice, who claimed that the agent had been the target of a "smear campaign" by merchants who wanted to discredit him and replace him with someone more "pliable." Despite Vanderslice's recommendation that he be returned to duty, Hepner was suspended, and he never returned to the Omaha Agency.[93]

J. B. Robertson, a former Omaha farmer who replaced Hepner as agent in 1856, appears to have been an extortionist and a thief. Robertson was universally disliked by the agency Presbyterians, who accused him of neglecting the Omahas and undermining their mission.[94] William Hamilton was convinced that Robertson played a role in an alleged plot to move the Omahas to Ponca lands to open their reservation to speculators. In Hamilton's view, tricking the Omahas out of their lands would be as simple as "mak[ing] a chief or two and brib[ing] one interpreter.[95] Robertson may also have misappropriated Omaha funds. Shortly after taking office, he deposited $2,000 with the Western Fire & Marine Insurance Company in Omaha at 3 percent interest per month. In September 1857, Robertson approached the company auditor, saying he needed the cash back because it was "government money, and if not paid would lead to his ruin and disgrace." When the company balked, Robertson threatened to have his son, who edited *The Nebraskian*, attack the firm in the press.[96] In addition, the construction of an agency building gave the dishonest agent another occasion to skim government funds—by charging $600 for a $450 construction job. Robertson was discharged during the summer of 1858, but a fourth charge finally attracted the government's attention. In 1866, the Omahas claimed that Robertson had kept part of the $25,000 provided them in the appropriation act of August 1851, and an investigation of the agent's books showed discrepancies. The Indians were right, and the government agreed to a $13,000 settlement for the stolen funds. In 1882, payment was still pending.[97]

Robertson's replacement, William F. Wilson, lost his position as Omaha agent on the strength of a quite possibly forged letter. On June 11, 1859, in a tribal council, the Omaha chiefs and headmen allegedly signed a petition to have Agent Wilson removed from office because he was "too old and infirm," had refused to pay their annuity at their village, and had exposed them to whiskey sellers. In addition, the Indians claimed that he replaced a competent engineer with an untrained one and refused to pay Indian employees. The Omaha chiefs later denied any knowledge of the letter, written by Henry Fontenelle, and categorically denied every charge that Fontenelle brought against Wilson. In a signed statement, Lewis Saunsoci accused Fontenelle of forging his signature, and the testimony of two white men from Decatur, Nebraska, who had spoken to Fontenelle in Omaha on the afternoon of the supposed council supported Saunsoci's charges.[98]

Why would Henry Fontenelle forge such a letter? At this point the plot takes an interesting twist. The chiefs, Omaha Hiram Chase, and agency farmer David Jones all testified that in mid-June, Nebraska Governor S. W. Black, Territorial Marshall William A. West, and "one Mr. Patrick" visited the Omaha village.[99] Governor Black passed himself off as the commissioner of Indian affairs while West claimed to be the new Omaha agent. The three men gave the Omahas money and asked leading questions whose "answers" appeared in the "petition." All the evidence indicates an attempt to discredit Wilson, who believed West wanted his job and had dictated the "petition."[100] Despite the three men's mysterious visit, letters of support from missionaries and local citizens, and his own believable defense in which he claimed to be the victim of a vendetta by a "corrupt" tribal faction, Wilson was summarily dismissed on October 17, 1859.[101]

Whereas some agents and many outsiders hoped to profit from the Omahas, missionaries hoped to change them. In 1846, the Board of Foreign Missions of the Presbyterian Church established a mission and a boarding school at Bellevue for the Otoes and Omahas. When the Omahas moved to their reservation in 1855, the Presbyterians and their ethnocentricity went along. Charles Sturges, an early mission school superintendent, told the Omahas in council that the missionaries had come "to tell them how to live and how to die," and he gave them the impression that their tribe would disappear if they did not educate their children and accept the white man's God.[102]

The churchmen criticized or ridiculed what they did not understand. Sturges complained that several "chiefs and men" wanted to observe the Sabbath but had no concept of time. One Indian recognized the Sabbath because that was the day the missionary came to see the Indians, and another counted on his fingers to represent the seventh as Sunday. R. J. Burtt of the Omaha mission thought the Omaha language "a very poor one," with a "scarcity of . . . words" to communicate religious ideas. Admitting that pride probably prevented the Omahas from being emotional, Sturges accused the Indians of underreacting to his gospel message.[103] Presbyterians also believed that the Omahas were immoral, a belief that seems strangely hypocritical in light of moral lapses by the churchmen. Burtt reputedly had an extramarital affair, causing La Flesche to remark that he had "as good a right to another wife as Mr. Burt [*sic*]."[104] In 1854, William Hamilton borrowed $1,800 from La Flesche with the understanding that La Flesche would earn 10 percent interest and would have the money back in six months. Three years later, La Flesche, who could not read English, learned that the note read 6 percent interest, not 10. Only the intervention of Sturges prevented La Flesche from suing Hamilton for his money.[105]

The Presbyterians, along with Omaha agents, advocated a program of forced acculturation by discouraging common ownership of property, by attempting to depose chiefs, and by curtailing hunts, even though the hunts were often the Omahas' only source of meat. Instead, missionaries encouraged private landownership, acquisitiveness, and detribalization of the Omahas.[106] But they directed most of their energy toward changing the Omaha children, believing that white ways learned at an early age would become permanent. In 1858, Sturges asked the government to force Omaha chiefs to send all children ages eight to fourteen to the mission school to "fill up [the] school and keep it so." Seven years later, Agent Furnas recommended that the treaty of that year include a provision requiring parents to educate children ages five to twenty or lose their annuities.[107]

The acculturation process began by missionaries giving their students English names to replace their difficult-to-pronounce and "heathenish" Indian ones. Traditional Indian dress was taboo, as noted by La Flesche's son Francis, who related an incident from his days at the mission school. Wanting to look his best, an Omaha boy arrived at school for the first time dressed in his "embroidered moccasins, his leggings and [his] little buffalo robe," and he was immediately sent to the storeroom, where La Flesche and a fellow student outfitted him with white-style clothing. His fine Indian costume was bundled up and returned to his parents. Since the government and the church considered the English language basic to civilization, children were forbidden to speak in Omaha, a rule "rigidly enforced with a hickory rod." But despite the rules and the rod, there remained, as Burtt noted, "a too general disposition to converse in their native language."[108] The Presbyterians meant well, and they hoped their presence would "humanize government policy" and help the Omahas survive. Board of Foreign Missions Secretary Walter Lowrie believed agriculture would solve all the Omahas' problems. All they had to do, according to Lowrie, was "to give up their hunting, and settle each on his own farm, and live like white men."[109] It would not be that easy.

In 1869, President Ulysses S. Grant's "Quaker Policy" brought Hicksite Friends to the Omaha Reservation as agents. Like the Presbyterians, these Quakers misunderstood and underappreciated Omaha culture and the huge problems confronting the tribe. Also, like the Presbyterians, they hoped to turn the Omahas into "civilized," Christian farmers. The Friends treated the Indians as "spiritual equals" but "cultural inferiors" who must learn white ways or perish. Important to their aims were the allotment of lands and the creation of individual farms, both of which contributed to the destruction of traditional Indian government and social structure.[110]

At first, Presbyterian missionary William Hamilton, Quaker Agent Edward Painter, and Painter's superintendent, Samuel M. Janney, had a good relationship, and a Quaker report in 1869 praised Hamilton's efforts, vowing that the Friends would work "shoulder to shoulder" with him to improve the Omahas.[111] But Hamilton soon fell out of favor with the Quakers and most of the Omahas when he interfered in tribal politics by defending La Flesche in his power struggle with conservative chiefs. Probably because of the relationship among Hamilton, La Flesche, and the mission boarding school, the chiefs in 1868 asked to have the school terminated and replaced with two or more day schools. Acting in concert with the request of tribal leaders and Superintendent Janney, Commissioner of Indian Affairs Ely S. Parker canceled the Presbyterians' school contract effective September 30, 1869.[112]

Although the Omaha chiefs requested the boarding school closing a year before the Quakers arrived, Hamilton blamed the Friends for the temporary demise of the school. The feud between the religious groups continued for years, finally degenerating into a war of words on the pages of Alfred B. Meacham's national Indian advocacy newspaper, *Council Fire*. In September 1879, Meacham published a letter sent by eleven Omahas, probably at the urging of Hamilton; they asked the government not to replace Quaker agent Jacob Vore with Barclay White, the current Winnebago agent. Apparently the Indians misspoke: what they meant to say was that they wanted no more Quaker agents because the Friends had closed the boarding school. Vore then attacked Hamilton, calling him anti-Quaker and accusing him of using "ignorant" Indians to convey his own message. Vore denied any Quaker involvement in the boarding school closing and referred Hamilton to his own 1869 report, in which Hamilton thanked Janney and Painter, both Quakers, for their support and kind words. In March 1880, J. Owen Dorsey announced that Hamilton was not sectarian and that all the Omahas had complained about Quaker agents.[113]

The Friends' stewardship among the Omahas was unsuccessful, but outside influences contributed significantly to their failure. For five years of their regime, Nebraska farmlands were attacked by grass-hoppers, and the Omahas' final buffalo hunt in 1876–77 was so unsuccessful that the starving Indians resorted to begging for food at Fort Hays, Kansas, where General John Pope issued them $340 worth of rations. But mostly, Quaker expectations were simply too high.[114] By 1876, Nebraska congressmen wanted only Nebraska citizens to serve as agents within the state, and as a result, the Senate rejected many Quaker candidates. One by one the Hicksite Friends lost their posts, until none remained in 1885.[115]

Of course, not all Omaha acculturation during the early reservation years was forced by whites. Tribal leaders roughly divided along "traditional" and "progressive" lines, with Joseph La Flesche and his followers representing the latter category. Letters translated by anthropologist Dorsey or those published by Meacham in *Council Fire* reveal the Omaha progressives' desire to "improve." Admitting they were a tribal minority, the letter writers all wanted to be farmers and follow white ways.[116] On the other hand, so-called Omaha reactionaries refused to leave their earth lodges and wanted no money spent on agriculture, physical improvements, or medical care. The parents of some children who wanted to attend school were afraid to send them for fear of being whipped. Hamilton believed these Omaha parents had been threatened by traditional chiefs under orders from former agent W. P. Callon and Superintendent H. B. Denman to keep the children away from the mission school. Tired of the Indians being pulled in several directions by interfering whites, Hamilton admitted it would be "a blessing to the nation if the white man were removed from the reservation."[117]

Of the tribal conservatives, Little Chief appeared to be the most troublesome to the agents; he controlled the more traditional Indians, obstructed justice, and threatened to drive whites off the reservation. The progressives hated him because he removed Indian children from the mission school, and both Agent Irish and Agent Furnas recommended that he be stripped of his title, since he impeded Omaha "progress."[118] But Little Chief was not alone; other tribes resented Omaha progressives as well. In a joint council, the Otoes cautioned Omaha chiefs not to try to become white men because they would fare badly. La Flesche disagreed: "Look back on the lives of your fathers and grandfathers; then look at yourselves, and see how far you have gone ahead, and seeing this, do not stop and turn back to them, but go forward. Look ahead and you will see nothing but the white man. The future is full of the white man and we shall be as nothing before them."[119]

As the Omahas "progressed," their government was modified to suit whites. Because tribal meetings were unproductive and "cumbersome," the agents organized a council of as many as nine "paper chiefs" whose tenure rested on good behavior and who could be "easily called together by the agent." Although chiefs were no longer independent, Quaker agents advocated abolishing the office altogether, since chiefs "insisted on special privileges and impeded tribal progress and 'republicanism.'" Most of the Omaha people must have agreed; in

August 1877, they petitioned the commissioner of Indian affairs to allow them to "remove [their traditional] chiefs and try some other way." They wanted to elect their leaders as white men did, but the embattled chiefs claimed that the "great Father made [them] chiefs" and that the people could not remove them from office. They were deposed, however. In March 1880, encouraged by Jacob Vore, their last Quaker agent, the Omahas elected seven chiefs with equal authority. This leadership committee would later be expanded to ten members. The new council of chiefs appeared to be democratic because it included representatives from the conservative and the progressive tribal factions as well as a group of impartial leaders. But because the council had been established by Vore according to his guidelines, Alice Fletcher and Francis La Flesche later claimed that "all governing power [became] centered in the United States Indian Agent." The era of the principal chiefs had ended.[120]

Amid the turmoil of the 1860s, the Omahas found themselves inundated by hundreds of destitute Winnebagoes fleeing the arid, desolate Crow Creek Reservation in Dakota Territory. A canoeload at a time, half-starved Winnebagoes arrived at the Omaha Reservation, and by May 1864, nearly twelve hundred of these strangers had moved onto Omaha lands.[121] Since 1832, when they had ceded their lands near Lake Winnebago in Wisconsin to the government, the Winnebagoes had been relocated, against their will, on several occasions. Their 1832 treaty had granted them lands in the "neutral ground," a forty-mile-wide tract running from the Mississippi to the Des Moines River. In 1837, they were given about eight months to relocate to their new home. Unfortunately, their presence on the neutral ground caused problems for the Sac, Fox, and Sioux tribes, who had been promised that the tract would be a buffer zone. The three tribes threatened to remove the Winnebagoes, by force if necessary. In 1842, the Iowa territorial legislature petitioned Congress to relocate the Winnebagoes because it feared an Indian war, which might endanger whites in Iowa. Congress and the Bureau of Indian Affairs agreed that this "degraded, intemperate, vagabond" people should leave the neutral ground, and in 1848, the Winnebagoes were removed to Blue Earth County in the Territory of Minnesota.[122]

White settlers in Minnesota became discontented with the Winnebagoes in their midst, and in 1860, claiming that the Indians' savage, idle, and roaming ways would never change, the Minnesota legislature demanded that the Winnebagoes move on. In 1862, the people of Minnesota had their way. After the violent Sioux uprising in the late summer and early fall, the Bureau of Indian Affairs moved the Minnesota Sioux, along with 1,945 blameless Winnebagoes, to the Crow Creek area in Dakota Territory. This was desolate country; the land was poor, and crops would not grow, since there was almost no summer rain. There was no game in the vicinity, and the Winnebagoes were constantly threatened by their Sioux neighbors. The unhappy Winnebago headmen approached an army officer camped near the Crow Creek Agency and confided to him that they were friends of the Omahas, spoke nearly the same language, and would very much like to join the Omahas on the reservation at Black Bird Hills if they could not return to Minnesota. The Winnebago agent at Crow Creek made no attempt to confine his charges to their reservation, and in small groups, they began to slip away.[123]

In a council with newly arrived Agent Robert Furnas, the Omahas agreed that the Winnebagoes could stay, but only if they obeyed stringent rules and if they paid their hosts out of their tribal annuities. Many of the very young and very old Winnebagoes froze to death during the following winter; they had arrived with nothing and had been issued no clothing since coming to the Omaha Reservation. Furnas could not understand Winnebago agent Saint A. D. Balcombe's lack of concern for the Indians in his care. Balcombe made no attempt to contact Furnas, who later learned that he had spent the winter in Sioux City, "forty miles from the nearest Winnebago," probably living off the Indians' clothing allowance, which had mysteriously disappeared.[124]

On February 6, 1865, over the objections of those who did not want to see their still-unallotted reservation reduced, the Omaha chiefs and headmen authorized La Flesche, Standing Hawk, Little Chief, Noise, and No Knife to negotiate with the United States to sell part of their lands for the Winnebagoes' use. The first article of the March 6, 1865, treaty stated the boundaries of the northern portion of the reservation to be conveyed to the Winnebagoes and provided that no Omaha improvements would be included. By the provisions of Article Two, the Omahas would be paid $50,000, to be used by their agent to improve what remained of their reservation. Article Three provided the Omahas with a blacksmith, a shop, a farmer, and mills for ten years longer and allowed them $7,000 for damages sustained during the Winnebagoes' stay on their reservation.[125] Article Four, which would almost immediately be questioned, abolished common land tenure on the remaining Omaha Reservation and provided for "regular and compact" allotments of 160 acres to each family head and 40 acres to each male over eighteen. The agency would occupy one quarter section, and all allotments would include some timber. Certificates would be issued for the tax-exempt allotments, which could not be sold or leased except to the government or to other Omahas. Finally, under Article Five, the Omahas could buy their land back if the Winnebagoes proved to be poor neighbors.[126]

The Omaha tribal representatives had no idea what was included in the 1865 treaty. When Superintendent Denman explained the treaty provisions, they were surprised and said they were unaware that allotment had even been mentioned. They objected strenuously to the changes in allotment terms in the new treaty, since land would now be parceled out without regard to family size. It was, they argued, unfair for a childless couple to have as much land as a family of ten. In February 1868, the Omaha chiefs asked to have their lands allotted according to the more generous terms of the 1854 treaty. Denman urged the Indian Office to change the mode of allotment, even if it took an act of Congress. In November, the Omahas once more voiced their objections, this time asking for a new treaty. But at his first council with the chiefs, in June 1869, Samuel Janney persuaded them to accept the 1865 terms. The Quaker superintendent must have been quite convincing, since the chiefs also offered to pay the surveyor from their "Winnebago fund."[127]

Early in 1866, Omaha leaders petitioned the commissioner of Indian affairs to survey and allot their lands promptly so that those who had chosen their acreage could begin working their farms in the spring. Exactly one year later, the U.S. land commissioner informed Indian Commissioner Lewis Bogy that the Omaha survey had been delayed

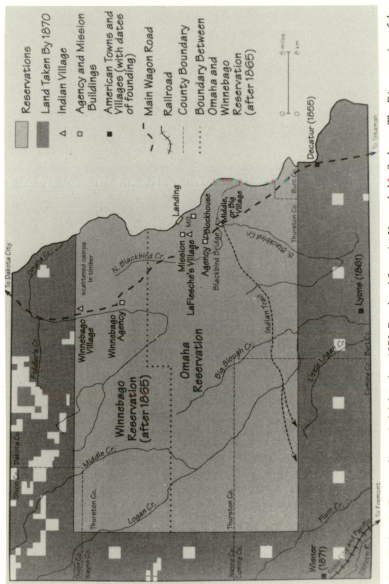

Map 7. Omaha Reservation and vicinity, circa 1870. Reprinted from *An Unspeakable Sadness: The Dispossession of the Nebraska Indians*, by David J. Wishart, by permission of the University of Nebraska Press. © 1994 by the University of Nebraska Press.

Reservations

Land Taken By 1870

△ Indian Village

□ Agency and Mission Buildings

■ American Towns and Villages (with dates of founding)

— — Main Wagon Road

⁓ Railroad

········· County Boundary

········· Boundary Between Omaha and Winnebago Reservation (after 1865)

0   5 miles
0   8 km

Winnebago Village

Winnebago Agency

Winnebago Reservation (after 1865)

Omaha Reservation

Mission

LaFlesche's Village

Agency

Blockhouse

Blackbird Bridge

Middle Cr. Big Village

Landing

Mill

N. Blackbird Cr.

S. Blackbird Cr.

scattered camps in timber

Omaha Cr.

Fiddler's Cr.

To Dakota City

Dixon Co. Dakota Co.

Middle Cr.

Thurston Co.

Logan Cr.

Thurston Co.

Wayne Co. Cuming Co.

Plum Cr.

Wisner (1871)

Sioux City and Pacific

Elkhorn R.

To Fremont

Big Slough Cr.

Indian Trail

Little Logan Cr.

Cuming Co. Burt Co.

Lyons (1861)

Thurston Co. Burt Co.

Decatur (1855)

To Tekamah

due to harsh winter weather, but he promised that it would be completed as soon as possible. The surveyor finally finished his fieldwork on June 27, 1867, and transmitted the survey to the land office in parts to speed up its verification.[128] Two months after the survey was completed, Agent Callon urged the government to get on with the work of allotting Omaha lands, since this would be a time-consuming process.[129]

The task of allotting Omaha lands fell to Callon's successor, Agent Edward Painter. Following clearly defined rules, he had assigned 160-acre parcels to 130 of the 278 heads of families by August 1869. A year later, 209 farms of 160 acres had owners, and 46 single Omahas had received their land. In July 1871, Painter finally sent his superior the complete roll of Omaha allottees, which included a few allotments to nonresident Indians, should they agree to return to the reservation. The Omahas whose land had been allotted received their certificates in March 1871, with the promise that the land was secure for them and their heirs.[130]

Painter had barely finished his work when problems arose regarding the allotments. Some were minor: because of the similarity of names and an inadvertent erasure, Little Buffalo received Sleeping Buffalo's claim; several Indians wanted to exchange their land for plots closer to the villages and the school; still others wanted to be near relatives and friends; and at least one Omaha built a house on the wrong allotment. But, more seriously, some land could not be farmed, and several allotments were being washed away by the Missouri River. Overall, the Omahas were unhappy with their inadequate 1871 allotments and worried about their futures, since they could no longer hunt and the Nebraska legislature had threatened to remove them from the state. Some Indians, especially La Flesche's faction, wanted written deeds to their lands so that they could not be driven to Indian Territory.[131]

After allotting the Omahas' lands, Painter could do no more. He had no funds to help the Indians improve their farms, and each received only $14 per year in annuities. Citing Article Six of the 1854 treaty, which allowed the Omahas to sell surplus lands, Painter suggested selling fifty thousand acres from the western end of the reservation to raise money for improvements. Both Painter and Janney worried that lack of capital for farms would cause the Indians to "regress." Approving their agent's plan, the Omaha chiefs asked that a delegation go to Washington to negotiate the sale.[132] The Omahas' proposition first came before Congress early in 1871, but because it was attached to a more complex and controversial bill, the tribe's request was denied.[133] Stressing the inadequacy of their $20,000 annuity, the Omahas in late October 1871 petitioned the new Congress for permission to sell the land, this time with the support of Interior Secretary Columbus Delano, Indian Commissioner Francis A. Walker, and the Quakers. In addition to approving the transaction, Congress allowed the Omahas a $30,000 cash advance, to be repaid from land sale profits.[134]

An act of June 10, 1872, ordered the fifty-thousand-acre western tract to be surveyed and appraised, after which the lands would be advertised for sale at no less than an average of $2.50 per acre. The resulting money would be deposited in the U.S. Treasury at 5 percent interest, payable semiannually, with the stipulation that no more than 25 percent of the land sale money could be used in any given year.[135] But sales were slow, since few investors wanted to pay the high per-acre price. Consequently, the Omahas saw little profit and were unable to "advance in civilization" in 1873. Instead, they went on a hunt.[136]

In 1873, the commissioner of Indian affairs called Omaha chiefs to Washington to transfer still more land to the Winnebagoes. Since the designated area included heavy timber and since the Winnebagoes had been stealing their horses, the Omahas initially resisted the sale. But when told by Agent T. T. Gillingham that chiefs who refused to negotiate would be deposed, they reluctantly agreed, under certain conditions: (1) they wanted more than $2.50 per acre; (2) the pony thefts must stop; and (3) Omahas whose allotments were on the land to be sold must be given titles or be allowed to choose other acreage.[137] In July 1874, all of the Omaha chiefs went to Washington, where they deeded 12,347.55 additional acres of their dwindling reservation to the Winnebagoes for $30,868.87, or almost exactly $2.50 per acre.[138]

To add to the Omahas' woes, the Omaha and Winnebago Agencies were consolidated under one agent in June 1879 and moved north to the Winnebago Reservation. Often, a month would pass between the agent's visits to the Omahas. In 1880, several Omaha leaders, unhappy with this turn of events, wrote to Commissioner of Indian Affairs Roland E. Trowbridge, asking him to restore their single agency. The

Omahas now had to travel a great distance to visit their agent. In the letter, White Horse complained that the agent was spending all of his time with the "disobedient" Winnebagoes and ignoring the "well-behaved" Omahas. But the Omahas' objections accomplished nothing; the consolidation had been a cost-saving measure, and so the change remained in effect.[139]

By 1881, the government still owed the Omahas $20,885 from the second Winnebago land sale. In a rational yet emotional appeal for payment, the Indians reminded Congress that much of the merchandise purchased from proceeds of the first sale was substandard. Also, the government-issue harnesses did not fit their small Indian ponies, and fifty of the one hundred cattle they had received had been kept by the agent and had been allowed to starve to death. The memorialists asked for itemized lists of articles purchased: "If we are not allowed to suggest or to direct how our money shall be expended, we . . . at least [want] the satisfaction of knowing what became of it when it is all gone."[140]

The Poncas' forced removal from Nebraska in 1877 prompted the Omahas to examine their own land titles. When lawyers told them they held worthless scraps of paper, they felt that the government had betrayed them. Joseph La Flesche addressed his fears to Alfred B. Meacham, of *Council Fire*: "We reserved for ourselves a very small part of the land. . . . But the white people wish to take that from us and send us to another land; that is very hard for us!"[141]

The Omahas did not suffer the Poncas' fate of removal, but the early reservation years left them in many ways poorer than they had been before their fateful trek to Black Bird Hills in 1855. They no longer feared the Sioux, but they did fear the future. For nearly thirty years they had been cheated, lied to, and forced to surrender many of their old ways. Promises had been made and broken, and their tribal government had been dismantled. No longer able to depend on the buffalo for food, they had been asked to farm without money or machinery. Worst of all, they had been unwilling participants in the rapid deterioration of their tribal land base. Yet to whites, the Omahas were "a steady and reliable set of men . . . advancing in the direction of citizenship."[142] Considered models of loyalty, self-reliance, and acculturation, they were deemed ready for allotments in severalty. But most were not ready, and even harder times lay ahead. In 1881, the Omahas would meet a determined "lady from Boston" who would study their culture, reallot their lands, and—for good or ill—lead them farther down the white man's road.

Chapter 4

A Model for Disaster
The Omaha Allotment Experiment, 1882–1887

I want title to my land, so that no one can take from my
children the land on which I have worked.

Wa-ha-sha-ga (James Springer), 1881

All friends of our race who urge land in severalty upon
us now will . . . see their error and repent of it when it
is too late to remedy the wrong they have caused to be
done to us.

An Anonymous Omaha, 1887

The Omahas had good reason to fear the future. Through the pleas of a
handful of tribal "progressives" and the lobbying efforts of an unlikely
mentor, they were awarded lands in severalty during 1882. But allotment
proved to be a continuation of rather than an end to their troubles. As a
result of the allotment legislation, they became lost in a legal no-man's-
land, subject to state laws but not protected by them. Lands on the
western end of the reservation were sold to white settlers, but little of the
money filtered down to the tribe. Attempts at self-government quickly
degenerated into tribal feuding, and controversy over a common pasture
permanently split the prominent La Flesche family. By 1886, the
Omahas were culturally adrift and unable to manage their own affairs,
but they were still considered successfully assimilated by many
reformers who refused to admit failure. Policymakers ignored agents'
reports that accurately portrayed the deteriorating conditions among the
Omahas, and despite the numerous problems, the Omaha "experiment"
became the blueprint for the 1887 Dawes Act, which allotted the lands
of many other tribes, often with equally disastrous results. Finally, with
the passage of the Dawes Act, the Omahas became citizens without
understanding the ramifications of citizenship.

Omaha allotment resulted from changes in public attitudes toward
Indian assimilation. Generally contemptuous of Indians, westerners

had historically opposed any efforts at assimilation, and until about 1880, easterners, far from the frontier and with little understanding of conditions there, saw Indians as romantic and exotic. But even staunch Indian advocates found it difficult to defend Native Americans in the 1870s, when a series of events, including the 1873 Modoc War in northern California and the 1876 Battle of Little Bighorn, turned public opinion against the Indians. Ironically, George Custer's monumental defeat created a climate more favorable to reform. Westerners criticized the U.S. Army for its failure to subdue the Sioux, but most eastern reformers abhorred the late General Custer's policy of Indian extermination.[1] Eastern reformers increasingly saw the army as the villain in this western tragedy and as an obstacle to Indian "civilization." After the Custer battle, many reformers feared that the army would "destroy the Peace Policy and probably the Indians." The army did place all the Sioux agencies under its control and, in a series of punitive campaigns, "forcibly disarmed and dismounted" hostile and friendly Indians alike. With their subjugation by the U.S. Army, northern plains tribes became people to be pitied, and their condition piqued interest in assimilation.[2]

As public anger over Little Bighorn subsided, the Ponca tragedy took center stage. Standing Bear's return to his Nebraska homeland in 1879 and the subsequent trial in which his right to sue in court was upheld made the Ponca chief an instant celebrity. But public sentiment in Nebraska did not support the Poncas, and in October 1879, Thomas H. Tibbles, a former abolitionist and onetime circuit rider who, as a reporter for the *Omaha Herald*, had been instrumental in Standing Bear's successful lawsuit, took the now famous chief on a lecture tour of the Northeast. Accompanying Tibbles and Standing Bear were Joseph La Flesche's highly educated daughter, Susette, and her half-brother, Francis La Flesche.[3] The Ponca chief's eastern trip "resembled a political campaign more than a state visit" and was designed to sway public opinion to obtain support for policy changes. Tibbles carefully selected his audiences, making sure they would be sympathetic. During the tour, Susette La Flesche downplayed her French and English ancestry, even appearing in buckskin and using her Indian name of "Bright Eyes" as she translated Standing Bear's remarks and made her own plea for liberty and equality.[4]

Standing Bear was well received in the East. In Boston, the cradle of the Indian reform movement, influential citizens urged the Poncas' return to Nebraska and at the same time recognized that injustice toward Indians resulted from their lack of legal status. With a zeal approaching that of the earlier abolitionists, eastern reformers urged that Native Americans be provided citizenship, legal protection, and individual land patents.[5]

Tibbles' lecture tour netted more than sympathy for the Poncas and other Indians. In Boston, Tibbles was approached by Alice C. Fletcher, an ethnologist and protégée of Frederic Ward Putnam, director of the Peabody Museum of American Archaeology and Ethnology at Harvard University. Fletcher wanted to study Indians firsthand, and despite Tibbles' insistence that she was not up to the rigors of camping on the prairie, she was determined to go. The tour group went back to the reservation, but when Tibbles and Susette La Flesche returned to Boston in 1881, Fletcher again pled her case. This time, they agreed to take her camping with the Sioux, and on September 1, 1881, she arrived in Nebraska carrying personal recommendations from the secretary of war, the interior secretary, and members of the scientific community. What Fletcher planned to do was unprecedented for a woman in the 1880s, and she knew there would be problems. She confided to a correspondent, "I know that what I am toward is difficult, fraught with hardship to mind and body."[6]

Tibbles and Susette La Flesche, who was now Mrs. Tibbles, escorted Fletcher north to the Omaha Reservation, where she was warmly welcomed by Joseph La Flesche and other tribal progressives who saw this "Boston lady" as someone who might be able to help them secure their land. Inevitably, the conversation turned to land titles, which the Indians saw as their only alternative to removal to Indian Territory, where they feared they would die as had so many Poncas.[7] As promised, after this short visit with the La Flesche family, Fletcher, accompanied by Tibbles, Susette, and Wajapa, a La Flesche family friend, set off for Sioux country. After briefly visiting the Poncas, the foursome continued on to the Rosebud Sioux Agency, then to Fort Randall, where Fletcher interviewed and was charmed by the captive Sitting Bull. After visiting the Yankton and Santee Sioux

Agencies with the inspector general, Fletcher rejoined the others and returned to the Omaha Reservation.[8]

When asked why she had come to Nebraska, Fletcher told her Omaha hosts that she hoped to learn their ways and to help them if she could. The Omahas indeed wanted her help. Since 1854, tribal progressives had fretted over the security of their lands, and the recent discovery that their certificates were worthless filled them with alarm. Thus Joseph La Flesche had sent Susette east with Standing Bear in 1879, and many Omahas had signed petitions and letters addressed to the "white people in the east," asking for aid in securing land titles. They had also sent letters to the reform newspaper *Council Fire*, with the intent that these be forwarded to the president, the secretary of the interior, and the commissioner of Indian affairs.[9] The desperate Omahas told Fletcher: "You have come at a time when we are in distress. . . . We want a 'strong paper.' We are told that we can get one through an act of Congress. Can you help us?"[10]

Having listened to the pleas of Joseph La Flesche and other leaders, the ethnologist decided that the only solution to the Omahas' problems was land in severalty. Fletcher later explained her decision to plead the Omahas' case before Congress: "While living with the tribe . . . I grew to know the fervor with which the people loved their land, and to see that over each fireside hung a shadow that would not lift—the fear of compulsory removal to the Indian Territory."[11] But like many other whites, Fletcher misunderstood the Omahas' desires. In asking for a "strong paper," most of the tribe wanted a secure title to their tribal lands so that they could remain in their ancestral home. Instead, Fletcher worked to destroy Omaha tribalism and to secure for individual Indians private property—their alleged ticket into "civilized society."[12]

After two meetings with Omaha headmen, Fletcher addressed a petition to the U.S. Senate asking that its signers be granted full title to their allotments. Fifty-three Omaha men signed the document, and Fletcher added personal statistics and remarks of each petitioner.[13] Fletcher mailed the petition on December 31, 1881, along with a letter explaining her own role. Insinuating that her short stay with them had made her an authority on the Omahas, she asked Commissioner of

Indian Affairs Hiram Price to "trust her interpretation of the situation." Admitting that the Omahas had two tribal parties, "one desirous of civilization [and] one that clings to the past," Fletcher assured the commissioner that the progressives were "the true leaders among the people."[14]

Fletcher remained with the Omahas all winter as they anxiously awaited news from Washington. Finally, in February, word came that the petition had come before the Senate. The eager Fletcher then wrote to Interior Secretary Samuel Kirkwood and Massachusetts Senator Henry L. Dawes, chairman of the Committee on Indian Affairs, asking them to support Omaha allotment legislation.[15] Too impatient to continue lobbying from Nebraska, Fletcher decided to conduct her Omaha campaign in person. During a three-month stay in Washington in the spring of 1882, she relentlessly lobbied government officials, one of whom called her "a dreadful bulldozer"; the wives and daughters of these officials persuaded them to hear Fletcher's plan.[16]

In her appendix to *The Omaha Tribe*, Alice Fletcher called her Washington allotment lobbying "a long, and for a time a single-handed campaign." Yet it was not that difficult. In fact, her campaign was "short and almost foreordained to succeed." Her timing was perfect; Washington was ready for a new Indian policy and was waiting for someone to force a bill through Congress. Fletcher did just that. A bill to sell part of the Omaha Reservation had already cleared one branch of Congress, and Fletcher wanted to ensure allotments for tribal members. Urged on by Commissioner Price, she managed to amend the bill so that the Omahas would receive allotments before any reservation lands could be sold to whites. In pushing for allotment, Fletcher stressed not what the Indians would lose but what they would gain—160-acre farms, citizenship, laws, schools, and the chance to become part of white "civilization."[17]

The bill did not pass unchallenged. In April 1882, several senators entered into a heated debate over the sale of Omaha lands. In his opening remarks, Nebraska Senator Alvin Saunders defended the sale of fifty thousand acres of the reservation. "This land has no settlers upon it . . . and is yielding nothing to the Indians, nothing to the government, and nothing to the country. It happens to be one of those few cases where I believe everybody is satisfied to have a bill of this kind passed."

Senator Dawes agreed with Saunders, after the Indian commissioner dismissed Dawes' fear that the loss of fifty thousand acres would leave the Omaha Reservation too small. The commissioner assured the senator that there was plenty of land, both for the present and for the future. In addition, Omaha tribal representatives had allegedly told Dawes that they "had more land than they could occupy" and wanted to sell "a portion of their real estate." The strongest objection to Omaha allotment came from Senator John Ingalls of Kansas, who disagreed with the twenty-five-year trust period and who questioned the constitutionality of depriving Nebraska of its tax revenues from Indian lands.[18]

The House Committee on Indian Affairs appeared quite proud of the Omaha act. Members told their colleagues they had drawn up a bill that met government needs and still safeguarded Omaha interests. The committee stated, "Great good will result to the Indians in the securing of title to their lands."[19] But the interests of the Omahas were already threatened. Ignoring Fletcher's and Omaha Agent George Wilkinson's recommendations that only those Indians who had previously worked their land should receive titles, the Indian Affairs Committee applied the bill provisions to every Omaha.[20]

As Fletcher had hoped, the Omaha allotment became law on August 7, 1882, as part of the act enabling the government to sell that portion of the Omaha Reservation west of the Sioux City and Nebraska Railroad right-of-way.[21] In passing this law, Congress made most Omahas private landowners, changed their legal status, and created a breeding ground for tribal dissension. But most tragically, it set in motion a process that would eventually leave many Omahas landless. Sections Five through Eight of the act established the terms and conditions of Omaha allotment. Section Five provided for an agent to allot reservation lands east of the railroad according to the following schedule: heads of families would receive 160 acres of land; each single Omaha over age eighteen would be assigned 80 acres; 40 acres would be allotted to each orphan under age eighteen; and other minors would also receive 40 acres. Heads of families would choose lands for their children, and orphans' allotments would be selected by the agent. Although these allotments superseded those of the March 6, 1865, treaty, Indians already holding lands from that agreement could remain on those lands if they so desired.[22]

The problematic Section Six provided that allottees would receive land patents to be held in trust for twenty-five years, during which time their lands could not be sold or encumbered in any way. At the end of the trust period, Omahas would receive their allotments, free and clear. According to Section Seven, the Omahas would be subject to the civil and criminal laws of the state of Nebraska, which in theory could not deny the Indians legal protection. By the provisions of Section Eight, lands remaining east of the railroad after all allotments had been made would be patented to the tribe as a collective unit and, like individual allotments, would be held in trust for twenty-five years, after which time the Omahas were to receive these lands minus acreage allotted to children born during the trust period. Finally, the last section of the act allowed Indians to take their allotments anywhere on the reservation, including west of the railroad.[23]

In early May 1883, Alice Fletcher, accompanied by interpreter Francis La Flesche, returned to the Omaha Reservation to allot the Indians' lands. Earlier that spring, Commissioner Price had named her an Office of Indian Affairs special agent, at a salary of five dollars per day plus expenses. Although somewhat wary of the challenge, she viewed her unusual assignment as a way to combine philanthropy and science at government expense. On her arrival, Fletcher called the Omahas together to explain the allotment process, then spent ten days familiarizing herself with survey procedures and land registration. Where she found no legal procedures, she created her own. After painstakingly collecting and accounting for all 316 of the 1871 allotment certificates, Fletcher reassigned as many families as possible to their same lands.[24]

Unfortunately, many of the allotments taken in 1871 were on Missouri River bottomlands that flooded frequently. After a tour of the reservation, Fletcher concluded that the Omahas' best land lay in the Logan River Valley, fifteen to twenty miles west of the Missouri. In addition, these lands were near the railroad. Fletcher explained to potential allottees that if they stayed on their original lands near the Missouri River, they would have to travel "miserable trails" to Decatur, Nebraska, or to more distant towns to sell their produce. To encourage the Omahas to choose rich prairie lands, Fletcher borrowed a tent and established her allotment headquarters on the banks of the

Logan River.[25] According to Agent Wilkinson, who greatly admired the forceful allotting agent, Fletcher's plan worked; he reported that a "large proportion" of the Omahas, including nearly all the progressives, decided to move to the Logan Valley.[26]

The first Omaha family to accept its allotments was the La Flesches. Taking Fletcher's advice, they chose land west of the railroad right-of-way. There they would be among whites when that area was opened to settlement and would also be near the small town of Unashtazinga ("little stopping place"), which would later become Bancroft. Ultimately, in the two townships through which the railroad passed and in the two townships immediately to the east, Fletcher made 326 allotments—69 to heads of families, 58 to single adults, and 199 to minors. She believed this "remarkable exodus" showed promise for the future, since the best land of the reservation was now in the hands of the most "progressive" Omahas. At a Board of Indian Commissioners meeting six years later, Fletcher revealed her elitist allotment strategy. "I give the best land to the best Indians I can find. I always help the progressive Indians first, on the principle 'to him that hath shall be given.'"[27]

Fletcher almost failed to finish her assignment. In July 1883, she was drenched in a sudden thunderstorm and became extremely ill with what the agency doctor diagnosed as inflammatory rheumatism. For five weeks she lay desperately ill at the Presbyterian mission and was then moved to the nearby agency at Winnebago. Realizing that tribal conservatives were using her sudden illness as proof that allotment was wicked, Fletcher began conducting business from her sickbed. With Francis La Flesche as her clerk, she made out allotments and, as a self-proclaimed judge, settled tribal disputes. By working in pain, Fletcher convinced many Omahas of her power.[28]

Fletcher continued her work, walking with the aid of crutches, but in December, allotments still had not been made to the most conservative Omahas. Twelve families, calling themselves "the Council Fire," had joined forces to fight allotment and to continue their traditional ways. Fletcher decided to compel these dissenters to take allotments. Probably under orders from Agent Wilkinson, tribal police rounded up the resisters and forced them to accept lands in the presence of Fletcher and other witnesses.[29] Having assigned these final parcels, Fletcher submitted her report and allotment schedule on June 25, 1884. The

Bureau of Indian Affairs approved her schedule on July 11 and directed the General Land Office to issue patents for 76,810 acres of the Omaha Reservation to 954 Indians. But despite Fletcher's efforts to encourage Indians to take lands farther west, near white settlers, only 877 of the allotted acres were west of the railroad. All the reservation land was now obligated; 50,000 acres would be sold to whites, and the remaining unallotted 55,450 acres east of the railroad would be held in trust for unborn children. Along with her allotments, Fletcher compiled a complete tribal registry, which she turned over to Agent Wilkinson. Hoping that the registry would answer future heirship questions, she instructed the Indians to report every birth, death, and marriage.[30]

Satisfied with a job well done, Fletcher left the Omaha Reservation in June 1884. But she left behind a divided tribe and covetous whites eager to occupy choice Omaha lands. In 1881, only a tiny minority of the Omahas had signed the petition asking for lands in severalty. Citing signatures on this and other petitions, Fletcher's biographer estimated that only one-fourth of the tribe supported allotment. One-third vehemently opposed it, and the rest, although not in favor, went along with the plan. At the 1884 Lake Mohonk Conference, Fletcher admitted that only one-third of the Omahas favored land in severalty.[31] And Fletcher must have been aware of the potential problems with whites near the reservation. In testimony before the Board of Indian Commissioners, she reported whites' constant complaints that she was "giving the very best land to the Indians," and she told of local white "committees" that had shadowed her as she made the allotments.[32]

In a letter to his half-sister Rosalie La Flesche Farley, Francis La Flesche explained that after allotment, the Omahas were "entirely under the law civil and criminal just exactly the same as if they were white men." Unfortunately, La Flesche was only half right. Despite being subject to Nebraska laws, the Omahas could not benefit from those laws because they had no legal officers—no sheriff or justice of the peace. And since they paid no taxes, they were discouraged from using state and local courts and were denied basic services. Neighboring whites resented the Omahas' tax-exempt status. So did the state of Nebraska, which claimed it was losing money and that it should be able to tax these lands. Senator Henry L. Dawes reminded Nebraska county officials that the land had been a reservation and had never been taxed, so there was no revenue loss under allotment status.[33]

Unhappy with their precarious legal position, the Omahas decided to establish an independent government. Fletcher did not think the Omahas would be ready for self-government until the tribal organization and the agency system had been destroyed, but in 1884, Omaha councilman Sindahaha presented the position of at least part of the tribe. He began by stating flatly, "In future, we wish no one here put over us by Government, but we wish to govern ourselves." Then he requested that the government pay the Omahas all money owed them and that it allow the tribe to handle its own affairs. Caving in to pressure, Fletcher wrote a sixty-page plan of government that recognized the ten-man Omaha Council, but she urged that most power be given to the three-man Indian Court of Offenses, designed to end "heathen" customs. Fletcher envisioned a simple form of county government, with a school superintendent, a superintendent of roads, and other officials. She further recommended that the lands being held for the next generation be fenced and used as a common pasture.[34]

During that same year, the Omaha leading men asked that all agency employees be discharged, a move supported by Agent Wilkinson. Noting that the desire for independence among some prominent Omahas had increased following allotment and that the Omahas had proved they could farm successfully, Commissioner Price agreed. On September 30, 1884, he instructed Wilkinson to release all Omaha Agency employees except the farmer, who would serve as a liaison, and those associated with the school. Wilkinson was also told to turn over to the Omahas the mills, shops, agency buildings, schoolhouses, and government livestock. The tribe was now on its own, and Price had high hopes for his Omaha "experiment." He was sure that it would succeed and that it would become a model for other tribes to emulate.[35]

But the Omahas could not manage on their own. In 1885, the agency farmer resigned, severing the tribe's tenuous link to the government. When neither newly appointed Indian Commissioner J. D. C. Atkins nor Alice Fletcher seriously considered an Omaha request that Fletcher become their "business manager," several Indian delegations visited Washington in April 1886 and gave Atkins mixed messages regarding Omaha needs. Fletcher and Francis La Flesche met with each delegation and worked out another plan for self-government that, for the moment, appeared to please everyone. But despite the seeming settlement, old tribal divisions rapidly resurfaced back in Nebraska. The Omaha Council of Ten split into factions. Whereas half of the leaders (Two Crows, Doubasmurri, Sindahaha, White Horse, and Chazininga) supported Fletcher's plan and the common pasture, the other five (Prairie Chicken, Wahininga, Wasagaha, Little Cow, and Kaiska) opposed the pasture, self-government, and the La Flesches. The five conservative councilors drafted a letter to Commissioner Atkins, accusing Fletcher of misrepresenting Omaha affairs and of playing favorites among their people. But they reserved their strongest criticisms for Joseph La Flesche, denigrating his mixed-blood ancestry and calling him a chronic troublemaker. The letter was signed by 150 men, nearly three times the number who had petitioned Congress for allotments five years earlier.[36]

The Omaha Reservation was in chaos. According to a Board of Indian Commissioners member who visited the Omahas in 1887, turning over the mills and the blacksmith shop to the Indians had been a disaster. William H. Waldby reported that the mill was falling down and the machinery had either broken or been carried off. Even doors and windows had been confiscated by tribal members. All that remained of the blacksmith shop was one anvil and the bellows, and the Omahas now had to hire their own blacksmith. In 1890, Agent Robert Ashley also questioned the wisdom of allowing the Indians to run the mill and shops, and a year earlier, Agent Jesse Warner, arguing that the Omahas still needed agency control, had described their situation as "trying to erect a new superstructure without removing the debris of the past."[37]

Along with tribal divisions and nonfunctioning mills and shops, a rift occurred in the influential La Flesche family. Former friends Alice Fletcher and Susette Tibbles sharply disagreed on self-government, the common pasture, and leasing of allotted lands, and their feud forced family members to choose sides. In addition, the family could not agree on citizenship. Joseph La Flesche favored self-government and doubted the Omahas' readiness to become citizens "in [their] present state." Five years earlier, Susette Tibbles had forcefully expressed her contrary views on citizenship in an introduction to one of her husband's books. "Allow an Indian to suggest that the solution to the vexed 'Indian Question' is *Citizenship*. . . . If it were not for the lands which the Indian holds, he would have been a citizen long before the Negro." In 1886, she saw citizenship as the proper alternative to the agency system, and she considered self-government a "great evil." Testifying before the Board of Indian Commissioners, she argued that citizenship could not hurt her people: "They cannot be in any worse condition than they are now."[38]

The major break between Alice Fletcher and Susette Tibbles occurred over the question of leasing Indian lands. By 1884, the Omahas' unallotted lands had become fair game for white squatters, and by paying the agent a fee, white men could graze cattle on the reservation. Roaming at will, these cattle trampled Indians' fields and gardens. The Omahas balked when Fletcher suggested they fence in their crops, so in her self-government plan, she had recommended fencing the unallotted lands and creating a common pasture. The plan worked; Indians could graze their cattle for free, and whites could graze their stock for a price. In July 1884, Rosalie La Flesche's husband, Ed Farley, requested permission to manage the common pasture. With Agent Wilkinson's blessing, he applied for a twenty-year lease on eighteen thousand acres of unallotted land at an annual rate of four cents per acre. This leasing arrangement was apparently unique on Indian lands. Farley bypassed Congress and dealt directly with the commissioner of Indian affairs while also entering into a partnership with the Omaha tribe, which would share the profits.[39]

Susette and her husband, Thomas Tibbles, took positions that alienated many Omahas, especially Susette's family. Crusading for immediate citizenship and against Omaha self-government, the Tibbles couple agitated for an investigation of the common pasture. The husband-and-wife team interpreted the no-lease provision of the 1882 Omaha Allotment Act as an infringement of Indian rights. Arguing that the Omahas should be allowed to lease their lands to whomever they wanted, Susette and Thomas actively opposed Rosalie and Ed Farley's management of the pasturelands. Although Susette probably knew that the Farleys kept accurate books and paid the tribe several hundred dollars per year, she claimed that Ed Farley cheated her people and that the Indians knew nothing about the operation of the common pasture or what their share should be.[40]

In 1883, many Omahas had taken allotments some distance from the Missouri River in areas where the land had never been farmed. To break and clear virgin sod, especially without proper equipment and animals, was hard work, and many Omahas wanted to lease their land to whites rather than farm it themselves. But by terms of the 1882 act, leasing the allotments was illegal. With their usual zeal, Susette and Thomas Tibbles worked for the Omahas' right to lease their individual farms. At rallies in nearby Bancroft and Pender, they raised enough cash from interested whites to plead their case in Washington. Thomas even tricked his father-in-law into initially supporting his scheme to promote leasing. After appealing to eastern reformers for Omaha leasing rights, Joseph La Flesche realized he had been deliberately confused. Fletcher fully supported the leasing of the common pasture—it had, after all, been her idea—but she was adamantly opposed to leasing Indian allotments. Assuming that only the best lands would be leased, Fletcher worried that with whites occupying the most productive farmland, the Omahas would become discouraged and would not "progress." When La Flesche saw that Thomas Tibbles was attempting to overturn the twenty-five-year trust period and, in the process, was personally attacking Fletcher, he withdrew his support for the campaign. He told his friend Two Crows, "I feel we have made a wrong move." It all came down to trust; increasingly, La Flesche distrusted Tibbles, and he felt Fletcher had never lied to him.[41]

To counteract the efforts to destroy the common pasture, Francis La Flesche instructed his father and other progressives to send Boston reformers a petition saying they did not want to lease the unallotted lands to outsiders because that would bring whites onto the reservation. Also, he told the tribal leaders to state that they wanted no input from Thomas Tibbles on the matter. In a warning that proved prophetic, Francis assured his father that whites would not pay a fair price and would be difficult to dislodge from Indian lands. He also wisely cautioned the Omahas not to involve themselves in any litigation, since whites controlled state and county officials and the Omahas would surely lose in court.[42]

Francis La Flesche detested Thomas Tibbles, whom he accused of spreading rumors about the propriety of his relationship with Alice Fletcher. Remarks made in a letter to his sister Rosalie in December

1886 reveal the depth of his animosity. La Flesche also never forgave the then-married Tibbles for his alleged affair with Susette La Flesche while they toured the East on behalf of the Poncas. Francis wrote, "Mr. T left his wife to die in Omaha while he made love to S."[43] Joseph La Flesche died in 1888, and for the last few years of his life he was torn between loyalty to his daughter and his son-in-law and loyalty to Alice Fletcher. The Fletcher-Tibbles controversy continued and finally resulted in a compromise: to Susette and Thomas Tibbles' satisfaction, the Omahas did become citizens with the passage of the 1887 Dawes Act, but the Council of Ten temporarily continued to oversee tribal affairs. Unfortunately, the rift in the La Flesche family never healed.

At twelve o'clock noon on April 30, 1884, 50,157 acres of Omaha Reservation land west of the Sioux City and Nebraska Railroad, with an appraised value of $512,670.24, was thrown open to white settlement.[44] According to the terms of sale, an individual purchasing Omaha land would be required to pay for it in three installments, beginning one year after the purchase was registered, and would be charged 5 percent interest, payable annually. Proceeds from land sales would be held for the Omahas in the U.S. Treasury, and the interest would be used to benefit the Indians.[45]

That was the theory. In practice, Congress repeatedly granted purchasers more time to pay for their acreage, always with the understanding that unless the annual interest was paid, buyers would forfeit their lands. With the Omahas' consent, the Indian Appropriation Act of March 3, 1885, extended the time of the first payment by one year, and in 1886 buyers, again with Indian permission, were granted an additional two years.[46] In September 1886, Francis La Flesche warned the Omahas that if they wanted to see any proceeds from their western lands, they should refuse to permit any further payment deferrals.[47] Nevertheless, in 1888, the tribe agreed to a further two-year extension.[48] That year, in response to a Senate resolution, acting Interior Secretary H. L. Muldrow asked the Bureau of Indian Affairs to produce figures regarding the sale of the roughly 50,000 acres of Omaha land. Acting Indian Commissioner S. M. Stockslager reported that nearly all of the land—49,630.62 acres, appraised at an average of $10.00 per acre—had been sold, but that as of December 31, 1887, only $154,654.62 had been deposited in the U.S. Treasury. Also in late

1887, $4,108.06 in interest remained unpaid, and no attempts had been made to force payment or to repossess the lands involved.[49] Despite the commissioner's adverse report, another extension was approved in 1890.[50] A final delay in 1894 allowed purchasers to defer their first payments until 1897, thirteen years after the land had first become available to whites, and only the intervention of Indian Commissioner Daniel M. Browning prevented Congress from approving the 1894 extension without the Omahas' knowledge.[51]

Because of these delays and delinquencies, the Omahas gained little from the sale of their western lands. In February 1886, Agent Charles Potter forwarded to Indian Commissioner Atkins a petition from 230 destitute Omaha heads of families, asking that the last nine $10,000 annuity payments from the 1854 treaty be paid in a lump sum so that they could afford essential improvements to their farms. The commissioner recommended that Congress pay the Omahas in two $45,000 installments, but Francis La Flesche, once more assuming his role as the "tribal conscience," cautioned his people that if they squandered the first payment, the second would be withheld.[52]

Congress rejected the Omahas' request, and in December 1887, 158 tribal members petitioned the government for the remaining $70,000. In their petition, the Indians agreed to accept half the proceeds in farm equipment but demanded the rest in cash.[53] Congress agreed to pay the remaining annuities in two $35,000 installments, but Nebraska congressmen and Senator Dawes suggested that an agent be appointed to make the payments in return for a 5 percent commission. Believing that to be a huge salary for a few days' work, four Omaha tribal leaders, probably coached by Francis La Flesche, asked their congressman to try to get them all their money.[54]

While the Omahas struggled to survive after allotment, reformers, congressmen, and government officials wrestled with the idea of granting Indians land in severalty on a much larger scale. Many backers of a general allotment act ignored reality or manipulated available data to support their positions. For example, in 1880, Acting Commissioner of Indian Affairs E. M. Marble claimed, "The demand for titles to land in severalty by the reservation Indians is almost universal."[55] Also in 1880, the House Committee on Indian Affairs reported favorably on Indian allotments. Communal life, they said, fostered "idleness, inefficiency, and dependency," especially among Indians. Citing the "encouraging" examples of several tribes, including the Omahas, who had been at least partially allotted, the majority of the committee agreed that these Indians' progress "clearly demonstrate[d] . . . the advantages to be derived by the Indians from holding their lands in severalty." The committee majority concluded its report by agreeing with Marble that the Indians of Nebraska and several other states were "exceedingly anxious" to have their lands allotted.[56]

Interior Secretary L. Q. C. Lamar insisted that tribal relations should remain intact during a slow transition to "civilization." Merrill E. Gates of the Board of Indian Commissioners disagreed. In a widely read pamphlet, Gates wrote that the greatest obstacle to assimilation was the tribe and asserted that the "best way to kill an Indian was to make him a white man."[57] Also to counter Lamar's views, in November 1885 Board of Indian Commissioners Secretary Eliphalet Whittlesey sent all Indian agents a questionnaire regarding allotments. He then carefully selected the most favorable responses for inclusion in his 1886 annual report, in which he claimed, "Not less than 75,000 [Indians] are asking for individual allotments . . . and nearly all of these are, in the opinion of their agents, far enough advanced to receive and care for separate homesteads."[58] But Lyman Abbott, the activist editor of *Christian Union*, offered the most extreme solution. He was convinced that reservations were a disaster: "I would, therefore, abandon this experiment, abolish the reservation, allow only time enough to work out the abolition, scatter the Indians among the white people, make their lands inalienable for a term of years, give them the rights of citizenship, and trust for their protection to the general laws of the land."[59]

Many concerned individuals and groups saw potential problems in severalty. Citing past failures and most Indians' opposition to allotments, they eloquently argued against the proposed General Allotment Act (the Dawes bill). Anthropologist Thomas Henry Morgan quoted former Interior Secretary Carl Schurz, who hoped that land in severalty would never become a reality because Indians were incapable of successfully dealing with whites. Schurz predicted that the result "of individual land ownership, with power to sell, would . . . be, that in a very short time [the Indian] would divest himself of every foot of land and fall into poverty."[60] After a chance meeting with aging former

Indian Commissioner George W. Manypenny, one reformer recalled the abject failure of early allotments. He reminded the Board of Indian Commissioners that those tribes that had been allotted under Manypenny's 1850s treaties were now "reduced in number; reduced in morals; without spirit," and he advised the board and the American people not to force severalty on any more unprepared Indians.[61]

Perhaps the most eloquent allotment opponent in the Senate was Henry M. Teller of Colorado. During the 1881 congressional debate over severalty, he reminded his colleagues that in the previous thirty-six years few tribes had chosen to be allotted and that those who did quickly lost their land. Declaring severalty "fundamentally wrong," Teller predicted, "When thirty or forty years shall have passed and these Indians shall have parted with their title, they will curse the hand that was raised professedly in their defense to secure this kind of legislation."[62]

Almost as though they had read different reports and experienced different history, a minority of the House Indian Affairs Committee disagreed completely with their colleagues. The dissenting committee-men pointed out that in 1862, Congress had provided that Indians, if they so desired, could take lands in severalty. If so many Indians favored allotments, they wondered, why had so few taken them? They urged Congress to proceed cautiously with severalty, and they criticized the application of the proposed law to "blanket Indians" as well as "those who [wore] the clothing of civilized life." Ridiculing the seeming hypocrisy of a land-in-severalty law, the minority on the committee accused Congress of treating Indians like adults by giving them land and expecting them to live off its profits and at the same time keeping them children by not allowing them to do as they wanted with their own property. Finally, opponents on the committee questioned the motives of Dawes bill supporters: "The real aim of this bill is to get at the Indian lands and open them up to settlement. The provisions for the apparent benefit of the Indians are but the pretext to get at his lands and occupy them. . . . If this were done in the name of Greed, it would be bad enough; but to do it in the name of humanity is infinitely worse."[63]

As late as the fall of 1882, after the Omaha Allotment Act had become law, even Senator Henry Dawes, who would later sponsor the general severalty bill, opposed the compulsory allotment of Indian lands. At that time, Dawes argued that Indians could not "be set up in severalty and left to stand alone any more than so many reeds."[64] But in the following few years, Dawes swallowed his own convictions and let events and activists such as Alice Fletcher dictate his actions.[65]

Because of her forceful personality and her experience in allotting Omaha lands, Alice Fletcher wielded considerable influence during the severalty debate. In 1884, Senators Richard Coke and Henry Dawes introduced a revised version of a severalty bill; it provided for a twenty-five-year trust period and tribal land patents for those Indians unwilling to accept individual allotments, and it required the consent of two-thirds of a tribe's adult males before a reservation could be allotted. Fletcher agreed with the twenty-five-year inalienability clause but objected vehemently to the other two provisions. As a member of a nine-person Lake Mohonk committee lobbying Congress for passage of the bill, she insisted that tribalism was an impediment to progress: "Under no circumstances should land be patented to a tribe. The principle is wrong." Citing the early resistance of most Omahas, she also thought that trying to get two-thirds of a tribe to consent to allotment would be a wasted effort. "The work must be done for them," she argued, "whether they approve or not." At Fletcher's insistence, the committee and the Lake Mohonk Conference voted to oppose any government recognition of tribalism.[66] In making final adjustments to his bill, Dawes heeded the voices from Lake Mohonk. The Dawes Act, as passed on February 8, 1887, contained the trust period, which Fletcher approved, but neither of the provisions she opposed. A controversial House amendment that became part of Section Six also granted the Omahas and other previously allotted Indians U.S. citizenship.[67]

Although the Dawes Act marked the culmination of years of work by numerous government officials, reformers, and private organizations, the stamp of Alice Fletcher was firmly imprinted on the bill in its final form. In recognizing her contributions, Senator Dawes said, "I stand in reference to that very much as Americus Vespucious [*sic*] stands to Columbus."[68] Fletcher called the Dawes Act "the Magna Charta of the Indians of our country." In an editorial in the Carlisle Indian School newspaper, *Morning Star*, she enumerated the reasons for her high praise: (1) each Indian was guaranteed a homestead; (2)

each Indian became a citizen; and (3) each Indian was now free from "tribal tyranny." She also mentioned, but did not belabor, the provision to open "surplus lands" to white settlement.[69]

But the so-called Indian Magna Charta had major weaknesses and created more problems than it solved. The Dawes Act left the Indians with title to their land but no power to use it, retaining just enough tribal interest to hold them back. The new law did not provide courts, education, or a public infrastructure, and tribal lands surrounding allotments would soon cause strife among Indians and invite greedy whites onto reservations.[70] Historian Wilcomb Washburn observed that had Dawes displayed more courage and greater understanding, his bill might have better protected Indians and provided fewer advantages to greedy whites. Or it may never have passed at all. As it was, "the losses were all on the Indian side."[71]

Because of Fletcher's high profile and reports of the Omahas' rapid progress after allotment, the Omaha tribe became the model for the more comprehensive Dawes Act. But had congressmen heeded the words of some Omaha agents and former agents, of the editor of *Council Fire*, or more important, of the Omahas themselves, they might have been less eager to allot additional tribes. A few reformers visiting the reservation, an eternally optimistic agent, and Fletcher herself, at first, spoke glowingly of the Omahas' condition. In 1883, before allotment was even completed, Agent Wilkinson saw a bright future for the Omahas. He believed that living near white settlements would teach the Indians the value of hard work. In 1884 and 1885, both Wilkinson and Fletcher reported that the tribe was doing well under allotment and its limited self-government. The agent insisted that closing their tribal shops showed the Omahas' determination to move forward, and he praised their progressiveness. In addition, Wilkinson assured the Indian commissioner that Fletcher's fine job of allotting and her sound advice would give the Omahas "an impetus which [would] never be lost." Despite serious problems on the reservation, Wilkinson predicted in 1885 that the Omahas would "soon become prosperous and profitable citizens."[72]

A year earlier, the Board of Indian Commissioners had admitted that many Indians were unprepared for allotment and would not be ready in the foreseeable future, but it had called the Omaha experience "instructive and encouraging." The board fully expected Omaha allotment to work, and just one year later, it proclaimed the Omaha experiment a success that proved "what [was] possible, and what, when protected by law, [would] always be successful."[73] Samuel B. Capen echoed the views of the Board of Indian Commissioners. In 1886, he told the Lake Mohonk Conference that the Omahas were on their way to civilization, had their land and were farming it, were receiving nothing from the government, and best of all, had done away with the agency system. He perceived this Omaha progress as a positive omen for the success of the impending Dawes Act.[74]

But these few voices were countered by a chorus of warnings that not all was well on the Omaha Reservation. As early as 1884, reports of Omaha difficulties surfaced, many of them on the pages of *Council Fire*. Stating that the Omahas had been more prosperous before allotment, a former agency employee told the editor that he hated to visit the Omaha Agency because everything had deteriorated.[75] Former agent Jacob Vore visited the reservation in 1884 and, in conversations with the Omahas, found that they were suffering. Their agent ignored them; their farmer—a doctor by profession—had proved incompetent; and the mission superintendent threatened parents in order to keep children in school. "We are not getting along well," several Indians confessed, "we are rather going back."[76]

Even Alice Fletcher worried about the Omahas. At a Washington, D.C., conference in 1886, she expressed optimism for their future, but when called on to report on her pet project in 1887, she felt differently. Having visited the Omahas earlier in the year, she found they were "doing very badly." She added: "They seem utterly at a loss how to get along. They don't seem able to work the land themselves. . . . White men are anxious to get leases, and almost all the Indians would lease their lands if they could." Letters from leading Omahas confirmed Fletcher's report but painted an even grimmer picture. *Council Fire's* editor, Thomas Bland, worried that the Omahas would soon be homeless, and he predicted a similar fate for every tribe touched by the Dawes Act.[77]

Claiming "that satisfaction of mind which results from telling the truth," Agent Charles H. Potter in 1886 filed a report that should have prompted legislators to delay passage of the Dawes bill. Potter stated that far from being solved, the Omaha problem was only in its first stages of solution and that the Indians' condition had been misrepresented. Angry because he was being held responsible for the sad state of affairs on the reservation, the new agent set the record straight. Without identifying names, but no doubt referring to former agent George Wilkinson, Potter charged that both the Bureau of Indian Affairs and the public had been "deceived in reference to the true condition of the Omahas." According to his report, the Omahas had also been deceived. When he explained their 1882 allotment to them shortly after his arrival, the Indians claimed that they had never agreed to allegiance to the state of Nebraska before the end of the twenty-five-year trust period and that the meaning of such allegiance had never been made clear to them. They refused to receive their land patents until Potter advised the Bureau of Indian Affairs of their feelings.[78]

Potter related the spring 1886 events surrounding the Omahas' request for a lump-sum payment of their remaining $90,000 in annuities. According to the agent, after neglecting their farms to hold feasts and councils, the tribe sent a delegation to Washington to discuss self-government, as well as the annuity payment. While the delegation was gone and for a time after it returned, the people refused to work. When Congress declined to appropriate money for a single annuity payment and the Omahas could muster no support for self-government, they became disheartened, and with the majority opposed to the conditions imposed on them, strong support developed for a return to agency employees and shops. In 1886, Potter had great concern for the Omahas' future. Their crops were failing, and they had no government, no interpreter, no law enforcement. He thought the Bureau of Indian Affairs would have to step in and dictate a system of government for the tribe.[79]

Amazingly, despite having received Agent Potter's discouraging report, Indian Commissioner Atkins lauded the Omahas' "success" and urged, "Indians everywhere . . . [should] adopt the same policy."[80] Atkins and Fletcher apparently shared the same blind optimism. Just a few weeks before the commissioner issued his favorable report in the fall of 1886, Fletcher visited the Omaha Reservation and found the Indians unable to handle their problems and quarreling among themselves as whites agitated for their land. As she was inclined to do, she turned this controversy into a positive sign. In her unrealistic view, this tribal "disintegration" denoted progress, and she believed other tribes would have similar experiences as the government "props" fell away.[81] Writing about the Omahas earlier in 1886, she had stated, "The people will succeed if given time."[82] The problems encountered by the Omahas after allotment in no way diminished Fletcher's enthusiasm for Indian land in severalty. In July 1887, when notified that she had been chosen to allot the Winnebagoes, she told her diary, "A great triumph!"[83]

Passage of the Dawes Act in February 1887 did not silence its critics. In the April edition of *Council Fire*, editor Bland discussed the tragic results of the Omaha allotment. In a statement highly critical of Fletcher's methods and her use of the Omaha experiment to encourage further land in severalty, he charged that the beneficiaries of Fletcher's work were not the Omahas but the "professional philanthropists, the land-sharks, the politicians who desired to catch the land-shark votes, and the railroads." Bland noted that at the Board of Indian Commissioners conference in January 1887, Fletcher had "virtually admitted the failure of her cherished scheme." Citing long passages from Agent Potter's 1886 report, Bland asked, "Can any intelligent friend of humanity look on this picture . . . and not sustain us in our opposition to the Dawes land-in-severalty bill?"[84]

Perhaps because of his outspokenness, Agent Potter submitted only one report from the Omaha and Winnebago Agency before being dismissed. In 1887, his successor, Jesse F. Warner, filed a report that was a masterpiece of constraint and compromise. Pointing to the large amount of publicity surrounding the Omaha experiment and the conflicting opinions as to its success, Warner granted that both supporters and detractors had good points. Admitting that the first few years after allotment promised little, the agent said that he could now see some progress, and he suggested that for the good of their people, the conservatives and the complainers should "return to their weed-grown farms" and "set an example . . . to others." Unfortunately, Warner lamented, it was too late to worry about whether the Omahas had been moved along too quickly; they were now citizens, and tribal government could not continue. In a thoroughly sensible statement, Warner suggested that in the future, other tribes should be given more time to accustom themselves to their changed status before being left on their own.[85]

It *was* too late to help the Omahas. Because of misconceptions regarding readiness for allotment, they had been forced into a situation that few of them desired or understood. Most Omahas in 1881 wanted only to remain in their Nebraska homeland; they had little desire to become individual landowners and even less to see a large portion of their reservation sold to white settlers. Generally unprepared for the consequences of allotment, they became confused and blamed one another for their problems. But the fault was not theirs; many mistakes had been made, most of them by Alice Fletcher. Often lost among the kudos that Fletcher received for her pioneering anthropological studies of the Omahas were the dire consequences of her Nebraska "field trip."

In part due to the attitudes of people such as Alice Fletcher, Indians in the 1880s came to be regarded as "children who needed to be encouraged to grow up." Fletcher had not always felt this way; she had gone west to study a people who had a different but "effective way of life." However, when she had to resort to force to complete the Omaha allotment, she began to see the Indians as children who could not make their own decisions. Fletcher came to perceive herself as a "mother" to the Omahas, calling them "her children—her babies."[86] At least one reformer noticed Fletcher's "curious feeling of ownership of the Omahas." Martha Goddard, the wife of Boston newspaper editor and prominent Indian advocate D. A. Goddard, observed that at the Lake Mohonk conferences, Fletcher refused to admit that others knew anything about the tribe and she ignored anyone else's comments regarding her pet Indians.[87]

In response to an 1886 letter of inquiry from Indian Rights Association Secretary Herbert Welsh, Goddard hinted at substantial wrongdoing by Alice Fletcher. From the tone of her letter, it is apparent that Goddard was on quite friendly terms with Thomas and Susette Tibbles, and so she may not have been totally objective, but her charges were too serious to ignore. Accusing Fletcher of being power hungry, Goddard argued that Fletcher had been given too much authority by the Indian Bureau. Welsh's confidante also charged that a "ring" of Fletcher's friends used her to profit from Omaha lands, but Goddard doubted that Fletcher gained personally, since "she care[d] for power, not for riches." Overall, Goddard found Fletcher's dealings with the Omahas "very questionable," and she called for an investigation into Fletcher's activities.[88]

Alice Fletcher did appear to enjoy the limelight, and she took great pleasure in being an "Omaha expert." Perhaps she was power hungry, as Goddard charged, but her "crimes" were more likely errors in judgment. Admitting that Fletcher often behaved rashly and made unwise decisions, anthropologist Nancy Oestreich Lurie observed that she may have acted more cautiously had her first Omaha contacts been "ordinary" Omahas rather than the acculturated, multilingual, mixed-blood La Flesche family. Fletcher did not seem to realize that they were atypical Omahas. In her haste to relieve the Omahas' distress, Fletcher gave herself too little time to familiarize herself with the Indians she was determined to help. "It is possible that if Alice Fletcher had first studied the Omahas thoroughly—as she later did—instead of plunging immediately into the matter of land, she would have sought some other solution to the Indians' economic problems than the one she brought with her into the field."[89]

Alice Fletcher did not deliberately undermine the Omahas' future. Because her dealings had been primarily with tribal progressives, she honestly believed that what she desired for the Omahas was what they wanted as well. Although the results were catastrophic, her intentions were good. Acknowledging her many shortcomings but defending her humanity, Lurie wrote, "Alice Fletcher, for all her misguided benevolence, must at least be respected for regarding the welfare of the people she studied as her primary obligation and for never forgetting that they were fellow human beings."[90]

Fletcher, "the lady from Boston," was of course not solely responsible for the Omaha "experiment" and its subsequent problems. In 1882, she had ridden the crest of the wave of assimilationist sentiment that had swept over Washington. Most reformers wanted to see the Omahas and other tribes allotted, and few later cared to admit that allotment had been a mistake. But the roots of the Omaha disaster actually went much deeper, back to the 1854 treaty that had begun their trek toward assimilation. No one else regretted his role in the 1854 treaty more than former Indian Commissioner George Manypenny. In 1885, he confessed:

When I made those treaties I was confident that good results would follow. Had I not so believed I would not have been a party to the transactions. Events following the execution of those treaties proved that I had committed a grave error. I had provided for the abrogation of the reservations, the dissolution of the tribal relation, and for lands in severalty and citizenship, thus making the road clear for the rapacity of the white man. . . . Had I known then as I now know . . . I would be compelled to admit that I had committed a high crime.[91]

The door was open to white greed, as the years following the Dawes Act would show. The Omahas, who were now citizens without recourse to law and were owners of valuable agricultural lands, would be victimized in the 1890s by unscrupulous whites hovering about the reservation fringes. Alcohol would once again become a major problem, and court battles would further divide tribal leaders. By 1900, due to an additional allotment provision and liberal leasing laws, the Omahas held little tribal land, and most of their individual farms were occupied by whites. Alice Fletcher was wrong: time would only make matters worse.

The "Venerable Man," the Omahas' Sacred Pole. This symbol of tribal unity has recently been returned to Nebraska after being stored for one hundred years at the Peabody Museum, Harvard University. Alice C. Fletcher and Francis La Flesche, *The Omaha Tribe*, Twenty-Seventh Annual Report of the Bureau of American Ethnology (Washington, D.C.: Government Printing Office, 1911), Plate 38.

Sacred Tent of the White Buffalo Hide. The hide of the white buffalo was sacred to the Omahas, and it occupied a place of honor inside this special tent, decorated with a stalk of corn. In 1884, arrangements had been made with the "keeper" of the buffalo hide to send it to the Peabody Museum at Harvard University for safekeeping, but the hide was stolen before this could happen. Alice C. Fletcher and Francis La Flesche, *The Omaha Tribe*, Twenty-Seventh Annual Report of the Bureau of American Ethnology (Washington, D.C.: Government Printing Office, 1911), Plate 27.

Logan Fontenelle. The son of a French fur trader and an Indian woman, Fontenelle was considered a chief by some of his contemporaries, though others referred to him as a "white man" or merely as an interpreter. Fontenelle died in 1855 in a Sioux ambush. Nebraska State Historical Society.

Part of an Omaha village, circa 1860. By 1860, some "progressive" Omahas had built frame homes and were "living like white men," but the majority of the people maintained their traditional ways. Alice C. Fletcher and Francis La Flesche, *The Omaha Tribe*, Twenty-Seventh Annual Report of the Bureau of American Ethnology (Washington, D.C.: Government Printing Office, 1911), Plate 23.

Joseph La Flesche, or "Iron Eye." Mixed-blood leader of the Omaha progressive faction, La Flesche was the father of several outstanding Omahas, including activist Susette La Flesche Tibbles and Dr. Susan La Flesche Picotte. His role in Omaha history remains controversial. This photo was made in Washington, D.C., in 1854. Nebraska State Historical Society.

Robert W. Furnas, Omaha Indian agent and governor of Nebraska. A former Civil War officer, Furnas was an opportunist involved in a highly suspect trading operation. His tenure as agent was marked by an ongoing feud with Joseph La Flesche. Despite his shortcomings, Furnas was an effective agent during a difficult time. Nebraska State Historical Society.

"Educated" Omaha Indian chiefs, date unknown. *Left to right*: Lewis Saunsoci, No Knife, and Joseph La Flesche. Saunsoci often served as an interpreter, and No Knife became a member of the Omaha Reservation police force. Nebraska State Historical Society.

Standing Hawk   Little Chief   Muttering Thunder

Omaha Indian Chiefs

"Uneducated" Omaha Indian chiefs, 1866. *Left to right*: Standing Hawk, Little Chief, and Muttering Thunder. Dressed in traditional finery, these conservative Omahas represent the tribal faction that wanted to hold on to the old ways. Nebraska State Historical Society.

Little Chief, conservative Omaha leader. An avowed enemy of tribal "progressives," Little Chief controlled the more traditional Omahas and wanted to rid the reservation of the white people. Indian agents recommended that he be stripped of his title of "chief." Alice C. Fletcher and Francis La Flesche, *The Omaha Tribe*, Twenty-Seventh Annual Report of the Bureau of American Ethnology (Washington, D.C.: Government Printing Office, 1911), Plate 31.

Ponca chief Standing Bear. The forced removal of the Poncas from Nebraska in 1877 prompted the Omahas to investigate the validity of their own land titles. Standing Bear's much-publicized trial would later make him a national celebrity. Alice C. Fletcher and Francis La Flesche, *The Omaha Tribe*, Twenty-Seventh Annual Report of the Bureau of American Ethnology (Washington, D.C.: Government Printing Office, 1911), Plate 5.

Alice C. Fletcher. Fletcher was the pioneering anthropologist responsible for allotting lands to the Omaha Indians in 1883–84. She repeated the process among the Winnebagos and the Nez Percé, although she later expressed doubts about the benefits of allotment. Nebraska Historical Society.

Wajapa, prominent Omaha and La Flesche family friend. A member of the Omaha "progressive' faction, Wajapa served as Alice Fletcher's guide when she toured the Sioux country in 1881. Alice C. Fletcher and Francis La Flesche, *The Omaha Tribe*, Twenty-Seventh Annual Report of the Bureau of American Ethnology (Washington, D.C.: Government Printing Office, 1911), Plate 29.

Francis La Flesche. An accomplished son of Joseph La Flesche, Francis was a writer, ethnographer, adviser to the Omaha people, and a devoted friend and protégé of anthropologist Alice C. Fletcher. Nebraska State Historical Society.

Chapter 5

A Beleaguered People
Liquor, Leasing, and Larceny, 1887–1905

> I never knew a white man to get his foot on an Indian's
> land who ever took it off.
>
> Henry L. Dawes, 1891

In 1896, Alice Fletcher reluctantly recognized the many cultural
problems that allotment posed for Indians.[1] Along with the loss of
traditional religion, the forced restructuring of the Indian family, and
the realignment of gender roles, Omahas suffered from exploitation by
greedy whites in the small towns that sprang up along the reservation
borders. Land "rings," merchants, bankers, and liquor sellers, particularly in Pender and Homer, Nebraska, took advantage of the Indians'
naiveté, leasing Omaha lands for a fraction of their value, charging
usurious interest, and selling the Indians whiskey for what little money
remained. In the years following the 1887 Dawes Act, the Omaha and
Winnebago Reservations became embroiled in controversy, especially
over the leasing of Indian lands, as agents either opposed or abetted
local real estate syndicates. Unfortunately for tribal unity, a few
Omahas, either for personal gain or under duress, cooperated with
whites in attempts to separate Indians from their lands. Indian Office
investigators and congressional delegations conducted inquiries and
filed reports, but the Omaha landgrab continued. With no farms to
work and with lease money in their pockets, idle Omahas became the
local bootleggers' best customers. Most local whites closed their eyes
to the tragedy of Omaha alcohol abuse, remaining concerned only with
the money that Indians pumped into their town economies. By the
early 1900s, few Omahas controlled their allotments, many drank
heavily, and almost no one seemed to care.

Omaha citizenship became an immediate problem after the passage
of the Dawes Act. Doubting their readiness, Senator Henry Dawes and
many reformers had objected to the House amendment that made the
Omahas and other previously allotted Indians citizens.[2] Dawes' con-

cerns were well-founded: in a letter sent through *Council Fire* to the commissioner of Indian affairs, 259 Omahas protested taxation and citizenship before the expiration of their trust period. Again in December 1887, claiming that their condition had been misrepresented, 158 Omahas signed a petition protesting their premature citizenship and resulting taxation. Pa-Hang-Ga-Ma-Ne said, "They have reported at headquarters that we live well; but we do not." He continued by asking Congress to "keep this thing citizenship away from us." Another Omaha reminded Congress that Fletcher had promised his people they would not be citizens or pay taxes for twenty-five years and that it was with this understanding that they had taken land patents. They had trusted Fletcher, but in less than five years, they now found themselves citizens, and many were unprepared.[3]

Dr. Susan La Flesche, Susette Tibbles' younger sister, believed that in some ways, citizenship had a positive effect on the Omahas. La Flesche observed that by being in closer proximity to whites, the Indians had learned about law and business and had become more independent.[4] But according to Susette Tibbles, it was not until their personal property was taxed that the Omahas realized that citizenship brought with it obligations and liabilities. Tibbles claimed that some whites who wanted Indians to remain noncitizens had told conservative Omahas horror stories regarding citizenship: that they would lose everything they had to taxes and that any crime was punishable by hanging. As a result, "nonprogressives" among the Omahas resented the young Indian assessors who came to evaluate their personal property. Some hid their horses, others destroyed the tax forms, and a few threatened to kill the messengers. However, when the recalcitrant Omahas learned that assessors would record their own estimates of present worth, they agreed to report their personal property.[5]

With citizenship, the Omahas became voters, and 70 to 80 percent cast ballots as soon as they were eligible. But beginning in 1892, many Omahas, in need of cash and seeing no difference in political parties as far as their welfare was concerned, sold their votes to the highest bidders, prompting Agent Robert Ashley to comment: "Full citizenship with the right of franchise . . . was a mistake. These people were not ready for it, and the evil and demoralizing effect of bartering in votes will outweigh all possible good."[6] Susette Tibbles claimed that whites treated the Omahas better after they could vote, but it appears in some cases that whites used enfranchised Omahas for their own purposes. For example, when saloons opened near the reservation, many Indians wanted them closed. But when Prohibition appeared on the local ballot, white liquor dealers tricked or coerced most Omahas into voting against it.[7]

Supporters of the severalty law did not anticipate Omaha voting irregularities and never foresaw the huge problems that would arise when the "ambitious little town of Pender" pushed a bill through the state legislature making nearly the entire Omaha Reservation one Nebraska county. Despite a reformer's suggestion that it would be more sensible to divide Omaha lands among four or five bordering counties, the reservation plus a small strip of white-occupied land on the southwestern border of the reservation became Thurston County on March 29, 1889.[8] Reservation lands were tax-exempt, yet the new county was required to build roads and schools and to provide courts. Since the county had no taxation right over Indian real estate, the Omahas' personal property was taxed at an exorbitant rate.[9] Anticipating their high tax bills, Silas Wood and Daniel Webster, along with over 150 other Omahas, had asked their eastern white friends to help stop organization of the county.[10] It had never occurred to Senator Dawes that virtually all the land of an entire county could become tax-exempt, and he urged the government either to pay Thurston County an amount equivalent to the Omaha taxes or to use tribal funds for that purpose. But even had this proposal been fair, Omaha annuity money was unavailable; the tribe had already received half of its remaining $90,000 and had been promised the rest.[11] Over the next twenty years, faced with large expenses and a tiny tax base, Thurston County would conduct a relentless campaign to tax Omaha real estate.

From the time the Omahas chose their reservation, whites had resented their ownership of some of the most fertile land in Nebraska. In the late 1880s and into the next decade, white settlers and land syndicates managed to move onto the reservation by leasing Omaha lands at ridiculously low rates. One scholar believed this systematic takeover of Indian lands was by design. Calling leasing an "inevitable corollary of the allotment system," Ward Shepard charged that leasing was more than a "mere afterthought."[12] Indeed, as early as 1888, Indian Commissioner John H. Oberly, in an attempt to cut Indian Office costs, campaigned for the legalization of grazing leases to provide tribal income and to reduce Indian dependence on government appropriations.[13] Reformers at the Lake Mohonk Conference supported leasing, arguing that Indians could not progress if they were forbidden to manage their own allotments and pointing out that leasing part of their lands would provide income to improve the rest.[14]

In the opinion of historian D. S. Otis, allowing Indians to lease their lands was the "most important decision as to Indian policy . . . after the passage of the Dawes Act," yet it met little opposition and generated almost no debate in Congress.[15] The only real objection to leasing came from Senator Dawes, who told the Lake Mohonk Conference in 1890 that a law allowing leasing would "overthrow the whole allotment system," since "the Indian would abandon his own work, his own land, and his own home." A year later, Dawes reminded the Lake Mohonk conferees that he had always opposed leasing of allotments because he knew that if an Indian gave up an allotment, he or she "would never get it back." These were strange words coming from a legislator who in March 1890 had introduced a leasing bill in the Senate.[16] Dawes explained that he had reluctantly changed his mind on leasing after seeing Indians, frustrated with trying to break prairie sod, turn their lands over to whites and return to their tepees. As an alternative, he suggested authorizing Indians to lease part of their allotments to white farmers and to use the rent money to have the rest of their lands cultivated.[17]

The perceived positive aspects of Omaha allotment had been used to promote the passage of the Dawes Act in 1887. Just a few years later, premature and unregulated leasing of Omaha allotments prompted the government to pass a law permitting the practice. In 1890 and 1891, the Bureau of Indian Affairs conducted three separate investigations into the largely illegal leasing on the Omaha and Winnebago Reservations. In his reports dated May 29 and June 2, 1890, Inspector W. W. Junkin observed that the Omahas were making little progress toward "civilization," a state of affairs he blamed on the presence of whites on the reservation. Whites rented grazing lands for eight to twenty cents per acre, and with few exceptions, the Indian landowners were idle most of the time. Junkin called for an end to this exploitation, and he unsuccessfully requested troops to drive every white person off the reservations.[18] A later report by Inspector A. M. Tinker stated that the more "progressive" Omahas did not want any lands leased, but some Indians had already leased both their lands and their homes and were living in tepees, "doing nothing." Tinker also reported that whites often refused to make their lease payments and allowed their stock to run free, breaking fences and destroying crops.[19]

In response to a January 1891 Senate resolution, Indian Commissioner T. J. Morgan directed Agent Ashley to investigate the leasing of allotments on the two reservations. On January 26, Ashley reported that without the knowledge of the Indian Office, some Omahas had been leasing their allotments to whites ever since they had received lands in severalty, and more were leasing each year. Before 1890, most leases were for grazing and for one year at a time, but more recent leases had been written for longer terms. According to the Thurston County clerk, 2,387 acres of Omaha land were leased in 1890, and fifteen lessees actually lived on the reservation. Ashley agreed with Junkin that both the Indians and their tenants knew that the leasing of allotments was illegal but that the practice continued. Omahas were quickly losing control of their lands, and their agent feared that soon all the best reservation lands would be farmed or used for grazing by white interlopers.[20]

In his 1890 annual report, Agent Ashley had suggested a solution to the problem of illegal leasing on the Omaha and Winnebago Reservations. Stating that at least 60 percent of allotted land belonged to women, old or ill men, or minor children, he urged that their lands be allowed to be leased with the oversight and consent of either the Indian commissioner or the local agent.[21] Inspector Junkin agreed that current laws were inadequate and that if the government wanted to allow leasing, it should be carefully controlled and fair rentals should be enforced.[22]

Realizing that leasing would occur legally or otherwise, Congress on February 28, 1891, passed "an act to amend and further extend the benefits of the act approved February 8, 1887" (the Dawes Act). Section Three of the new law stated that if an Indian, because of age or disability, could not personally occupy or improve an allotment, he or she might lease the land for a term not to exceed three years for farming or grazing and ten years for mining.[23] But able-bodied Indians also wanted to lease their lands, and as a result, in August 1894, the leasing act was amended. The words "or inability" were added, and lands could now be leased for five years for farming and grazing and ten years for "business purposes" or mining.[24]

It was easy for whites to persuade Indians to lease, and the term "inability" covered many conditions, including simple laziness. C. C. Painter, of the Indian Rights Association (IRA), predicted that this change in the leasing law would result in innumerable leases and would harm Indians more than annuities ever had: "There has never been a time when the situation has been so full of danger to the Indian with reference to his land as now."[25] The changes were so heavily criticized that in June 1897, the words "or inability" were removed, farming and grazing leases reverted to three years, and a five-year limit was set on business and mining contracts.[26] Congress could not decide on a definitive policy, however. The legislative tinkering continued, and in May 1900, "inability" once more became grounds for leasing. Lands could now be rented for five years for "farming only," business and mining leases remained at five years, and grazing lands could be leased for a maximum of three years.[27]

Leasing almost totally demoralized the Omahas in the late 1880s and 1890s. Cattlemen encouraged strife within the tribe, and the promise of "grass money" was more attractive to many Indians than the prospect of working a farm. In a letter to his half-sister Rosalie Farley, Francis La Flesche described the scenario should white men be allowed to lease Omaha lands. He predicted that the Indians would do nothing to better themselves and that at the expiration of their trust period, his people would be unprepared for their new responsibilities.[28] Unfortunately, the always perceptive La Flesche was correct. By 1892, 90 percent of the Omahas and Winnebagoes had leased either all or part of their lands and were getting by on rent money. Many Omahas had deserted their allotments, leaving white lessees to farm the land, and had either moved in with relatives or were living on their children's allotments on the poorer lands.[29]

In reply to an 1892 survey distributed by Commissioner Morgan, Agent Ashley stated that illegal leases were "doing more to retard the progress of [the Omahas] . . . than all other causes combined." Ashley had seen far too many Omahas begin to farm, then lease every acre they owned for a little cash, on which they hoped to survive without working. Those allottees who held desirable lands near towns came under tremendous pressure to lease. The agent explained how land companies, in conjunction with local townspeople, "feasted, cajoled, and incited" the Indians to try to gain control of their valuable lands.[30]

By 1894, allotment advocates who had held high hopes for the Omahas were bitterly disappointed. Whites now lived on lands that reformers had once envisioned as flourishing Indian farms, whereas many of the Omahas remained camped along the Missouri and drank heavily. The Omahas received higher rents for their lands than did the Winnebagoes; according to C. C. Painter, this simply gave them "greater facilities for debauchery." Some Omahas themselves abused the system by claiming unallotted lands for nonexistent children or by making more than one claim for a single child. In Painter's judgment, many Omahas had been "irreparably damaged" by leasing, and all had been slowed in their quest for "civilization." Furthermore, he did not foresee the lessees vacating Omaha lands in the near future.[31]

White tenants did stay, and leasing proliferated on the Omaha and Winnebago Reservations. On the two reservations in 1894, 223 leases were approved, and in 1896 and 1897, over 220 more Omahas rented their lands. The year 1900 was a banner one for whites who wanted Omaha lands. When Indian Commissioner William A. Jones submitted his annual report, 543 farming and grazing contracts had already been approved, and 135 more were pending. In 1901, 284 more Omahas leased; another 293 parcels fell into white hands in 1903, and between October 1903 and August 1905, Commissioners Jones and Francis Leupp reported an additional 466 contracts. Prices for Omaha lands ranged from twenty-five cents per acre per year for grazing to $2.50 per acre for choice farmland; in 1903, allottees could command $3.00 per acre for their best lands. By 1904, the leasing of 55,560 acres of Omaha land netted the tribe and individual Indians $43,763.63.[32]

In fiscal year 1898, Omaha Agent W. A. Mercer began collecting rents for leased lands, much to the dissatisfaction of whites who had for years taken advantage of the Omahas' unfamiliarity with business matters. Mercer estimated that Indian income would more than double under the new system. Because many Omahas had in the past agreed to accept whatever rentals the white lessees offered, Mercer's successor, Charles P. Mathewson, also predicted a large increase in Omaha income with rentals going through the agency.[33] Although he collected land rentals, Agent Mercer thoroughly disapproved of leasing, considering its income "a premium on laziness and a discouragement to industrious effort and self-support among the Indians." The outspoken agent recommended that Indians be forced to live on and farm their allotments, and he advocated banning all whites from the reservation until the Omahas could support themselves.[34]

By 1900, leasing had gotten out of hand, and reformers as well as officials in the Indian Office recognized that the system was corrupt and detrimental to Indians. The once supportive Lake Mohonk Conference included in its 1900 platform an official stance on the leasing issue. Since "the habit of leasing allotments convert[ed] the lessor from an industrious worker to an idle and improvident landlord," the conferees urged that leasing be strictly limited to those Indians who could not work their lands and that guidelines be rigorously enforced.[35]

The Indian Rights Association assigned blame, charging that greedy agents played a large role in the proliferation of leases of Indian lands. A potential lessee would allegedly approach an agent, offer a ridiculously low rental, then promise the agent a bonus if he would recommend the lease. Bonuses paid on thousands of acres could net an unscrupulous agent an income much larger than his government salary.[36] Commissioner Jones hinted that there may have been some truth in the IRA's charges. Although the interior secretary theoretically approved all leases, in reality the work was done by agents, many of whom came from the areas around the reservations they served and who wanted to remain on good terms with their constituents. Consequently, if an acquaintance of an agent asked for a lease, the request was usually approved. Jones admitted that there would be fewer leases if agents were chosen from outside the local communities.[37]

The Omahas also recognized the ill effects of leasing. In 1900, an allottee asked Francis La Flesche to deliver a message to whites that "the leasing business [was] ruining the Omahas in every way." He worried that his people had become shiftless; many of them "loaf[ed] about the towns" and drank to excess. Instead of working their farms, they used rent money to pay railroad fares to visit other tribes.[38] In an effort to make them more responsible, Agent Mathewson suggested that in the future, "progressive" Omaha allottees should have their lease money paid to them directly instead of through their agent. He reasoned that with such a short time left in their trust period, they should gradually take charge of their own affairs.[39]

When the Omaha Agency once more became independent of the Winnebago Agency in 1904, its newly appointed superintendent found the Omahas idle and demoralized and living almost entirely on lease revenues. Remembering when these Indians were "self-supporting, industrious, and thrifty," John F. MacKey saw the tribe going steadily downhill as the result of leasing.[40] Events on the Omaha Reservation demonstrated that allotment was much different in practice than in theory. In reality, the allotted Indian was allowed to turn over his land to whites and "go on his aimless way." In 1900, Commissioner Jones blamed the allotted Indians' problems on the leasing acts passed after the original 1891 law. Had the statute stood as originally written, Jones would have had no complaints; but he believed that the term " 'inability' . . . opened the door for leasing in general," making it in many cases "the rule rather than the exception." Jones was convinced that leasing had hurt the Indians. "By taking away the incentive to labor it defeats the very object for which the allotment system was devised, which was, by giving the Indian something tangible that he could call his own, to incite him to personal effort in his own behalf."[41] Twelve years later, Indian Commissioner Robert G. Valentine charged that the purpose of the Dawes Act had been "perverted" by the 1891 leasing law. After the leasing act, allotted Indians were free to lease their lands and "live . . . after their former fashion."[42]

Local white involvement in Omaha affairs during the 1890s is perhaps best illustrated by two leasing controversies, both of which made their way into the courts. In one case, local businessmen attempted to discredit an Indian lessee and her husband in order to take over the Omahas' common pasture, and in the other, a controversial agent tangled with a local land syndicate over reservation leasing irregularities and unauthorized tenants. At least two groups of whites in newly organized Thurston County hoped to profit from Indian lands. One group specialized in cheating the Winnebagoes, allegedly leasing

Indian land at ten cents an acre and then subleasing to farmers for ninety cents more. The syndicate interested in Omaha lands was led by Pender businessman William E. Peebles, a political supporter of Nebraska Senator John M. Thurston and a would-be Omaha agent.[43]

Since the summer of 1884, Rosalie and Ed Farley had unofficially but successfully managed the Omahas' unallotted common pasture. In 1890 Peebles, along with A. C. Abbott, D. N. Wheeler, George F. Chittenden, and Harry F. Swanson, all eager to profit from Omaha lands, devised an elaborate scheme to nullify the Farleys' lease. When the Omahas appointed Wajapa, Henry Blackbird, and Omaha Agency clerk Thomas McCauley to go to Washington in December 1890 to discuss allotments with Commissioner Morgan, Peebles, the front man for the "Pender ring," saw his chance to undermine the Farleys' contract. Peebles decided he should accompany the Omaha delegates as their "guide." On Christmas Day, he sent Thomas McCauley "credentials" for himself and for the Indian delegation with instructions for the clerk to have all the Omaha leading men sign the form, then to deliver it to him in Pender. The credentials consisted of a sheet of cheap stationery on which Peebles had introduced himself as a "true friend" to the Omahas, one in whom they had complete confidence. Attached to the bottom was a sheet of paper containing six names: Fire Chief, White Horse, Wajapa, Two Crows, Sindahaha, and Prairie Chicken. When Rosalie and Ed Farley learned of the scheme, they confronted the clerk, who tried to burn the offending papers. The rescued documents contained no signatures, since the leading men were totally unaware of Peebles' plan.[44]

Peebles did nevertheless accompany the delegation to Washington, and the tribal leaders suspected a Pender plot to gain possession of their unallotted lands. With this in mind, and with Peebles out of town, the headmen asked Rosalie Farley to meet with them earlier than planned to draw up a new lease for five years, renewable yearly at fifteen cents per acre. Instead of a large number of Omahas signing this lease, a small delegation acted for the tribe, probably to minimize outside influence. The twenty signers included three leading men whose names Peebles had attached to his fraudulent credentials.[45]

In the spring of 1892, through Agent Ashley, Rosalie Farley signed a new lease on 2,632 acres of land for five years, this time renewable yearly at twenty-five cents per acre. Future events would hinge on a clause stating that the lease would be canceled if and when the pasturelands were allotted.[46] When the suspicious Indians refused Peebles' counteroffer to lease the lands at fifty cents per acre for seven to eight years, the Pender ring tried another tactic. Working through Henry Fontenelle and a few others, Peebles and his cronies allegedly persuaded some Omaha councilmen to sign a widely distributed circular stating that the Farleys' lease had expired, that an allotting agent was en route to Nebraska, and that all cattle would have to be removed from the pasture. Although several councilmen denied signing the circular and Fontenelle admitted using their names without permission, many stockmen did remove their herds.[47]

But most Omahas, recognizing who was behind the controversy, supported the Farleys and encouraged them to continue accepting cattle. Failing in their attempt to ruin the Farleys' business, Peebles and Wheeler, once again using a few Omahas as a front, filed suit in federal district court during early 1893, charging Rosalie Farley with defrauding the Omahas. The suit, nominally brought by "Fire Chief, White Horse, et al.," claimed that the Omahas had not authorized Agent Ashley to negotiate the 1892 lease and that the lease was delaying allotments and therefore hindering tribal progress.[48] The Pender conspirators also apparently sent a letter to the commissioner of Indian affairs, using Fire Chief's and White Horse's names and inquiring as to the legality of the Farleys' lease. When confronted, Fire Chief said Peebles and his friends had "badgered him" into signing the letter.[49] Fontenelle finally tipped his hand and gave his reason for cooperating with the men from Pender. In a statement revealing his intense jealousy, Fontenelle fumed, "We want to *break* the *La Flesche family*, no matter *what* they always have their hands into it."[50]

As a result of the lawsuit against Rosalie Farley, the Omahas became furious with the Omaha councilmen, whom they accused of working for Peebles rather than for the tribe. They were especially angry that the council had pledged several hundred dollars in tribal funds to pay attorneys from Sioux City to file the lawsuit, which they did not support. At a tribal meeting in late May 1893, the people united in denouncing the councilmen who had allowed themselves to be used by Peebles. As the meeting adjourned, someone suggested that all those who disapproved of what had been done and who agreed not to pay the Sioux City lawyers should rise. Every man came to his feet. Early in September, the Omahas elected a new council; only old Two Crows was retained. But the new councilmen refused to take office until the old ones had finished with the lawsuit and had dealt with Peebles.[51] Later that fall, the commissioner of Indian affairs instructed Agent William A. Beck to withdraw the Omahas' lawsuit against Rosalie Farley, but Farley, in the meantime, had sued Peebles and his partners for conspiracy to destroy her cattle-grazing business.[52]

Rosalie Farley's conspiracy case against Peebles and other members of the Pender ring was heard in the district court for Cuming County at West Point, Nebraska, beginning on December 18, 1893. According to Farley and the Nebraska Supreme Court, the trial was a mockery of justice. Because they were unprepared, defendants Peebles and Wheeler did everything they could to delay the trial—even resorting to the fabricated excuse that their star witness, Henry Fontenelle, was dying. When the trial did get under way, the Pender gang claimed that the Omahas had asked for help because they believed the Farley lease was fraudulent and was delaying further allotment.[53]

As the trial progressed, the irregularities multiplied. Fontenelle, White Horse, Sindahaha, and Big Elk lied on the stand, and during the trial, Sindahaha confessed to Farley that he was "under obligations" to the Pender men, as apparently was presiding Judge W. F. Norris, who may have owed the Penderites a political debt. During jury selection, the prosecuting attorney asked prospective jurors if they had any bias against Indians. They all said they did not, yet in his summation, Peebles' attorney appealed to racial prejudices, reminding the jurors of every atrocity ever committed by Indians.[54] Despite the defense attorney's diatribe, the jury could not reach a verdict and asked to be excused. Judge Norris refused to dismiss the panel and instead instructed them to find against Rosalie Farley. A month later, ignoring these irregularities, the court refused to grant a new trial.[55]

The Farleys' attorneys thought that had Judge Norris not made his improper speech to the jury after its long deliberation, the case would have resulted in a "hung jury," and a new trial would have been automatic. But having been refused a second trial, they took the case to the Nebraska Supreme Court, where they believed Rosalie Farley would receive a fairer hearing.[56] On February 16, 1897, the state supreme court overturned Judge Norris' ruling due to numerous errors in the conduct of the trial at West Point.[57]

Fontenelle's campaign to discredit the La Flesche family continued after the conspiracy trial. In the spring of 1896, the Farleys leased tribal lands for agricultural purposes—apparently quite legal according to the 1894 leasing act revisions. But Fontenelle drummed up opposition and sent a petition opposing the lease to the Indian commissioner. Even though two other lessees paid less, in his petition Fontenelle charged that the Farleys were not paying the Omahas enough. Because of Fontenelle's "checkered past," Agent Beck expected the commissioner to disregard the petition, but to be safe, Beck countered with a petition of his own, signed by numerous Omahas who supported the Farleys.[58] There must have been some concern in Washington regarding the contract, for the Bureau of Indian Affairs did send an inspector to Nebraska to look into the agricultural lease. The *Lyons (Nebraska) Mirror* recognized the financial benefit to the Omahas but had concerns that the lease, like all other large leases, would violate the spirit of the Dawes Act by encouraging Indian indolence.[59] The government inspector must have been satisfied, for in late June 1896, Alice Fletcher informed Rosalie Farley that Indian Commissioner Daniel M. Browning had reported favorably on the new lease and was prepared to recommend it to the interior secretary.[60]

The entire history of the Farley leases is problematic. On the one hand, Rosalie and Ed Farley apparently ran an honest business and regularly shared their profits with the Omahas. On the other hand, the Lyons newspaper was correct: the leases did contribute to Omaha idleness. Perhaps the Omahas considered the Farley enterprise the lesser of two evils. They did not want Pender "land sharks" taking over the reservation; Rosalie La Flesche Farley, although married to a white man, was one of their own, and most Omahas trusted her.

When cavalry officer William A. Beck took over as Omaha and Winnebago agent in the summer of 1893, he was warmly welcomed by the citizens of Pender, who feted him at the local hotel. However, the honeymoon ended abruptly when Beck refused to cooperate with a powerful local land syndicate. The Fluornoy Livestock and Real Estate Company had leased nearly fifty thousand acres from individual

Indians for "a few cents per acre" and had subleased to farmers at a much higher rate, pocketing the difference. Without having access to the actual contracts, the IRA's C. C. Painter estimated that the Fluornoy Company netted $60,000 to $75,000 per year while each Indian received from ten to twenty-five cents an acre for the land.[61] Beck reported the leasing irregularities to his superiors, and on July 17, the Indian Office directed him to inform illegal tenants that they must either make legal leases or leave the land by December 31. By about October 1, all illegal lessees had been notified.[62]

Taking Beck quite seriously, the Fluornoy Company brought an injunction against the agent, preventing him from interfering with their leases, and by January 1, 1894, four other land companies had followed suit. After a long delay, Judge Elmer Dundy of the Eighth Circuit Court ruled that the injunction should be permanent.[63] In return, Agent Beck took the injunction to the Eighth Circuit Court of Appeals. Painter, along with everyone on or near the reservations, waited anxiously to see if Judge Dundy's restraining order against Beck would be lifted. If not, Painter feared that few allotted Indians would ever possess their own lands. The good news for the Omahas and Winnebagoes came in early December 1894. Arguing that the injunction was too broad and that the Fluornoy Company had knowingly violated the law, the appeals court lifted the restraining order. In his opinion, Judge Amos Thayer criticized Judge Dundy: "It is not within the legitimate province of a court . . . to assist a wrongdoer . . . in retaining the possession of property which it has acquired in open violation of an Act of Congress."[64]

The Fluornoy Company appealed Judge Thayer's ruling to the U.S. Supreme Court and, while awaiting a decision, continued to make illegal leases with the Winnebagoes. In April 1895, an assistant U.S. district attorney sought unsuccessfully to get a restraining order against the Fluornoy Company, and at about the same time, the land syndicate proposed a compromise by which, in return for an end to litigation, it would vacate the reservations by January 1, 1896. Beck refused to compromise, and the battle went on. The agent expanded his police force, hiring sixteen additional men. Then in a series of events that would be almost comical if the situation had not been so tragic, the Thurston County sheriff tried to arrest an Indian policeman, and tribal police arrested the sheriff, who in turn organized a posse to arrest Beck.[65]

In May, Agent Beck called for fifty more Indian policemen to counter opposition from the land company and its subtenants. The extra men went on duty July 1, and the War Department supplied Beck and his small "army" with seventy Springfield rifles and ammunition. Now well-armed and with an adequate force, the agent set about evicting illegal tenants. But shortly after he began, the Nebraska district court issued an injunction to stop the removals, and men from Pender armed themselves to arrest the Indian police force. Beck now requested federal troops to protect his policemen and asked the Bureau of Indian Affairs if he should obey the restraining order. The Indian Office ordered him to abide by the state court ruling, and the evictions stopped.[66]

According to Commissioner Browning's version of the controversy, Beck's purpose in trying to remove the Fluornoy Company and its tenants was to allow the Indians to get a fair rental for their lands. Besides cheating the Omahas and Winnebagoes and making a huge profit in the process, the company paid the Indians little or nothing from 1893 to 1895. Beck's campaign was against the land company— the middleman—not against the settlers who occupied the land. From the beginning, he had advised the sublessees to sign legal leases. The problem was that many farmers had signed promissory notes with the land company, which had sold the notes to bankers, who now wanted to be paid. If a farmer signed a legal lease, he would have to pay double rent, which he could ill afford, and the land company naturally discouraged proper leases, since that would eventually cut profits.[67]

The near-violence between Beck and the Fluornoy Company brought the Nebraska congressional delegation to the Omaha and Winnebago Reservations in July 1895 to conduct what was termed an "informal investigation." According to Rosalie Farley, the "so-called" congressional investigation was really promoted by "Peebles and the Fluornoy Co. land swindlers." Regardless of who instigated it, the "investigation" was definitely more than a chat between congressmen and Indians, since the resulting reports of wrongdoing on the reservations made the front pages of the *Omaha World-Herald* and the *Omaha Daily Bee* and appeared in Commissioner Browning's 1895 annual report.[68]

On the evening of July 23, the Pender opera house was the scene of a town meeting as the congressional delegation met with settlers who had leased lands on the two reservations. Peebles made the first accusations—against Agent Beck—when he presented a memorial from sixty settlers who had invested everything they had in the land and now resented paying "tribute" to the agent's friends. Fred Jennewein, secretary of the Farmers' Society, charged that in granting leases, Beck favored "middlemen" John Beck (his son), Winnebago traders Thomas and John Ashford, F. B. Hutchins of Sioux City, Joseph Blenkiron of Bancroft, E. J. Smith of Herman, and John Beck's brother-in-law, Charles McKnight, of the Winnebago Agency.[69] Beck was obviously not the crusader that Commissioner Browning had portrayed in his report. From the testimony of many farmers who had leased from the Fluornoy Company, it appears that Beck conducted a scheme in which he would have his Indian police evict a Fluornoy lessee, then would re-rent the land to the farmer through one of his middlemen. All of the paperwork and personal negotiating was conducted through Beck's Omaha clerk, Thomas L. Sloan, perhaps to disguise the agent's involvement in leasing irregularities. Beck's scheme resulted in settlers paying double rent, but most had no choice, since they had crops in the ground and no other income.[70]

Jennewein's damning testimony especially impressed the delegation. He claimed that John Ashford had told him of holding a lease to Jennewein's land from Agent Beck. For $1.25 an acre, Ashford would "fix things so that he would have no trouble with his land." Jennewein agreed to pay, since he already farmed 320 acres and could not afford to be evicted. At least fifty other settlers had been approached by middlemen and ordered to pay "protection money" to avoid eviction. Based on the settlers' testimonies, the congressional delegation informally charged Thomas Sloan and the middlemen whom the farmers had accused with "speculating on leaseholds."[71] The delegation declined to charge Agent Beck with any wrongdoing. Perhaps because he represented the government, they gave him the benefit of the doubt.

The hearings at Winnebago on July 24 were well attended by men from Pender. Although billed as an "Indian council," to Rosalie Farley it smacked of a political meeting, with all of the congressmen except Senator William V. Allen favoring Peebles and the illegal lessees. On

July 25, Peebles packed a hearing in Pender with white settlers and "his Indians." Three tribal representatives sent by the Omahas to defend Agent Beck were never heard; they sat by the door all day but were not allowed into the meeting room. Denied a hearing before the delegation, over fifty Omahas wrote to Commissioner Browning expressing their support for Agent Beck and thanking him for his efforts on their behalf. At a mass meeting the following day, citizens of Bancroft also endorsed Beck's actions, and by July 28, fifty more Indians had signed the tribal letter.[72]

Omahas on both sides of the still-smoldering pasture allotment question did testify before the congressmen, and Rosalie Farley accused the pro-allotment Indians of working in concert with Peebles and against Agent Beck. This is highly likely, since the Omahas presenting evidence against the agent were the same ones who had testified on Peebles' behalf at West Point.[73] On the other side, speaking against allotment of the common pasture, Wajapa compared himself to a man with his back against a wall, and he asked the government to keep whites from taking Omaha lands. He admitted that his people did "not know how to take care of [their] possessions" and "could not keep the land if [they] had it." He also insisted that it was not the Indians but someone pulling strings in the background (probably a reference to Peebles) who wanted Omaha lands allotted. After Wajapa spoke, Representative George D. Meiklejohn tried to weaken his testimony by pointing out that he was Rosalie Farley's uncle and therefore would not want the pasture allotted.[74]

Frequent tribal spokesman and allotment proponent Daniel Webster revealed further details of Peebles' plot to have the pasture land allotted. Webster told the congressmen that over dinner in Pender, Peebles had told him of the plan to quickly allot the common pasture with only the councilmen's knowledge and had asked him to attend a late-night meeting at Fire Chief's lodge. Webster admitted that he liked the plan but was afraid he would be punished if he participated. Peebles then allegedly offered Webster $300 in expense money to go with him to Washington and asked to be paid if he was able to push the allotment through. Webster refused this offer as well.[75]

Silas Wood testified that he had originally supported allotment of the common pasture but had changed his mind when he had realized that it would bring a white takeover of the land. Wood recounted a dream in which the "Great Spirit" warned him not to disturb the land because there was a snake hidden there and it would bite. To Wood, the snake was the white man, who wanted the Omahas to own land so that he could take it away. Wood also foresaw, with a great deal of accuracy, whites getting Indians drunk and having them sign contracts. In addition, he charged that it was the old men of the tribe, the ones who cared little for the children's futures, who wanted allotments.[76]

White Horse, one of Wood's "old men," admitted that he thought little about future generations. He cared only for those Omahas living at the time, and he strongly supported allotment and the Omahas' right to lease to whomever they pleased.[77] As he had so often done before, Henry Fontenelle hurt his own cause. When asked his opinion, he appeared to have no objections to the approval or rejection of allotments by the interior secretary, but he bristled when Senator Allen suggested that the agent should control leasing. Fontenelle then launched a personal attack on Agent Beck, clouding his entire testimony.[78]

Fontenelle was not alone in his criticism of Agent Beck. Sindahaha pointed out that technically the Omahas had no agent but that Beck nevertheless tried to manage tribal affairs. He accused the agent of being short-tempered and impatient and looked back fondly to the days when Indian agents were friendly and gave good advice.[79] S. A. Combs, of Homer, Nebraska, wrote to Senator Allen to inform him of the corrupt nature of Beck's administration. He called Beck rotten and disreputable and said the agent's son, John, was a "drunken, gambling . . . vagabond" who ran a house of prostitution using Indian women. Combs reminded the senator that John Ashford had been convicted of selling liquor to Indians. On the whole, he considered the people surrounding Beck a "gang of scoundrels."[80] On the other hand, Daniel Webster believed that Beck looked out for the Indians' welfare and that those who fought the agent were out to ruin the Omahas.[81] Agreeing with Webster, Wajapa considered Beck a good man falsely accused.[82]

When asked to testify regarding the common pasture, Beck lashed out at his Indian detractors and the Pender ring, stating that the reason for the allotment push was that the now-defunct firm of Wheeler and Chittenden had advanced Indians from $20 to $50 on the promise that when the Indians received allotments, the firm would be able to lease them. Beck pointed out that oddly, all of the Indians signing illegal promissory notes requested lands in the Farley pasture, certainly not the best lands available. The agent viewed these dealings as yet another attempt to destroy the Farleys' lease through its allotment clause.[83]

After listening to hours of testimony on all aspects of the controversies, the Nebraska congressional delegation filed a report on July 25, 1895, recommending that all settler evictions be halted, that the Fluornoy Company lessees be allowed to harvest their crops unmolested, and that the agency be investigated.[84] In addition to their joint report, Senators Allen and Thurston and Representative W. E. Andrews sent personal letters to Acting Interior Secretary John M. Reynolds, condemning the conduct of the Omaha and Winnebago Agency and urging a congressional inquiry into events there. Senator Allen expressed his belief in Beck's honesty but charged that the agent was surrounded by "a class of men whose conduct ought to be investigated." Allen believed that the trader, his brother, and others holding government jobs intended to gain control of a huge tract of Indian land.[85]

There clearly were no heroes in the Omaha and Winnebago leasing controversies of the 1890s—only victims and villains. The Indians were systematically cheated of their lands, and white settlers were cheated of their leasing payments. Peebles and his cronies, the Fluornoy outfit, Agent Beck and his alleged agency "ring," and even Rosalie and Ed Farley all wanted one thing—profit. During those troubled times, the widening split in Omaha leadership became a chasm as Indians threw their support to opposing factions. Unfortunately, testimony and support could be bought, and allegiances were often based on favors given and received. The land syndicates knowingly broke the law, Omahas perjured themselves and claimed fraudulent allotments, and Agent Beck apparently saw an economic opportunity too tempting to resist.

By late 1896, Beck knew that he would soon be replaced as the Omaha and Winnebago agent. Through his stormy term of office, he had been protected by his close ties to high-ranking Interior Department officials and to Secretary of War Daniel Lamont, but now Lamont was gone, and Senator Thurston was agitating for a new agent.[86] On May 17, 1897, the army ordered Beck to rejoin his cavalry unit in Montana.[87]

The leasing troubles on the Omaha Reservation, though serious and detrimental to the Indians, were not unique. As on the Omaha Reservation, the leasing issue elsewhere caused tribal divisions, mainly over the distribution of "grass money." To the south, Texas cattlemen ignored Kiowa and Comanche reservation boundaries and grazed their cattle on Indian lands. By the 1890s, informal grazing had evolved into formal leasing, with Interior Department support. A few Kiowa and Comanche leaders, particularly the mixed-blood Quanah Parker, profited by cooperating with cattlemen and encouraging leasing.[88]

Another case in point was the Cheyenne-Arapaho Reservation in Indian Territory. By 1876, cattle grazed legally and illegally on the reservation. Agent John D. Miles encouraged the leasing of Indian lands to help the Indians economically, and most Cheyenne and Arapaho leaders supported his efforts. However, Cheyenne warrior societies opposed white intrusion onto their lands and urged their people to keep the reservation "Indian." Convinced that the problems among the Indians were caused by the cattlemen and fearful of Cheyenne attacks on white settlers, President Grover Cleveland ordered all cattle not belonging to Indians to be removed from the reservation. By late 1885, the Cheyenne-Arapaho agent reported that the last of the cattle were gone.[89]

In 1897, with Beck's days as Omaha agent numbered, the *Thurston Republic* and, according to the newspaper, nearly every Indian and white in Thurston County endorsed William Peebles as his replacement. Though the paper acknowledged that the Indians should have some input into the choice of a new agent, the *Republic* paternalistically insisted that the Thurston County whites, burdened with the task of helping twenty-five hundred Indians become "intelligent and civilized," should be the ones to ultimately decide. Oddly, the paper contended that over 80 percent of the Omahas supported Peebles, even after many of them had agreed to testify against him in the Farley leasing case.[90] On March 2, Peebles passed through Omaha on his way to Washington, reportedly armed with a petition signed by practically every Republican in Thurston County, endorsing him as the new agent for the Omahas and Winnebagoes.[91] Despite his campaign, Peebles did not get the job. On about June 6, 1897, Beck was relieved by another army officer, Lieutenant William Mercer of the Eighth Infantry.[92]

But Peebles did not give up; about a year later, he arranged a meeting between Senator Thurston and several Omahas and Winnebagoes. He must have hoped that their planned "speeches" would enhance his chances of replacing Mercer. However, one Indian, claiming that Lieutenant Mercer had done nothing for him as agent, said he wanted Peebles, who had promised him a new house in return for his support. Another admitted that he disliked Mercer because he refused to put his friends on the tribal police force. Peebles, of course, had promised to do so if the Indian backed his campaign. The Indians' painful honesty helped end Peebles' aspirations.[93]

While the Omahas were expressing their opposing views on further allotment of their lands before the congressional investigators, the question had already been answered for them. Many Omahas did not understand why children rather than wives should inherit land or why wives did not receive lands of their own under the terms of the 1882 Omaha Allotment Act. Because of Indian complaints, as well as Peebles' incessant lobbying, the Omaha Allotment Act was amended as part of the Indian Appropriation Act of March 3, 1893. Under the terms of the new legislation, children born between the time of the original allotments and March 3, 1893, would receive eighty acres of land instead of forty, each Indian woman would be given eighty acres, and any other allottee who had received only forty acres would have that amount doubled.[94] The Dawes Act had been amended two years earlier to provide acreage to every Indian, and the change to their allotment act finally gave the Omahas the amounts of land granted to others in 1891.[95] All of these additional allotments were to be taken from the remaining tribally held lands. In a master stroke of poor planning, the 1893 amendment did not address Omaha children born after March 3, 1893, thus leaving these children landless.

No action was taken on the new law for six years, but controversy over its passage arose almost immediately. Within weeks after the second allotment act became effective, Indian attorney Thomas Sloan began distributing allotment numbers to young Omahas, who promptly agreed to lease their prospective lands to Wheeler and other Pender men for fifty cents an acre for terms of from five to seven years.[96] In the early confusion, some allotments were claimed by two or three different Indians, and because of the chaotic conditions, a group of Omahas prepared a petition asking the Indian commissioner to put the allotments on hold.[97] Other problems surfaced: some Indians began to doubt the benefits of the bill, and Ed Farley claimed that the act was illegal because there was not enough land to allot.[98] Francis La Flesche agreed; early in 1898, with the new allotments imminent, he advised his sister Rosalie to "quietly" and "quickly" file papers with Agent Mercer for her children. Like Farley, he did not believe there was enough land to go around. La Flesche was happy to see the lands allotted, however, because he hoped it would end intertribal land squabbles and "bring all land matters in[to] the Courts—where they belong[ed]."[99]

On April 24, 1899, Special Agent John K. Rankin arrived at the Omaha Agency to assign the new allotments. By August, the process was well under way, and Rankin had nearly finished his work by January 1900. In all, he made eight hundred new allotments involving about fifty thousand acres.[100] Most of the allotments under the 1893 act were granted to women and minor children and were therefore legally subject to leasing. These lands had been leased as pasture, and because many of the new allotments were approved after planting time and had not been broken, they continued to be rented at pasture rates for another three years.[101]

The only land that Rankin failed to allot was about five thousand acres that remained in dispute due to outstanding claims by mixed-bloods. This litigation had been ongoing for years, with no determination. In the event that the mixed-blood claims were disallowed, Agent Charles Mathewson thought an act of Congress would be required to either allot or sell the disputed lands. In 1904, the courts finally rejected the fifteen-year-old claims. The lands left unallotted pending the outcome of the litigation were later sold, and part of the proceeds were distributed among the tribe's landless children.[102]

As they had in the past, agents, reformers, and occasional visitors to the Omaha Reservation varied greatly in their assessments of Omaha "progress" in the 1890s. In 1891, Connecticut Women's Indian Association leader Sara T. Kinney compared the "savage" Omahas of a decade earlier with the Omaha citizens of the early 1890s, who, she assured Lake Mohonk delegates, were "self-supporting" and "self-respecting." In Kinney's opinion, the Omahas were doing quite well.[103] A year later, Charles C. Painter challenged congressional rumors that the Omahas were in serious trouble. Every Omaha, Painter insisted, had a "comfortable house on his own land." But when he visited the reservation in 1894, Painter was shocked to find the Indians in a "deplorable condition."[104]

The year 1893 marked the beginning of the troubled tenure of Agent Beck. Beck never minced words, and the first paragraph of his first report on the Omahas summed up their situation:

> The Omahas are presumably self-supporting and have been instructed by whites in the surrounding towns that they have all the rights and privileges of the United States. Hence they assume . . . an independent attitude toward the agent, regarding him somewhat as one who interferes with their transactions rather than one to whom they should look for guidance. As a result of this they use too much intoxicating liquor, lease their lands, and generally are worsted in their transactions with the white element with whom they deal.[105]

In an impassioned speech at Lake Mohonk in 1895, Senator Henry Dawes accused the Bureau of Indian Affairs of allotting the Omahas' lands and then turning its back on them. They had had a bright future in 1882, with fifty thousand spare acres and $90,000 in the treasury drawing 6 percent interest. But the government abandoned the Omahas. Twelve years into their trust period, they were much worse off than when first allotted. They were being paid just enough in rents to keep them in whiskey, and they still knew nothing about citizenship. Would a delegation of Omahas, asked Dawes, have asked Congress to "undo" their allotment act if the government had acted properly in their behalf?[106]

In the 1890s, nearly every concerned agent and reformer cited the Omahas' growing dependence on alcohol. This had not always been the case; under Joseph La Flesche's firm hand, alcohol abuse among the Omahas had been nearly nonexistent. But drinking increased among the tribe members after they became citizens. Whites assured the Indians that as citizens, they could buy whiskey wherever whites could, and liquor sellers were prepared to supply the Omahas with all the whiskey they wanted.[107] In 1892, Agent Robert Ashley reported a general decline in the Omahas' condition, caused mainly by the "alarming" increase in alcohol abuse. But he also said that the "better element" within the tribe was trying to stop the abuse of liquor, even asking that money from tribal land leases be set aside to prosecute whiskey peddlers.[108]

One contemporary journal held the Omahas up as an example of a promising tribe that seemed "almost shipwrecked and ruined by the . . . presence of liquor sellers around and among them."[109] Rather than helping the Omahas at a time when they needed guidance, neighboring whites took advantage of them. "Grocers," who were really liquor sellers, settled around the reservation and to a great degree succeeded in corrupting the Indians and snatching their lands.[110]

Despite the damage being done by liquor vendors hovering about the borders of the Omaha Reservation, local law enforcement officers were unable to put a stop to the whiskey trade, in part because of the ambiguous wording of an 1874 federal law and its interpretation in two landmark court cases. Section 2139 of the revised statute stated: "Every person, *except an Indian, in the Indian country*, who sells, exchanges, gives, barters, or disposes of any spirituous liquor or wine to any Indian under the charge of an Indian superintendent or agent, or introduces or attempts to introduce any spirituous liquor or wine into the Indian country, shall be punishable by imprisonment for not more than two years, and by a fine of not more than three hundred dollars" (author's emphasis).[111]

In 1876, Judge Casius Foster of the U.S. District Court for Kansas handed down a verdict that would reverberate far beyond the borders of that state. The case involved the sale of liquor in Kansas to two Pottawatami Indians under the jurisdiction of an Indian agent. Judge Foster's decision hinged on the phrase, "except an Indian, in the Indian country." Did this mean where the Indians actually lived or where the sale took place? After criticizing the wording of the law, Judge Foster gave it a very broad interpretation, ruling that the defendant, a Mr. Downing, had committed no crime because the liquor had not been sold on a reservation ("Indian country").[112]

Judge Foster knew when he made his ruling that he had given whiskey dealers free rein to sell their wares on the borders of Indian reservations, but he hoped that liquor trade such as Downing's would be punishable under state laws. As a result of the *Downing* decision, the offending phrase "except an Indian, in the Indian country," was omitted from the next statute revision, and law officers in Nebraska and throughout the West were forced to admit that they could not convict "off-reservation vendors" under federal law.[113]

A second alcohol case, argued before the Supreme Court in 1877, further pointed out the difficulty in defining "Indian country." In *Bates v. Clark*, the Supreme Court ruled that an army officer in Dakota Territory had wrongfully seized a supply of whiskey, believing it to be in Indian country. The court, no doubt influenced by the *Downing* case, argued that because the Indians had relinquished title to the area where the liquor was confiscated, that area no longer constituted Indian country.[114]

The Bureau of Indian Affairs also had to deal with local prejudices to stop the flow of liquor to Indians. Officials and residents of western towns wanted to see drunken Indians punished but refused to testify against liquor suppliers, arguing that "it was not their business to aid in their prosecutions." Most Indians also declined to testify against liquor dealers. As citizens, they believed they had every right "to drink whiskey as the white people [did]," and they did not want to betray their sources. Commissioner Jones admitted that those who complained of liquor law violations may have had good reasons not to testify. They feared unpleasant publicity or even bodily harm, so Indian agents were left to bring charges or to look the other way, since they had neither the time nor the resources to gather evidence.[115] Jones did not believe agents alone could handle the problem. In 1901 and again in 1902, he asked Congress for a special $5,000 to $10,000 fund to pay detectives to obtain evidence against liquor dealers. Congress refused to appropriate the funds, and the angry commissioner denounced the lawmakers' decision, since the Justice Department did not have the money to prosecute whiskey sellers before violations got out of hand.[116]

Even when apprehended and convicted, liquor dealers received little punishment. Agent Beck had as many whiskey sellers arrested as possible, but $25 fines and court costs did little to stop the lucrative trade. Beck was angry that local courts and the U.S. district court cared so little about the damage being done to the Omahas. Omaha Superintendent John F. MacKey, like Beck and his other predecessors, saw no solution to the Omahas' alcohol problems. Indians would not testify against suppliers; local whites ignored laws prohibiting liquor sales to Indians; and even when convicted, liquor traffickers were undeterred by the light sentences imposed by the district court.[117]

It was nineteen years after *Bates v. Clark* before Congress passed a liquor law that satisfied reformers and the Bureau of Indian Affairs. Early in 1896, in response to the alarming increase in alcohol use by Omahas and other Indians and in a further effort to curtail the liquor traffic, Nebraska Third District Representative George D. Meiklejohn sponsored a bill "to prohibit the sale of intoxicating liquors to Indians providing penalties therefor [*sic*], and for other purposes." Although prompted by conditions among the Indians in his home district, the congressman's proposed legislation would pertain to Indians throughout the country. Commissioner Browning, Indian agents, the Indian Rights Association, and Indians themselves all heartily endorsed the "Meiklejohn Bill," which they considered necessary to prevent further Indian degeneration.[118] Realizing that they had problems, 183 Omaha men and 52 Omaha women signed a January 31 letter to Commissioner Browning urging him and all "friends of the Indians" to secure passage of the bill.[119] The bill, which became law on January 30, 1897, made it a crime for anyone to sell or supply liquor to any Indian allottee whose land was held in trust, or to any Indian supervised by the government, and provided for the following punishments for those convicted of liquor peddling: imprisonment for not less than sixty days; fines of not less than $100 for a first offense and $200 for subsequent offenses.[120]

For about two years after its passage, the Meiklejohn law, combined with vigorous enforcement, reduced the flow of alcohol onto the Omaha Reservation. But in July 1899, the Justice Department removed its local deputy marshal, and the Indians began drinking again. When admonished by Dr. Susan La Flesche, unapologetic Omahas told her: "We can get all the whiskey we want, for the white men are selling it to us. . . . The government says we can drink again." Agent Charles Mathewson continued to report liquor offenses, but few traffickers were prosecuted.[121]

Despite the concerted efforts of Agent Mathewson, other agency employees, the federal court, and the local justice of the peace, the

Omahas continued to have easy access to liquor. Mathewson put the blame on the small town of Homer, which he claimed supplied 90 percent of the liquor coming onto the reservation. Located only a few miles from the northern border of the Winnebago Reservation, Homer, with its two saloons and its "army of 'boot-leggers,'" provided all the whiskey the Indians could afford. Mathewson accused the town citizens of putting greed above the Indians' welfare. They could, he insisted, stop the liquor traffic, but they chose not to, since drunken Indians were big spenders in Homer.[122]

In the report of his 1904 investigation into affairs on the Omaha and Winnebago Reservations, Supervisor A. O. Wright charged, "There is no place in the United States where the defiance of the law has been so public and the sale of liquor to Indians has been so thoroughly organized as in Homer, Nebraska." A part of the town scenery was its "bull pens"; these areas, located behind saloons, were hidden by high wooden fences and were accessible either from the saloons or from back alleys. When Omahas and Winnebagoes came to town, Indian "runners" brought them to the saloons, where they were seated at tables in the bull pens. Bootleggers then bought whiskey from the saloons, served it to their bull-pen "customers," and charged the Indians 20 to 25 percent commissions. Indian runners were paid in whiskey, and each bootlegger hired two, since one or the other was nearly always intoxicated.[123]

Before 1903, Homer merchants rented buildings to saloonkeepers, but even after they discontinued the practice, businessmen did little to stop liquor sales. Many claimed to fear the bootleggers, some of whom were not above "burning them out or stabbing them in the dark."[124] In 1904, Pender attorney E. J. Smith asked Homer merchants C. J. O'Connor and Thomas and John Ashford to donate money toward hiring someone to halt liquor traffic in the town. The merchants agreed to contribute, but anonymously, because they feared reprisals by bootleggers. Smith, O'Connor, the Ashford brothers, and a U.S. deputy marshal paid the Dakota County, Nebraska, sheriff to make the arrests, since the deputy had been unsuccessful in his attempts.[125] But even with many Homer bootleggers behind bars, investigator Wright did not see Homer as a permanently "dry" town. There was too much profit to be made.[126]

On April 10, 1905, the U.S. Supreme Court overturned Kansan Albert Heff's conviction for selling liquor to a Kickapoo Indian allottee, and in doing so, it nullified the Meiklejohn law. The court ruled that when allotted, Indians came under the jurisdictions of the states; because they were no longer wards of the federal government, they were free to buy whiskey, just as whites could.[127] The *Heff* decision made it even more difficult to stop liquor sales to Omahas. Superintendent MacKey did state that to their credit, some towns bordering the reservation offset the court ruling by refusing to license new saloons or by licensing them with the condition that they sell no liquor to Indians. One Nebraska town had selfish reasons for curtailing the growth of saloons. According to South Dakota Indian Superintendent John Flinn, the town jail in Homer was overcrowded with drunken Indians, so "kind hearted" bartenders dragged their Omaha and Winnebago customers out of the saloons and laid them in rows on the sidewalks. According to Flinn, Homer's citizens became tired of having to "stumble over a corduroy road composed of newly born American citizens."[128]

Indian's Friend saw the *Heff* decision as the "death knell" for the Omahas and Winnebagoes. According to this organ of the National Indian Association, as a result of the Supreme Court ruling, the "already besotted" Omahas would soon be exterminated, and Superintendent John H. Wilson of the Winnebago Agency predicted that in a few years, "every able-bodied man on the reservation [would] drink himself to death."[129] In 1904, *Omaha Daily Bee* editor Edward Rosewater had proposed a ten-mile "prohibition zone" around the reservations to cut off the Indians' whiskey supply. At the time, Superintendent MacKey had scoffed at the idea. "The zone," he argued, "would have to be 100 miles each way, and then a troop of United States Cavalry would be needed to patrol the lines of the reservation."[130] But in the opinion of the U.S. district attorney, Rosewater's plan, which never reached the floor of the state legislature, would have passed had Nebraska lawmakers been aware of the recent Supreme Court decision.[131]

With fewer saloons in Nebraska, bootleggers now plied their wares on the Iowa side of the Missouri River, and Indians crossed the river in boats to buy whiskey. Unfortunately, the Iowa liquor dealers appeared to be doing nothing illegal. On July 26, 1905, Omaha Agency Superintendent MacKey appealed to Iowa law enforcement officers for help in stopping liquor sales on the eastern banks of the Missouri River. Deputy U.S. Marshal J. A. Tracy in Sioux City responded that it would be difficult to prosecute liquor traffickers such as William Wise, the most flagrant offender, because he had an Iowa liquor license and the recent Supreme Court ruling protected him. Tracy advised MacKey to provide him with names and facts, especially the names of any unallotted Indians, and said he would discuss the case with the U.S. attorney for Iowa.[132] To comply with Marshal Tracy's request, Omaha notary public Carey La Flesche took the statements of over a dozen Indians and whites who either had witnessed clandestine Iowa liquor sales or had themselves bought whiskey from Iowa dealers.

Three Poncas, visiting on the Omaha Reservation, testified that two white whiskey peddlers had pitched a tent on the Iowa side of the river, setting up a more or less permanent operation.[133] Walter Adair of Decatur, Nebraska, swore that on August 2, 1905, he came upon this camp, occupied by William Wise and two other men whom he did not know. Early in the afternoon Little Rabbit, an Omaha, motioned to Wise from the Nebraska side of the river. Wise rowed across the river and brought the sixty-year-old Indian to his camp, where he filled a bottle with whiskey. He then returned Little Rabbit to the Omaha Reservation.[134] Five days after Adair testified, Little Rabbit admitted that he had bought $1.25 worth of whiskey from Wise and a second man on August 2.[135] On the same day that Little Rabbit made his purchase, Omahas Arthur Mitchell and George Ramsey had bought a half-gallon jug of whiskey from the Iowa peddlers.[136]

Wise and his companion undoubtedly knew that the Iowa state line was located in the middle of the Missouri River. When fourteen-year-old James Wood and his friend Jeremiah Parker purchased liquor for young Wood's father, the boys paid on the Nebraska side of the river, then the peddler simply rowed Parker fifty yards out and handed him his whiskey.[137] But Wise became even bolder. On August 22, Charles Funkhouser testified that two weeks earlier, he had seen a white man row across the Missouri and deliver twelve jugs of whiskey to two Omahas who were waiting on the Nebraska side, within the boundaries of the reservation.[138] The identities of the Iowa peddlers were never in doubt. Nearly all who testified assured Superintendent MacKey that they either recognized William Wise or could identify him and his partner, believed to be Charles Allen.

J. A. Singhaus, a Tekamah, Nebraska, attorney and a U.S. commissioner, seemed eager to prosecute William R. Marr of Decatur for bringing whiskey onto the Omaha Reservation, and he offered his help in suppressing the Iowa traffic as well. Singhaus issued arrest warrants for Wise, Marr, and Allen, but Marshal Tracy in Iowa could not apprehend them with a warrant from Nebraska.[139] On August 18, Tracy received Iowa warrants to bring in the three whiskey peddlers, and on August 21, he took Wise and Allen into custody. Unable to post bond, the two men were jailed in Sioux City.[140] State jurisdictions now came into play; Wise and Allen were not brought to Nebraska for trial until the federal judge for the Northern District of Iowa issued a removal order. Marr remained free in Nebraska, but Commissioner Singhaus claimed that he could arrest the liquor dealer at any time. The commissioner also intended to prosecute the Indians named in affidavits as having brought liquor onto the reservation.[141]

As a final move to halt the Iowa-to-Nebraska liquor traffic, Singhaus suggested that Superintendent MacKey destroy what remained of Allen and Wise's camp on the Iowa side of the river "in such a way that it could not be shown who did it."[142] Thanks to the cooperation of the Iowa authorities, the whiskey peddlers doing business on the eastern bank of the Missouri were now virtually out of business. But it remained difficult to prosecute liquor traffickers. Even when indicted, few were punished, since appeals were pending in one or two cases and the courts were waiting to see how these proceeded.[143]

Leasing irregularities on the Omaha and Winnebago Reservations did not end with the Beck-Fluornoy era. In the early 1900s, six or seven speculators made enormous profits by gaining control of leases for over forty thousand acres of Indian land, then subleasing the lands at a 50 to 200 percent profit. Much of this land fell into the hands of four area men—F. B. Hutchens, C. C. Maryott, brother of the Omaha Reservation trader, and the O'Connor brothers, Indian traders at the Winnebago Reservation.[144] Like Agent Beck before him, Omaha and Winnebago Agent Charles P. Mathewson was accused of favoring leases to middlemen. Individual allottees were effectively locked out of the leasing process and could not choose their own renters, since

Mathewson favored leasing in large tracts and insisted that he had too little time to approve contracts negotiated by Indians.[145]

Apparently patience with shady dealings grew thin in early 1902. On February 24, editor Edward Rosewater charged Mathewson and trader C. J. O'Connor with "gross mismanagement" at the agency and showed Commissioner Jones "documentary proof" of wrongdoing.[146] A week later, a delegation of Omahas and Winnebagoes, unhappy with affairs on their reservations, arrived in Washington to protest Mathewson's leasing policies.[147] But the actions of one of Mathewson's clerks brought an investigator to the agency. When Special Agent Eugene McComas arrived in Nebraska, he had with him an extensive list of Indian leases to middlemen, complete with rentals paid. Mathewson must have known that McComas possessed damaging evidence; the *Pender Times* reported that the agent had hired Indian attorney Thomas Sloan to defend him, if necessary.[148]

McComas was considered a problem for Indian agents "on the ropes." Taking his assignment seriously, he refused to allow Mathewson to "wine and dine" him. As he left the agency after completing his investigation, he declared the leasing operation on the reservations to be in "bad shape." Although Commissioner Jones declined to release the contents of the special agent's report until it could be reviewed, the *Omaha Daily Bee* reported that McComas would recommend the dismissals of the agency farmer and the chief agency clerk, as well as the removal of Agent Mathewson. In addition, the paper stated, the investigator would likely tell the Indian Office that the Omahas received too little compensation for their lands.[149] Sensing that they were on shaky ground, members of the new Pender "ring" dispatched Agent Mathewson, C. J. O'Connor, and their "troubleshooter," E. A. Wiltse, to Washington to try to "offset any bad effect" that McComas' visit may have had on their operation.[150]

In May, the Interior Department sent another inspector, Special Agent Frank C. Churchill, to the Omaha Reservation. From the outset, locals complained about the way Churchill conducted his investigation. Although he possessed widespread evidence against "parties on the reservation," he chose not to act on his knowledge. Churchill began his interrogations behind closed doors, and when Rosewater complained, the investigation came to a halt. None of the parties involved held out much hope for a "fair and impartial report."[151]

Early in 1903, it appeared that the dishonest Mathewson would no longer have a job. Since no Nebraska congressmen lobbied for an agent for the Omahas and Winnebagoes, Congress failed to appropriate money for his salary in fiscal year 1904. Mathewson's position was eliminated effective July 1, 1903, and the agency was turned over to bonded school superintendents, the first of which was to be the newly unemployed Omaha and Winnebago agent.[152] Mathewson's appointment as superintendent was in keeping with an Indian Office custom of giving agents jobs "equally as good" as their old ones. The advantage to Mathewson was that as a civil servant, he could now be removed only for misconduct. Behind the scenes, the land syndicate front man Wiltse had urged Nebraska Senator J. H. Millard to back Mathewson for the superintendency. The syndicate was naturally delighted with Mathewson's assignment, but most Thurston County residents opposed the appointment of such a person to a secure civil service job.[153]

Mathewson and his middlemen gave the impression that they were still in business, but they knew that their gravy train had been at least partially derailed. Under a new 1902 Interior Department rule, in the future no one person would be allowed to lease more than one section of farmland, and already several hundred leases had been disapproved. In reporting the new ruling, the *Pender Times* editor remarked, "Now it's Rosewater's turn to smile."[154]

Edward Rosewater could smile for a while, but the Omahas had not seen the last of the Pender ring or other local sharks bent on taking advantage of Indians. And in 1902, the U.S. government had passed the first in a series of laws that would drastically reduce Omaha real estate holdings through land sales. Little by little, Congress would make it easier for whites to separate Omahas from their allotments, as heirship rulings and competency commissions made more and more Indians eligible to sell their lands. In 1894, the Board of Indian Commissioners had voiced its concern that the twenty-five-year trust period to protect Indian lands from sale could be overridden by special legislation. They foresaw a great temptation for Indians to sell their allotments, leaving many homeless: "We are getting possession of

Indian lands quite fast enough by the purchase of large unallotted tracts, and we can surely leave the unallotted lands to their owners until a generation shall be educated to appreciate their value, and use them for their own and their children's benefit."[155]

For the Omahas, this progressive vision was not to be.

Chapter 6
The Final Assault
Taxation and Land Sales on the Omaha Reservation, 1902–1916

There is not a wild Indian living who knows what a
fee-simple is . . . and there are certainly very few
Indians, civilized or uncivilized, who understand it.

Henry M. Teller, 1881

So soon as the proper official declares that an Indian is
competent to administer his own affairs, let that Indian
have . . . a patent in fee for his allotment, and let him
shift for himself.

James McLaughlin, circa 1909

Just as the Board of Indian Commissioners had feared, during the early
decades of the twentieth century new laws were designed to relieve
tribal members of their lands or incomes. Even more threatening was
the fact that the interior secretary was given discretionary power to
issue land titles to Indians whose lands were still held in trust. In many
cases, inherited lands were sold as quickly as heirs received them, and
in 1910, a government competency commission issued hundreds of
fee-patents to Omahas, sometimes to Indians who did not want them
and almost always to recipients who did not understand what they
were. In addition, the taxation of Omaha lands became a major issue.
Thurston County organizers knew as early as 1889 that their county
was composed of over 90 percent Indian trust lands and that their tax
base would be small. Almost from its inception, the county waged a
campaign to tax Omaha lands, and most Nebraska senators and representatives were happy to support tax legislation that would keep their
white constituents happy at the Omahas' expense. Land fraud continued on the reservation, and unfortunately, some of the best-educated
Omahas, who could have become effective advocates for their people,
often chose to align themselves with those who victimized the Indians.
By late 1916, the Omaha land base had been drastically reduced. All

the property that remained in Indian hands was taxed, and despite the disastrous results of the 1910 competency commission among the Omahas, a new commission was hard at work on other reservations, issuing thousands of fee-patents that would soon be in the hands of white settlers and speculators.

On his way back east after conducting his 1902 investigation of the Omaha Agency, Special Agent Eugene McComas told reporters that the situation regarding traders near the reservation was "as near a hold-up as is possible to imagine." According to McComas, traders were allowed to attend Indian "paydays," and most Omahas left the agency with little or nothing.[1] In addition to the inspector's report, remarks made by a Catholic priest and published in the *Washington Post* prompted the Bureau of Indian Affairs to send another investigator in 1904. On his arrival in Nebraska, Inspector A. O. Wright was met by Father Joseph Schell, self-proclaimed missionary to the Winnebagoes and author of the inflammatory statements in the Washington newspaper.[2] In oral testimony, Father Schell accused Homer, Nebraska, merchants John and Thomas Ashford and C. J. O'Connor of cheating the Omahas and Winnebagoes and of contributing to their dependence on alcohol. For instance, the priest accused the businessmen of charging the Indians 100 to 1,500 percent interest on loans, and he claimed that they loaned the Indians "whiskey money." According to Father Schell, drunken Indians were led into banks to sign notes for three times the loaned amounts, and he insisted that Indians were "hunted down" and forced to buy goods at exorbitant prices when merchants learned they were expecting money. Finally, Schell charged that Homer merchants drove out other tradesmen who attempted to sell Indians goods at reasonable prices.[3]

Shortly after his first contact with Father Schell, Inspector Wright began to suspect the priest's motives. Schell presented Wright with affidavits, allegedly from Indians, but when Wright informed the priest that his Indian witnesses must testify in person, they never appeared. When questioned, several Indians swore that Father Schell had written the affidavits and had had them sign the documents when they were drunk.[4] Gradually, Wright learned the true story behind the priest's accusations. Apparently, Schell had reached Homer in April 1903, claiming to be the new missionary to the Winnebagoes. He took over the Catholic church in Homer and demanded $4,000 from town citizens to repair the church, to build a parsonage, and to pay his salary. When the Ashford brothers and O'Connor refused to donate 80 percent of the money, Schell threatened to put them out of business. The priest intimidated other merchants as well. When Homer butcher William O'Dell was called to testify before Inspector Wright, Father Schell warned him that he too would soon be bankrupt if he did not incriminate O'Connor and the Ashfords.[5]

Obsessed with his vendetta against local merchants, Father Schell portrayed them as greedy and grasping, never missing an opportunity to exploit their Indian customers. In their own testimony, the merchants agreed with Schell's accusations, to a point. O'Connor confirmed that he did go to the agency to collect debts when the Indians received lease money or other income, because he wanted to be paid while his debtors still had some money. But he denied doing what the priest called "snapping" checks from Indians. On the contrary, O'Connor testified that many Omahas voluntarily gave him their checks so that he could deduct their payments.[6]

Trader Thomas Ashford Jr. verified that on occasion he had loaned drunken Indians enough money to reclaim their horses from livery stables, but he swore that he had never knowingly loaned any whiskey money. However, he knew that Indians sometimes borrowed money for "food," then used it to buy liquor.[7] In response to Father Schell's charges of price-gouging, all of the merchants admitted charging "high-risk" Indians more for their purchases, but reservation trader George C. Maryott defended his pricing policy, explaining that he had to transport goods over eighteen miles of bad roads. Maryott believed the Indians took advantage of his "generosity," buying goods in town when they had cash and dealing with him only when they needed credit. Without exception, the merchants admitted to charging clearly illegal interest rates for small loans, but they called the extra charges "premiums," necessary to cover collection costs.[8]

Although he realized that the local tradesmen were looking out for their own interests, Inspector Wright defended the merchants, even after they had pleaded guilty to many of the charges. Wright insisted that while on the reservations, he never saw an Indian forced to surrender a check; traders were simply urging their customers to pay debts, and sometimes they even gave Indians gifts for prompt payment. The inspector also observed that merchants were not the only ones to crowd around the agency on paydays; lawyers collected fees in this way, and the justice of the peace became a familiar figure as he waited to collect fines. Wright explained to his superiors that many Indians' reluctance to pay their bills led merchants to take chattel mortgages on their work horses; when an Indian exhausted his credit, the horses became collateral. As for Father Schell, Inspector Wright recommended that in the future, the priest should be barred from all Indian reservations.[9]

In 1906, Congress finally agreed with Indian Commissioner William Jones that the liquor traffic among Indians was out of control. Between 1906 and 1916, federal lawmakers appropriated nearly $300,000 to suppress liquor sales, but it was too little money spread too thinly, and like weeds, bootleggers and liquor dealers resurfaced on the Omaha Reservation.[10] With little help forthcoming, Omaha and Winnebago Superintendent Albert H. Kneale took matters into his own hands in 1910. Faced with rampant alcohol abuse on the two reservations, Kneale called on Ed Brents, "Special Officer for the Suppression of the Liquor Traffic among Indians," to help him stop liquor sales. Together, they devised a plan in which they would accompany two Winnebagoes "of pronounced Indian type" to bars in towns near the reservations. After being served whiskey, the Indians would turn their purchases over to Brents, who would then label the bottles with date and liquor seller. During their "sting operation," not one saloon refused to sell the Indians liquor. Because there was a Nebraska law prohibiting liquor sales to Indians, Kneale and Brents presented their evidence to the Thurston County attorney in the hope of getting convictions. To their surprise, the county attorney, who was himself part-Indian, refused to press charges, arguing that the state law was unconstitutional because it discriminated against Indians. Actually, according to Kneale, the attorney did not want to see the law enforced because that would mean he "could not even purchase a drink [himself]."[11] Having failed in Pender, the two investigators took their case to the U.S. attorney in Omaha, who cooperated fully. A grand jury heard the case and handed down indictments that resulted in several arrests. Kneale and Brents had largely curtailed Indian liquor sales in saloons, but they were unable to stop bootleggers.[12]

Thus liquor continued to reach the Omahas. In a January 1915 report, Kneale's successor, Axel Johnson, accused "notorious character" Will Estill of selling whiskey to Indians in order to separate them from their lands, and he charged that George F. Phillips, who had been under investigation for two years, was still distributing lemon extract among the Omahas.[13] Phillips was arraigned on July 12, 1915, at Pender for selling intoxicants to the Indians.[14] The previous year, Estill had been exonerated of liquor trafficking charges and had lashed out at those who had initiated the charges and allegedly conspired against him. In a series of scathing letters, he accused the government's star witness of perjury, claimed that a special investigator had conducted a personal campaign against him, and implicated Omaha Agency clerk W. A. Martindale in a plot to convict him of whiskey dealing.[15] Two Indian Office inspectors apparently agreed that Estill had been the victim of a conspiracy. E. B. Linnen and E. M. Sweet Jr. defended Estill, calling him "an honest and upright man" while accusing Martindale of discriminating against him in the granting of leases.[16]

Due to budget constraints, in October 1914, the Indian Office had recalled its special deputy assigned to help halt liquor traffic among the Omahas. Now it would be up to a deputy at Sioux City, Iowa, and a part-time officer to stop the whiskey flow. This arrangement proved ineffective, and in November 1915, Omaha Superintendent Johnson requested and received an additional enforcement officer.[17] In April 1916, Superintendent Johnson himself was commissioned "Deputy Special Officer" for the balance of the fiscal year.[18]

Johnson and other superintendents ignored few sources in their campaign against illegal whiskey. The Interior Department received permission to search mail vehicles entering reservations, and in November 1915, Johnson informed Chief Special Officer Henry Larson that he wanted to cancel the leases of those people who had brought liquor onto the reservation. Larson supported Johnson's efforts, and an assistant Indian commissioner reminded the superintendent that Omaha leases contained no provisions for such cancellations but added that he had no objections to Johnson's inserting such a clause in future leases.[19] In June 1916, liquor arrests were made in Winnebago and Rosalie, Nebraska; instead of being fined, offenders were put to work on a county road gang.[20]

In the meantime, a series of U.S. Supreme Court rulings contradicted the *Heff* decision of 1905 and supported the earlier Meiklejohn antiliquor law. In one of these cases, attorney Thomas Sloan attempted to persuade the high court to negate an Eighth Circuit Appeals Court conviction of tribal member Simeon Hallowell for bringing liquor onto his allotment. Sloan failed, and the ruling stood.[21] On June 25, 1916, the Supreme Court overturned the controversial *Heff* decision, stating that the ruling had not reflected the true intentions of Congress when Congress had passed the 1887 Dawes Act. Now it was once again illegal to sell liquor to allotted Indians.[22] Liquor traffic enforcement officers rejoiced at the news of the high court ruling. Henry Larson predicted that keeping allotted Indians under federal protection would increase the number of whiskey traffic convictions, and the special officer in Sioux City looked forward to "lots of fun" as more arrests were made.[23]

But on the Omaha Reservation, the traffic continued, and concerned Thurston County residents received little help in combating the problem. In August 1916, a vice-president of the Farmers State Bank of Rosalie asked Johnson to send a "good Indian or two" to testify against a "new crop of boot legers [*sic*]."[24] The *Walthill (Nebraska) Times* editor, sharply critical of Third District Representative Dan Stephens, accused the Nebraska congressman of dragging his feet regarding the stationing of a special agent on the Omaha Reservation to stop bootlegging. The irate editor believed that as a Democrat in a Democrat-controlled Congress, Stephens could get the agent if he really wanted to.[25] It would obviously take more than zealous agents and a Supreme Court decision to solve the Omahas' alcohol problems.

Buried in the 1902 Indian Appropriation Act was a section that would bring about the first phase of wholesale land loss among the Omahas. Section Seven stated, "The adult heirs of a deceased Indian to whom a trust or other patent containing restrictions upon alienation has been or shall be issued for lands allotted to him may sell and convey the lands inherited from such descendent." Buyers of "heirship lands" would receive unencumbered titles as though the allottees' patents had been unrestricted.[26] This law allowing Indians to sell heirship lands was a natural progression from the 1890s leasing laws. The number of acres lost to Indians through the sale of inheritances was only a tiny percentage of the total lands turned over to whites, but heirship sales devastated Indian futures. Combined with the later sales of surplus lands, the loss of inherited acreage left many allottees' grandchildren nearly landless.[27] Congress passed the 1902 heirship law because (1) it did not want deceased Indians' lands lying untilled, (2) it hoped Indians would apply their heirship proceeds toward improving their own allotments, (3) some people did not want Indians to become heirs to large estates because this would encourage idleness, and (4) perhaps most important, whites wanted the land.[28]

Shortly after passage of the bill, Commissioner Jones' office fielded many inquiries from whites living near reservations, and he hoped that delays in implementing the law would give Indians time to learn their rights, to ascertain the true value of their lands, and to decide whether they really wanted to sell.[29] Reaction to the new law was overwhelmingly favorable among whites on and around the Omaha Reservation. Agent Charles Mathewson considered the law a wise one for the Omahas, whose trust period would expire in a few years. Mathewson thought that selling heirship lands would provide "a valuable lesson in the management of their own affairs."[30] The *Pender (Nebraska) Times* viewed the legislation as a step toward equalizing the tax burden in Thurston County; white county residents hoped that the trust limitations of about forty thousand heirship acres would be lifted as allottees died and their lands were sold.[31]

Before the rules governing the sale of heirship lands arrived at the Omaha and Winnebago Agency, attorney Thomas Sloan procured a copy and released some of the guidelines. The entire procedure would be controlled by the agent, who was supposed to look out for the Indians' welfare. Any contracts were to be witnessed by two prominent Indians, and before any action could be taken, each land tract had to be probated in county court, a process that, optimistically, would take three months. Lands of minors could not be sold without a court order and then would go to the highest bidder. Buying heirship lands could be risky, since Indian land titles were often contested and since, under Nebraska law, heirs could come forward after probate to claim their rights.[32]

Whereas Thurston County whites extolled the virtues of the new law, the Omahas, whose lives would be most directly affected, opposed it.

At a general council in late July 1902, 149 of 150 Omahas in attendance signed a protest and vowed not to sell their lands. In specific terms, the council outlined the Omahas' trampled rights, identified the guilty whites, and voiced annoyance with certain Omahas who had aided whites in their schemes. In addition, the council members claimed that the May 27 act had been passed without their knowledge and that they wanted it repealed. In summing up their protest, the Omahas declared:

> All proceedings tending to the destruction of our rights, happiness and prosperity . . . are hereby disapproved. That the Act of Congress of May 27, 1902, providing for the sale of the lands of deceased Indians of our tribe, is hereby disapproved and not binding on our people. . . . That our tribal council . . . are hereby invested with power to . . . obtain relief from the wrongs we have so long suffered, even to the bringing of suits or actions . . . in any court of justice, against any person or persons who violate our rights.[33]

At about the same time that the Omahas issued their protest, Edward Rosewater of the *Omaha Daily Bee* accused the Thurston County "land lease ring," allegedly presided over by Superintendent Mathewson, of putting up $500,000 to purchase Indian heirship lands. A provision of the statute requiring purchase money to be deposited before a sale allegedly played right into the syndicate's hands and effectively shut out those settlers who would buy lands if they could do so in installments.[34] Recognizing that ordinary farmers would have difficulty raising the full purchase price of a parcel of land, Nebraska congressman John S. Robinson asked Commissioner Jones to amend the rules to allow mortgages.[35]

In September 1902, the Interior Department changed the heirship land rules to require sealed bids, with sales going to the highest bidders. In response to criticisms of the original rules, Interior Secretary Ethan Hitchcock nullified deeds already issued and ordered the land resold. The *Pender Times* gleefully reported that speculators in Omaha lands had lost several thousand dollars that had been paid to Indian heirs as bribes.[36] Despite the pleas of newly elected Nebraska Third District Congressman John J. McCarthy, Commissioner Jones and Secretary Hitchcock refused to back down regarding the new rules. On one day in early September 1903, Hitchcock disapproved thirty-one heirship land sales in Thurston County. Heretofore, according to the Pender newspaper, land transfers had been "going through as though greased." The *Times* surmised that the interior secretary had found something badly amiss and that he planned to conduct an investigation.[37]

The *Times* was correct. Hitchcock returned the money for the rejected land sales and promptly dispatched an Interior Department inspector to Nebraska. Hitchcock had discovered that Omaha and Winnebago Superintendent Mathewson had continued his association with the land syndicate.[38] The inspector remained at the Omaha and Winnebago Agency for about a month, vowing to "weed out the whole outfit." At a meeting with the inspector in late September, the Omahas vented their anger at the superintendent and his cronies. However, outspoken tribal member Silas Wood, who was eager to sell his land, defended Mathewson and accused attorney Hiram Chase of lowering Indian land prices by telling prospective buyers that the titles were no good. Shortly after the Omaha meeting, Superintendent Mathewson, pleading ill health, suddenly resigned. But given his history, few believed that his sole reason for leaving was his health. Rosewater, who had been "hounding" Mathewson for two years, took credit for his early departure.[39]

The requirement for sealed bids was the first of several adjustments to the Indian heirship act. On September 16, 1903, the Bureau of Indian Affairs ordered the "newspaper of widest circulation in the county" to publish an updated weekly list of available Omaha heirship lands. The *Pender Times* printed the list and went a step further by publishing a map of the Omaha Reservation showing Indian allotments and inherited lands available for purchase. Regular *Times* subscribers could buy a copy of the map for just one dollar.[40] In 1904, Commissioner Jones suggested that cash from sales of inherited lands be deposited in individual Indian accounts in national banks near reservations so that each Indian could gain business experience by personally withdrawing $10 from his or her account each month. By June 30, 1905, Omahas had deposited $62,164.40 in either Pender National Bank or Security National Bank of Sioux City.[41] However, after taking office, Indian Commissioner Robert Valentine became convinced that

Indians had become dependent on their monthly stipends and had ceased to "progress." Accordingly, in March 1909, he instructed super-intendents and agents to stop these small payments. The commissioner claimed that with the stipends discontinued, more Indians began working their lands.[42]

On October 28, 1905, all agents received instructions to insert in deeds for inherited Indian lands a clause prohibiting the use or sale of alcohol on those parcels. The proviso proved unpopular with land buyers, and due to protests from whites living on or near the Yankton Reservation in South Dakota, the Bureau of Indian Affairs asked its attorneys to review the amendment. After reviewing the clause, the legal department advised that it be removed because it would slow land sales and reduce prices and would have little impact on liquor traffic, since it pertained only to heirship lands. The attorney general's office agreed, and on February 3, 1906, the liquor restriction ended. During fiscal 1906, sales of inherited Omaha lands dropped sharply, a decline that Commissioner Francis E. Leupp attributed directly to the liquor clause, which was in effect for part of the year.[43]

The first Indian heirship lands subject to the law of May 27, 1902, and the amended rules of October 4, 1902, went on sale on March 4, 1903; by June 30, 1904, 142 tracts of land on the Omaha and Winne-bago Reservations, comprising 9,542 acres, had been sold for a total of $239,284.50, or an average price of $25.08 per acre.[44] Between July 1904 and August 1905, another 50 Omaha parcels totaling 3,126 acres sold for about $26.00 per acre, and by August 1906, despite the short-lived liquor clause, another 18 tracts changed hands.[45] According to the Indian Office plan, Indians would use the proceeds from sales of heirship lands to improve their allotments, but little of the money was used for its intended purpose. The Omahas were the only tribe for which figures on these expenditures were reported, and of the $147,150 realized between 1902 and 1904, less than 20 percent went toward improvements.[46]

Unfortunately, much of the Omahas' heirship land money made its way into the coffers of local merchants who, anticipating heirs' sudden windfalls, had extended credit to the unsuspecting Indians. Many Omahas went deeply into debt, and in 1905 and 1906, over four hundred claims were paid from heirship land proceeds on deposit in local banks.[47] Ten years later, little had changed. In a 1915 report, Superintendent Johnson stated that the Omahas still had no understanding of a credit economy and that many of them would "sign any paper" to obtain goods or money on credit. An Omaha would mortgage his horses, his tools, and even his crops, and in order to pay his debts, he would often have to sell his land. In Johnson's opinion, unless the credit system among the Omahas stopped, the tribe would face financial ruin.[48]

Heirship lands composed only a small portion of the Omaha Reservation, but a 1906 law placed much more Omaha land in jeopardy. Confusion over Indians' rights as citizens and the differing degrees of acculturation among allotted Indians had necessitated a modification of the Dawes Act. The Indian Office saw a need to manage the affairs of the "helpless class" and at the same time discontinue its role as guardian of an increasing number of "competent" Indians. The 1905 *Heff* decision had basically given allotted Indians equal rights with whites. As a result, Congress worried that it could no longer protect Indians and that the Supreme Court ruling would slow the pace of allotment. Representative Charles H. Burke of South Dakota argued that the *Heff* ruling had "demoralized" Indians. To prevent further degeneration and to return Indians to U.S. jurisdiction, Burke introduced sweeping Indian legislation that would become known simply as the Burke Act.[49]

To circumvent the effects of the *Heff* decision and to prevent future liquor sales to Indians, the 1906 Burke Act would allow the interior secretary or the president to shorten or lengthen trust periods for individual Indians based on their ability to manage their own affairs. Any Indian categorized as "competent" could then be issued a patent in fee simple with *no restrictions as to sale, encumbrance, or taxation.*[50] Although the Burke Act tried to combat the disastrous effects of the *Heff* decision by delaying citizenship until Indians who were assigned allotments after 1906 actually received titles to their property, this open-ended proviso would later justify the disastrous 1910 competency commission and the tragic loss of Omaha lands.

The Burke Act enjoyed nearly unanimous support in Congress and among officials in the Bureau of Indian Affairs. Indian Commissioner Leupp argued that before the passage of this law, the only way a self-sufficient Indian could be released from the "shackles of wardship" was through special legislation, and Leupp saw that route as an open invitation to "graft and blackmail." The commissioner enthusiastically supported fee-patents and predicted that "the Burke law, wisely administered," would do more to end the Indian problem "than any other single factor in a generation of progress."[51] The pragmatic House Committee on Indian Affairs backed the bill because it would reduce the paperwork involved in approving individual allotments. That responsibility would now fall to the Bureau of Indian Affairs, which Burke insisted knew "best when an Indian [had] reached such a stage of civilization as to be . . . capable of managing his own affairs."[52]

Reformers were less than enthusiastic about the new law. Though the members of the Board of Indian Commissioners did not question the good intentions behind the bill, they did see it as a step backward for Indians. They argued that the interior secretary could not possibly know each Indian's circumstances. Therefore, it appeared to be left to an Indian who wanted citizenship to convince the Bureau of Indian Affairs that he or she deserved it. The commissioners also believed it was wrong "to make citizenship for an Indian depend upon his keeping on the pleasant side of the local officials at the agency."[53] Samuel Brosius of the Indian Rights Association complained that Indians denied citizenship until their trust periods expired were also being denied the opportunity to learn valuable lessons on surviving in a white world. In addition, it seemed incongruous to Brosius that some tribal members would become citizens subject to state laws while others would remain under federal jurisdiction.[54] Unfortunately, no one seemed concerned about the possible ramifications of the removal of restrictions on Indian lands.

To receive a fee-patent under the terms of the Burke Act, an allottee was required to submit an application to his or her superintendent, who would then forward it to the Bureau of Indian Affairs along with his own evaluation of the Indian's competency. People believing that a patent should not be issued had thirty days to come forward and give their reasons for objection.[55] Commissioner Leupp was happy to see that the process was "well safeguarded." At this early date, he really believed that the procedure would work properly, since superintendents, agents, or inspectors would thoroughly investigate each case.[56]

But in determining applicants' competency, agents and superintendents held personal opinions that no doubt influenced their recommendations. Although Leupp later admitted that mistakes had been made and that more would be made in the future, he insisted that most resulted from misinformation received from sources other than Indian agents.[57]

By December 1908, 123 Omahas had been issued titles to 6,882 acres of land under the terms of the Burke Act. According to Superintendent John M. Commons, many Indians had sold their lands, some had mortgaged them, and a few had retained their allotments. But he believed that about 75 percent of the Omahas who had received fee-patents had used good judgment in handling their affairs, and he recommended that the patents continue to be issued gradually, to prevent the issuance of a huge number at the termination of the trust period. Commons had correctly heard that whites around the reservation anticipated "something of a harvest" when the trust period expired in 1909.[58]

But much to the dismay of Thurston County land-seekers, the trust period for the "old" Omaha allotments assigned by Alice Fletcher in 1883–84 did not expire as scheduled in 1909. A campaign to extend the trust period had begun in January 1904, when 397 Omahas, claiming old age or bad fortune, petitioned the government to prolong their trust relationship. The petitioners feared that because of their lack of business acumen, the very young and the very old would continue to be preyed on by greedy whites and, without their trust umbrella, would soon lose their lands. The list of petitioners included some surprises, such as former agency clerk Thomas McCauley, who undoubtedly was able to manage his own affairs. But the most glaring name among the signers was that of attorney and judge Hiram Chase, obviously a "competent" Omaha.[59]

The editor of the *Pender Times* called Chase's participation in the petition hypocritical. By signing the document, Chase had placed himself among those Omahas who considered themselves unprepared to continue without government support. Yet Chase had held public office in Thurston County for ten years as county attorney and judge and was currently campaigning for reelection to the bench. The *Times* sarcastically asked its readers if they were willing to pay an "admittedly incompetent" Indian a salary for two more years. Without using the actual words, the irate editor accused Chase of tax evasion. While holding public office, Chase owned and received revenue from over six hundred acres of land but in ten years had been billed for only $84.50 in taxes, some of which remained unpaid. The newspaper predicted that the thoroughly political Omaha attorney would issue an election-eve statement that he was in favor of paying taxes, knowing that he would not have to if the trust period continued.[60]

Provisions of the 1906 Indian Appropriation Act giving the president power to extend the twenty-five-year trust period of any Indian outside Indian Territory enraged the *Pender Times* editor. Accusing the Nebraska congressional delegation of being "asleep when this section passed," he complained that whites in Thurston County had hoped that their tax burden would be lightened when the trust period expired. The county, he feared, would now "be left shackled in the hands of the Secretary of the Interior."[61] At least one Omaha questioned the tribal trust extension request. In a letter to the *Times*, Levi Levering argued that retaining an Indian agent would retard Omaha progress and merely "create [an] office for an old worn out politician."[62] Suspicious superintendent John F. MacKey doubted the tribe's motives. He believed the Omahas wanted a trust extension so that they could fall back on "Uncle Sam" if they failed as farmers. They were, he charged, perfectly willing to assert their rights as "citizens" when it served their purposes, but if it meant avoiding responsibility, they chose to remain simply "Indians."[63]

Superintendent MacKey's replacement, John M. Commons, agreed completely with the Omaha petitioners. Like them, he feared that Omaha senior citizens and minors would become landless if the trust period ended, and he recommended that it be extended a few years for some and indefinitely for others.[64] Commons gained an ally in Commissioner Valentine, who in March 1909 instructed the superintendent to provide lists of all minor, elderly, and handicapped Omahas so that their lands could be protected. A few weeks later, he amended his instructions to include the lands of deceased Omahas whose heirs included minors.[65]

By May, Commons had compiled a detailed list of Omahas in each category requested by the commissioner. He included the names of 92 "old and incapable" Indians, 13 Omahas whom he considered "old but capable," 8 disabled tribal members, and 33 younger Omahas who had requested extensions over the superintendent's objections. Commons also forwarded a list of the 115 Omaha minors who would not turn twenty-one until after the trust period was due to expire. These were all "new," or Rankin, allotments, which had been legislated by the 1893 amendment to the Omaha Allotment Act and assigned in 1899–1900; Commons provided each minor's annuity number, allotment number, and the date on which he or she would reach majority. He also included the names of 17 Omahas between the ages of twenty-one and twenty-five and recommended trust extensions for each.[66] Commons' reply also contained a list of 164 deceased allottees with minor heirs, along with a recommendation that these lands remain in trust until each heir reached majority. The superintendent did not consider trust extensions necessary for 5 minor heirs who had white fathers.[67]

In his attempt to protect as many Omahas as possible, Commons added three categories not requested by Commissioner Valentine. He hoped that thirty-seven parcels of heirship land for which heirs had not yet been determined would remain in trust, along with the inherited land sale proceeds that were deposited in area banks.[68] In June, Commons forwarded a list of thirty-one land parcels that had been sold or that were currently advertised for sale, asking that these lands and monies also be held in trust until sales were completed or proceeds paid to Indian sellers.[69]

Just a month before the scheduled end of the trust period for the "old" Omaha allotments, Thurston County taxpayers eagerly anticipated two-thirds of the Omaha Reservation lands coming onto the tax rolls. The Pender newspaper flatly stated that the end of the trust period would place 150,000 acres of land "into the hands of the whites, who have awaited this move." The *Times* admitted that the recent law allowing the president to grant trust extensions clouded the issue, but its editor believed that most requests for extensions would be denied and the trusteeship would end on schedule.[70] As the July 10, 1909, deadline approached, the reservation was overrun by land speculators who tricked many Omahas into signing away their lands. Pender businessmen and two Indians formed a syndicate to buy up Indian lands as they were removed from trust. Omahas Thomas Sloan and William F. Springer, along with Will Estill, Llewelyn C. Brown-rigg, and Garry P. Meyers, stockpiled currency so that they could purchase land immediately after midnight on July 10. Estill and Springer alone invested nearly $20,000 of their own money and borrowed another $15,000 to finance land contracts with about forty Indians.[71]

In a series of letters to the interior secretary and Commissioner Valentine, Dr. Susan La Flesche Picotte accused these same men of interfering with an agency investigation conducted by E. B. Linnen. Picotte claimed she could prove that Sloan, Estill, and their cronies had incited the Indians to complain about Superintendent Commons' job performance. While Commons lay seriously ill, Estill, Springer, and Brownrigg had allegedly rounded up Indians and had taken them to Inspector Linnen to prefer charges, after telling the Indians exactly what to say. Picotte pleaded with Valentine not to remove Commons, who had become a great protector of her people.[72] But the syndicate apparently succeeded in its campaign to discredit the crusading superintendent, for he was transferred a few months later.[73]

Due to the rampant irregularities on the reservation, on July 3, 1909, President William Howard Taft extended the trust period on nearly all of the original Omaha allotments for ten years. This was done with the condition that competent Omahas would continue to be singled out and given fee-patents. The Pender speculators who had entered into premature land contracts lost huge sums of money when Taft ordered the extension, and to cut their losses, they urged Omahas still under trust agreements to apply for land titles.[74] Thurston County taxpayers felt betrayed by the president's action, and their frustration surfaced on the front page of the *Pender Times*, whose editor charged fully competent Omahas with shifting the burden of taxation to local whites when they could have taken title to their lands and paid their share.[75]

To placate angry Nebraskans, Assistant Commissioner of Indian Affairs Fred H. Abbott offered assurances that every effort would be made to "free" the lands of competent Omahas.[76] The method used to free Omaha lands was both arbitrary and unfair. To expedite fee patenting, Commissioner Valentine had proposed special "competency commissions" on the Kiowa Reservation in Oklahoma, among the Yakimas in Washington, and at the Umatilla and Santee Reservations. But the very first competency commission operated on the Omaha

Reservation. Because the Omahas had been allotted their lands for twenty-five years, and because many of them worked farms, they were considered the nation's most competent Indians, and Valentine wanted to see them completely independent. In addition, the commissioner believed that allowing capable Indians to sell the land they did not actually farm would be the best way to end the destructive practice of leasing.[77] Local whites, eager to purchase Omaha lands, supported Valentine's idea, since they knew that at least some of the Indians would sell the lands either to speculators or to current lessees.

Because he believed the local superintendent had too narrow a view and could not possibly represent all the interests involved, Valentine doubted the agent's ability to judge Indian competency. He therefore appointed a three-man commission to determine which Omahas could handle their own affairs. On October 10, 1909, Indian Office traveling auditor W. W. McConihe, former Omaha superintendent Andrew G. Pollack, and prominent Thurston County newspaper editor H. P. Marble began their work among the unfortunate Omahas.[78] All Indians over age eighteen were to be presented forms containing seventy-five questions regarding their financial and physical condition, their education, the current use of their lands, and most important, whether or not they desired fee-patents. Two local businessmen were to certify each Omaha's fitness for landownership, and the commissioners would then add their own comments. By February 1, 1910, McConihe, Pollack, and Marble had supposedly questioned 605 Omaha allottees.[79]

In early March, the commissioners submitted their report to Valentine. Based on testimony and their questionnaires, they had divided the Omahas into three classes. Class One Indians were declared fully competent to receive fee-patents; those in Class Two could lease their lands and handle their own funds, but their allotments would remain in trust. Class Three included "wholly incompetent" Indians "who should remain under the supervision and jurisdiction of the Government for a further period of tutelage."[80] On February 28, an Omaha newspaper had estimated that approximately 250 Indians would receive titles to their lands. A week later, McConihe put the number at 300 and assured his superiors, "Everything is working out beautifully."[81] On March 10, 1910, 294 Omahas officially became "compe tent," and on that same day, the Land Office issued 244 fee-patents for

20,199 acres of Indian land.[82] Later that month, Superintendent Kneale received the official list of Omahas whom the Indian Office considered ready to receive their titles. At the request of the Indian Office, Kneale published the list in local newspapers, along with each Indian's acreage and a warning that any contract to buy or sell these Indians' lands would be void if the patent had not yet been recorded by the General Land Office.[83]

In choosing competent Omahas, the three commissioners often violated their own rules. Self-sufficiency and knowledge of English were essential criteria, yet allottees who could not read, write, or speak English and who could not manage on their own received fee-patents. In addition, the commissioners never met some of the Indians whom they ruled competent.[84] Historian Richmond R. Clow further argues that many Omahas who agreed to accept fee-patents did not really understand the meaning of their assent. Allottees' forms were filled out by the commissioners; there was no place on the competency form for an Indian to sign, and it is unlikely that taxation, mortgages, and other landowning obligations were explained to confused Omahas. Clow also asserts that Omahas may have accepted fee-patents because they would agree to anything to keep their lands.[85] Of the 258 Indians who actually appeared before the commissioners, 53 stated that they did *not* want fee-patents. But their lands, totaling 4,002 acres, were patented against their objections, meaning that one of every five Omaha allottees interviewed by the three commissioners was "forced to accept a fee-patent to his or her land."[86]

The commission's arbitrary division of Omahas into three competency classes caused controversy from the beginning. On March 11, 1910, approximately 500 Indians attended a tribal meeting to voice their objections to government interference in their affairs. Many of the 243 Class Two Omahas believed they were as capable as the Omahas labeled Class One. For their part, Class One allottees felt they were being discriminated against. They believed it was unfair to tax only the lands of "competent" Indians, and at the council, many demanded to be declared Class Two so that they could keep their allotments, tax-free. Not surprisingly, land-hungry Thurston County whites tried to persuade the three commissioners to include more Omahas in the Class One category.[87]

With the issuance of deeds imminent, on March 31 the Omaha Reservation teemed with speculators—from Winnebago, Sioux City, and other "nearby financial centers"—who hoped to snap up the lands of those Indians on the "competent list." However, the deeds had not yet been filed with the General Land Office, and by early April, speculation was rife as to the status of the Indian patents. None had been delivered, and no announcement had been made; everyone remained in the dark. Rumors claimed that fifty deeds had been registered in Pender, but no one knew for sure, and "everyone . . . [had] the headache from sustained deep thought on the subject."[88] Finally, Superintendent Kneale announced that all patents had been delayed pending an investigation into possibly illegal land contracts. Chief Superintendent E. P. Holcomb, Special Indian Agent W. W. McConihe, and Interior Department Inspector E. B. Linnen conducted the inquiry, which resulted in grand jury land-fraud indictments against seven local men and former Superintendent John M. Commons, now a resident of New Mexico.[89]

According to the charges, the defendants had induced Indians to sign away lands that were still in trust. In some instances, Indians were persuaded to sell their property at prices far below true value; the speculators then transferred the deeds to third parties at over double the price. In other cases, unsuspecting Omahas were led to believe they had signed leases when in fact they had sold their lands for "a mere pittance." Many allottees, on receiving their fee-patents, found that deeds, sometimes for the lands on which they were living, had been filed as much as a year earlier. By the time third, or even fourth, parties took over the lands, it had become difficult to trace the transactions. Consequently, the Indian Office intended to cancel every patent obtained by fraud and to invalidate the resulting deeds. The seven Nebraska defendants—H. L. Keefe, W. T. Diddock, E. S. Kelly, Will Estill, E. W. Rossiter, and James J. Orr, all of Walthill, and Frank Coddington of Decatur—all pled "no contest" to illegally trafficking in Omaha lands and were fined from $25 to $300 each. There is no indication of the disposition of John Commons' indictment, but the indictment itself shows that he may have been less concerned with Omaha rights than Dr. Susan Picotte believed. The unsuspecting Omahas who had sold their lands prematurely found themselves reclassified as "incompetent."[90]

The work of the Omaha competency commission was a complete failure. A carefully researched list of land transactions involving both "old" and "new" allottees who received fee-patents in March 1910 and shortly thereafter reveals a pattern of forced patents, mortgages, and quick sales. Many allottees sold their lands outright within weeks of receiving them. For example, Ernest Merrick, Thomas White, Charles Thomas, and Mary Esau Walker were issued patents on March 10, and all had sold their allotments, totaling 280 acres, by March 31. By October 5, Will Estill alone had purchased the lands of at least four Indians, one of whom had not given his consent to receive a fee-patent. James Porter, Edward Esau, Madeline Tyndall, and John Sheridan were among those Omahas who answered "no" to the question "Do you desire a fee-patent?" Tyndall subsequently mortgaged her land eight times before selling it in 1913; Esau's land transaction record shows fifteen mortgages in four years; Porter had already borrowed on his land when he sold it in August 1911; and Sheridan's record reveals ten loans in just two years. He sold his land for a mere dollar.[91]

An appalling number of Omahas mortgaged and remortgaged their lands. Roce Grant received his fee-patent on September 1, 1910, and had already borrowed on his acreage five times when he sold it the following June. Etta Webster (Warner), Eugene Pappan, and Jackson Wolf each had thirteen or more loans on their records, and Daniel Webster, who had not consented to a fee-patent, had twenty-one unpaid mortgages on his land when he sold it for one dollar in October 1916. Homer Walker borrowed on his land seven months before he received it, and he later mortgaged it seven more times. Amos Walker told the competency commission he was too old to receive title to his land. The commissioners said he was intelligent and issued him a fee-patent anyway. Walker leased his land for three years, then took out fifteen different mortgages. Maggie Walker, either his wife or daughter, sold the land in 1916, again for just one dollar. Upton Henderson received a fee-patent on March 10, 1910, mortgaged his land eleven times, then sold it for one dollar in 1916. Henderson was blind.[92]

The Bureau of Indian Affairs ignored the disastrous results of its policies among the Omahas, just as it had so many times before. Many tribal members had already sold or mortgaged their lands when Commissioner Valentine appointed another competency commission in

1910 on the nearby Santee Sioux Reservation. But Valentine soon questioned his own decision. The Omaha experiment had obviously failed, and the Santee commissioners were using similarly slipshod methods. Given the "carelessness and incompetence" of the commissioners on the two reservations, Valentine reluctantly decided that fee-patents were not in the best interest of the Indians: they were "at cross purposes with other efforts of the government to encourage industry, thrift, and independence." He subsequently canceled plans for further commissions and disregarded the Santee report. The Indian Office now temporarily returned to reviewing fee-patents on a case-by-case basis.[93]

Concerned with the possible damage done by his competency commissions, in April 1912 Valentine asked Indian superintendents to tell him what effects fee-patenting had had on their charges. He especially wanted to know how many Indians had sold their newly acquired lands to whites.[94] Later that year, S. A. M. Young sent Commissioner Valentine the bad news regarding the Omahas. Young reported that 90 percent of the Omahas who had been issued fee-patents by the commission had sold their lands, 8 percent had mortgaged them, and only 2 percent still retained their allotments. One inspector stated the obvious: "The work of the 1910 commission was not a success." But rather than condemning the commissioners, he placed the blame on Thurston County whites who had badgered the Omahas to apply for fee-patents before they were ready.[95]

Citing "mental wear and tear" and "the struggle between all kinds of opposing forces," a weary and ailing Robert Valentine resigned as commissioner of Indian affairs in September 1912.[96] With Valentine gone from the Indian Office and with President Woodrow Wilson's election, "progressivism" replaced humanitarianism in Indian affairs. Progressives, who were determined to force Indians to make it on their own, turned to a much more liberal fee-patenting policy. Against the objections of some officials in the Bureau of Indian Affairs, new Indian Commissioner Cato Sells and Interior Secretary Franklin K. Lane instituted a "policy of greater liberalism," in which all able-bodied adult Indians of less than one-half Indian blood would be given complete control of their properties and those with more than one-half Indian blood would receive fee-patents if found competent. To accomplish this goal, Sells reinstated competency commissions. Between

1917 and 1920, the Bureau of Indian Affairs issued over seventeen thousand Indian land patents.[97]

Commissioner Sells did not stumble forward blindly. In December 1914, recognizing that "a more liberal policy with regard to the issuance of patents in fee [had] been followed at the Omaha and Winnebago reservations than elsewhere," he asked Omaha Superintendent Johnson and Winnebago Superintendent Young to study the effects and results of fee-patenting on their reservations and to report to him as soon as possible. The commissioner wanted facts and figures, but he was also concerned with moral issues and wanted Johnson's and Young's recommendations as to whether a future fee-patenting policy should be liberal or restricted.[98] Superintendents at the Santee, Sisseton, Yankton, and Pottawatami Agencies each received a copy of Sells' letter to Johnson and were also asked to forward reports.[99]

In reply to Sells' request, Johnson submitted a detailed report that included a list of 140 male Omaha patentees divided into four categories: (1) those who had retained their lands; (2) those who had sold their lands but used the proceeds wisely; (3) those who had little or nothing to show for the sale of their allotments; and (4) those who had signed away their holdings or had squandered their payment due to the influence of alcohol. Of the 140 allottees listed, 18 Indians, or fewer than 13 percent, had kept their lands. Ten had used their land proceeds wisely, and a disturbing 112, or 80 percent, had nothing left. In at least 16 of these latter cases, liquor was to blame.[100]

Johnson believed that the liberal granting of fee-patents demoralized both Indians and whites. The large amounts of Indian land that could be alienated attracted unscrupulous whites, who relieved the Omahas of their lands by committing fraud, by using whiskey, and by encouraging Indians to go into debt. Knowing that they were being cheated discouraged the Indians, as did the increased use of alcohol. Superintendent Johnson stated emphatically that the liberal issuance of fee-patents would result in Indian land loss. But, he cautioned, if the government insisted on pursuing that policy, patents should be issued gradually and only on the recommendations of local superintendents, who could best judge Indians' competency.[101] In their investigative report of March 1915, Indian Office inspectors E. B. Linnen and E. M. Sweet Jr. agreed that to keep the Omaha land base from eroding further, the office should be very cautious in its issuance of fee-patents.[102]

Just a few days before Superintendent Johnson submitted his disturbing account of the Omahas, Superintendents Young of the Winnebago Agency and E. D. Mossman of the Sisseton Sioux Agency had filed almost identical reports. Like the Omahas, few Winnebagoes retained their lands or used their land proceeds wisely, and like their Indian neighbors, many lost their property due to alcohol.[103] Fee-patents had been issued on the Sisseton Reservation over a period of years, but in late 1914, Superintendent Mossman told Sells that of 222 Indians who had received titles to their lands, only *nine* had successfully kept them. The "most intelligent class" among the Sissetons opposed fee-patents and saw them as a means to make paupers of the Sioux. Mossman agreed, and he believed that granting a large number of fee-patents at one time would cause a "feast of graft." He had recommended that only a handful of Indians receive land titles during his superintendency, and he planned to continue that policy.[104]

Totally ignoring the disastrous results reported by Johnson, Young, Mossman, and Yankton Sioux Superintendent A. W. Leech, Interior Secretary Lane proceeded with his renewal of a liberal fee-patenting policy: "It is the judgment of those who know the Indian best, and it is my conclusion . . . that we should henceforth make a . . . *systematic* effort to cast the full burden of independence and responsibility upon an increasing number of Indians of all tribes." Citing the powers granted to him by the 1906 Burke Act, Lane promised to use that authority "as soon as the machinery of administration [could] be set in motion." Reaction to Lane's plan was mixed. Local superintendents were no doubt in a position to "know the Indian best," and most of them opposed Lane's new policy. The Indian Rights Association called for the repeal of the Burke Act and for the establishment of a permanent, nonpolitical competency commission with regional branches to minimize delays in fee-patenting.[105] But Lane's policy was encouraged by the Indians of the Cheyenne River Reservation in South Dakota and especially by tribal member Henry C. Lafferty, who, in a series of letters to the secretary, urged him to "hurry up the process of removing restrictions and cutting red tape." Any doubts that Lane may have entertained were erased when he received a petition from thirty-two of Lafferty's tribespeople, supporting his plan.[106]

A few days after receiving the Cheyenne River petition, Lane appointed Interior Department Inspector Major James McLaughlin and Frank A. Thackery of the Pima Indian School in Arizona to ascertain "just what Indians should be allowed to handle their own affairs." At each reservation, the two would be joined by the local superintendent as the third member of the competency commission.[107] Thackery apparently had doubts about his new role. In a letter to Matthew K. Sniffen of the Indian Rights Association, he inquired about the workings of a competency commission and asked, "Do you think it would be advisable to force citizenship upon thoroughly competent Indians who do not desire it?"[108]

Lane and Sells' new policy produced the exact results expected by Indian officers in the field. Delivery of fee-patents at the Yankton Agency invited a "mad rush by land buyers," and Superintendent Leech feared that the secretary would "feel very much disappointed over results [there]."[109] When the competency commissioners, accompanied by Secretary Lane and a film crew, arrived on the Santee Sioux Reservation to conduct an elaborate citizenship ceremony, they discovered that at least twenty-five Santee patentees had already arranged to sell their lands for about one-half their value. Unperturbed, Lane withheld the patents in question and continued with the ceremony, before a "large and appreciative audience."[110] In Thurston County, land speculators became even bolder under the liberalized fee-patenting rules. Through an Indian Office informant, they knew when each Indian patent would be issued and were able to snap up the land before the local superintendent had received the government paperwork. Real estate brokers often used liquor to pry Omahas loose from their lands and on several occasions actually held drunken Indians captive until their fee-patents came through, then induced them to turn over their deeds for practically nothing.[111]

In 1916, Superintendent Leech expressed his concern for Yankton Sioux children, who would likely become landless because of wholesale fee-patenting on their reservation.[112] Likewise, seven years earlier, shortly before the trust period for the old Omaha allotments was due to expire, Interior Secretary James R. Garfield had suddenly realized that over five hundred Omaha children had not been issued allotments. The oversight dated back to the 1882 Omaha Allotment Act and the government's failure to issue a trust patent for the unallotted tribal lands. Section Eight of the original act provided that each Omaha child born before the end of the trust period (July 10, 1909) should receive an allotment from these "excess" lands, but for some unexplained reason, these allotments were never made. The only lands allotted to Omaha children after 1882 were the additional acreages provided for in the act of March 3, 1893. Now the Interior Department determined that each child born after March 3, 1893, was entitled to forty acres of land.[113]

The government had a problem. In 1909, there were 520 living Omaha children who had been born after 1893 and only 4,500 acres of unallotted land. It appeared that Secretary Garfield had two choices; he could allot 40 acres to only 112 children, leaving the rest landless, a plan fiercely fought by Omaha parents; or he could divide the acreage equally, giving each child only 8.6 acres of sometimes marginal land, too little to farm or to lease. But Omaha Superintendent John Commons offered a third alternative. Why not, he asked, sell the 4,500 acres, which were worth approximately $100,000, and give each child an equal share, about $192?[114] Garfield took Commons' advice, with the stipulation that each young Omaha's money would remain in the U.S. Treasury at 5 percent interest until he or she reached age twenty-five. This plan would net an Omaha fifteen-year-old the grand sum of $285.[115]

The Interior Department had not yet finished with these unfortunate Omaha children. True, the proceeds from 4,500 acres of land would be divided 520 ways, but before one Omaha child received one cent, the $3,000 cost of implementing the land sales would be deducted from the profits, meaning that landless children would pay for a twenty-five-year-old government error.[116] In early 1910, a new interior secretary, Richard. A. Ballinger, found another way to reduce the children's share of the land proceeds. Since young Omahas would benefit most from increased property values after the completion of an ongoing reservation drainage project, Ballinger proposed that the $600 cost of the project be subtracted before the children received their shares.[117]

Having disposed of the embarrassing problem of children's allotments, with the Omahas' concurrence, Congress passed an act on May

11, 1912, "to provide for the disposal of the unallotted land on the Omaha Indian Reservation." Not all of the land would be sold: 49 acres was reserved for the Indian agency; the Omahas could select 10 acres to be used as a tribal cemetery; and the Presbyterian Church retained 10 acres. Two acres of the grounds of the old Presbyterian mission would be deeded to the Nebraska State Historical Society, and a 164-acre townsite would be surveyed and platted. The act authorized the interior secretary to survey, appraise, and sell 40-acre tracts of the remaining land. No one person could purchase more than 160 acres, and Omahas whose allotments were being eroded by the Missouri River could choose new farms from the unallotted lands. Their original allotments would then be sold.[118]

There was some question as to which Omahas could apply for new allotments to replace eroded ones. The Interior Department finally ruled that those allottees whose lands had entirely disappeared and those who had inherited lands subject to erosion could exchange their lands. Those whose property was close to the river but not actually in danger could not.[119] The problem of lands in litigation added to the confusion over the sale of the remaining unallotted lands. In March 1914, Assistant Indian Commissioner C. F. Hauke informed Superintendent John Spear that six of the seven applications for new allotments on grounds of erosion were for lands currently involved in lawsuits. Hauke assured the Omaha superintendent that as soon as court decisions were received, the Indians involved would be notified. In the meantime, to expedite land sales, he urged those allottees to make other selections.[120] In early 1915, new Omaha Superintendent Axel Johnson inquired about the disputed allotments. Hauke reminded Johnson that nothing could be done regarding substitute allotments for the six applicants until the lawsuits cleared the courts. Once more, he urged the Indians to choose other lands.[121]

The six Omaha allottees would have a long wait. In 1914, attorneys John L. Webster and Hiram Chase filed twenty-one suits with the federal district court, which would determine ownership of the remaining Omaha tribal lands. Webster and the U.S. attorney agreed that regardless of the outcome, when the court handed down its rulings, they would take one decision to the circuit court of appeals as a test case. The others would await the appeals court verdict. In March 1915, *two* cases came before Appeals Court Judge Walter H. Sanborn. Interestingly, one involved land claimed by Hiram Chase.[122] Chase asserted that as the sole heir of his mother, Clarissa Chase, he owned the forty acres assigned to her in 1870 by the terms of the 1865 treaty. Another Omaha, Rose Wolf Setter, claimed the same land as the widow and sole survivor of Reuben Wolf, who had been allotted the forty acres in 1899 and had received a trust patent for it in March 1902, under the 1882 Omaha Allotment Act. The questions involved were whether the land assignment in 1870 was a title or merely permission to occupy the land and whether the provisions of the 1882 act superseded all other agreements.[123] The Eighth District Court had found in favor of Rose Wolf Setter, but in April 1915, Judge Sanborn overturned the earlier decision and awarded the disputed land to Chase, ruling that his mother did have title to the allotment.[124]

When the attorney general's office informed Assistant Indian Commissioner E. B. Meritt of the appeals court decision, Meritt voiced his disagreement. He believed that the 1882 act took precedence over the earlier treaty and that Rose Wolf Setter should have the land. Because of his disagreement and the far-reaching implications of the ruling in this case, Meritt recommended that the attorney general take the matter to the U.S. Supreme Court.[125] In his objections, Meritt faulted Judge Sanborn for not following the opinions of two earlier cases involving the Omaha Thomas Sloan. Sanborn had reviewed the Sloan cases but had decided that they were too dissimilar to the Chase litigation to be cited as precedents.[126]

On July 21, 1915, First Assistant Interior Secretary A. A. Jones asked the attorney general to present the Chase–Wolf Setter claims to the Supreme Court. On April 24, 1916, the high court heard the arguments but refused to render a decision. Instead, the justices asked for the court of appeals records so that they could further review the case.[127] Finally, on November 5, 1917, more than three years after the suit had first been filed in district court, the Supreme Court rendered its verdict. Stating that Chase's mother merely had the right to occupy the forty disputed acres, the court ruled in favor of Rose Wolf Setter. As a result, future reservation land disputes would be decided in favor of Omahas who were granted allotments in 1882.[128]

While Omaha allottees remained on their eroding lands and awaited the Supreme Court decision, the Nebraska State Historical Society enlarged its reservation preserve, and tribal leaders ensured their people adequate burial grounds by correcting a deficiency in the 1912 land sales act. Neither the tribe nor the historical society was content with the terms of the May 1912 act. Walthill attorney Harry L. Keefe complained that the two-acre Presbyterian mission site earmarked for transfer to the society did not include a historic springhouse and cemetery. Keefe hoped to enlarge the historical society tract so that these points of interest could also be preserved, and he asked the Omaha Agency clerk to bring his request to the attention of the Bureau of Indian Affairs.[129] On learning of Keefe's request, Commissioner Sells asked Francis La Flesche to attend a tribal meeting and ascertain whether his people would agree to enlarge their land donation to the historical society.[130]

In late November 1913, Keefe informed Sells that, on behalf of the historical society, he wanted to buy the entire forty-acre tract surrounding the mission. He pointed out that this land was unfit for farming, and he suggested that the Omahas could "well afford to give the 40 acre tract to [his] society." But even without a donation, the attorney was confident that the historical society could raise enough money to make the purchase.[131] Sells in turn notified the Omaha superintendent that he would try to enact legislation to include the springhouse and cemetery in the society's land patent but that he saw no need to rush, since the Nebraska legislature would have to approve funds for the historic site.[132] Unless Keefe and the historical society wanted to pursue the mission preservation immediately, Sells suggested issuing the patent when all the lands were ready for sale.[133] The Omahas apparently refused to give up the additional thirty-eight acres without compensation, for in January 1915, the Nebraska State Historical Society agreed to buy the extra land. Keefe appeared especially anxious to secure the property. He told Superintendent Johnson that if the land could be made available before the rest of the unallotted parcels, he and two other society members would buy it and be reimbursed later. He intended to ask the legislature to designate the entire forty acres as a "historical monument."[134]

In the original draft of the 1912 act to sell unallotted Omaha lands, the tribe was to be allowed only a seven-acre burial ground, but before the bill became law, the interior secretary agreed to grant the Indians an additional three acres for cemetery purposes.[135] Before Congress even considered the 1912 legislation, the Omahas had outgrown their cemetery, and they had been burying their dead, without congressional approval, on an adjoining tract to the north of the original burial grounds. In December 1914, Superintendent Johnson, at the tribe's request, asked the Bureau of Indian Affairs to approve their use of the entire cemetery tract, which now comprised eighteen acres. The Omahas' request arrived too late to be included in the 1916 Indian Appropriation Act, but Assistant Commissioner E. B. Meritt promised that, if necessary, his office would support special legislation to provide the extra land.[136]

But the Omahas were still not satisfied, and in April 1915, in council with Superintendent Johnson, they asked for a total of forty-eight acres on which to bury their dead. Assistant Commissioner Meritt, who had been involved in all the cemetery negotiations, questioned whether the tribe really intended to use the entire acreage as a cemetery.[137] At a second tribal council in early June, the Omahas made their final request to the Bureau of Indian Affairs, this time asking for a total of seventy-eight acres of burial grounds, to be located in two different areas of the reservation. Although exasperated with the Omahas' increasing burial site demands, Meritt acceded to their request and prepared legislation for introduction at the next session of Congress.[138] The Interior Department agreed that the Omahas' present burial grounds were inadequate, and in July 1916, at the urging of Secretary Lane, Congress approved a bill to set aside seventy acres of Omaha Reservation land as a tribal cemetery.[139] Like any other lands withdrawn from sale for special purposes, the extra cemetery acres reduced each Omaha child's share of land sale proceeds. But enlarging the burial grounds benefited the young as well as the old by ensuring that Omahas would be buried on their own lands, with their own people.

From the time the Omahas had settled on their reservation, whites in northeastern Nebraska had resented their occupation of that valuable land and had tried to buy it, lease it, or cheat the Indians out of it. Any land that whites could not wrest from the Omahas they attempted to tax. These were trust lands and, as such, remained tax-exempt, but as the Board of Indian Commissioners had predicted, Omaha trust status was violated time and again by special legislation. The formation of

Thurston County in 1889 marked the real beginning of the campaign to tax Omaha lands, and some Nebraska senators and congressmen became willing county allies by sponsoring Indian tax bills.

For the first three years of its existence, Thurston County made no attempt to tax Omaha lands, but county revenues did not meet expenses. In April 1892, in a bizarre plan to induce the government to make up the revenue shortfall, county officials entered into a contract with the ubiquitous Pender "businessman" William E. Peebles. Peebles agreed to lobby Congress for money for Thurston County in lieu of taxes not forthcoming from Indian trust lands. In return for successful passage of a tax relief bill, Peebles would receive 10 percent of any money Congress appropriated. Peebles' strange contract did not sit well with the House Committee on Indian Affairs. On July 26, 1894, the county received a telegram from Peebles canceling his contract and asking the county commissioners to officially inform Nebraska Third District Congressman George D. Meiklejohn that a deal no longer existed between him and the county in the event that a tax bill passed.[140]

However, invalidating the Peebles' contract with the county had not ended the efforts to tax Omaha lands. Perhaps in response to Peebles' lobbying, on September 6, 1893, Representative Meiklejohn had introduced a bill "extending relief to Indian citizens and for other purposes." Unfortunately, the "other purposes" included taxing the Omahas.[141] Commissioner of Indian Affairs Daniel M. Browning opposed Meiklejohn's bill, mainly because it provided that the land taxes would be deducted from the tribal trust fund, without Indian approval. The bill failed to pass, but its introduction foreshadowed the coming struggle between the white minority and the overwhelming Indian majority in Thurston County.[142]

Thurston County's tax problems were real. On March 2, 1900, the *Pender Times* published a supplement illustrating the unique tax situation in the county. According to one chart, only a little over 7 percent of the taxable real estate in the county lay within the Omaha and Winnebago Reservations, yet these lands composed 91 percent of the county. A high crime rate on the reservations necessitated large Indian court costs, which white taxpayers resented paying. Not surprisingly, the county wanted to tax the other 91 percent of its land.[143] Early in

1902, nervous Omahas were led to believe that a law to tax their lands was currently before Congress. When confronted by concerned Indians, Congressman John S. Robinson assured them that no such bill had been introduced and that, even if it had, it could not become law without violating treaty rights.[144]

The Omahas must have been relieved to learn in 1903 that in a landmark taxation case, the U.S. Supreme Court had ruled that James A. Rickert, treasurer of Roberts County, South Dakota, could not tax Indian lands held in trust by the government. In deciding in favor of the federal government in *United States v. James A. Rickert*, the high court also ruled that Roberts County could not tax improvements, farm implements, cattle, and other personal property provided to Indians by the government as part of their treaty or trust agreements. The court declared simply, "A state cannot impose a tax which will substantially impede or burden the functioning of the Federal Government."[145]

Ignoring the high court decision, Thurston County officials stepped up their taxing campaign. On June 13, 1905, the County Board of Equalization passed a resolution requiring that all funds from heirship lands deposited in individual Omaha accounts be added to the tax list, and it ordered Superintendent MacKey to turn over Omaha deposit records. MacKey refused, and on June 14, the County Board of Equalization met again and instructed County Assessor Thomas Pollack to go to the Omaha Agency and bring back a list of the names of all Omahas having money on deposit in banks or in other institutions. Pollack apparently got the names, for on June 19, the board had in its possession a printed list, along with increases in assessment due to heirship deposits.[146] All this activity did not go unnoticed. In late July, the U.S. district attorney filed suit in circuit court, asking Judge W. H. Munger to grant a temporary injunction prohibiting Thurston County from pursuing its taxation policy. A deputy U.S. marshal then notified the county clerk and treasurer that they could not tax or attempt to tax money in Omaha accounts.[147]

In September 1905, the government once more took its complaint against Thurston County to the Eighth Circuit Court, this time to request a ruling on the legality of taxing Omaha heirship funds. After hearing the arguments, Judge Munger, citing the freedom given Indians by the *Heff* decision and arguing that money from heirship lands was deposited to the credit of individual Indians, ruled that these accounts could be taxed "the same as the property of any ordinary citizen." Interestingly, Omaha attorney Thomas Sloan represented Thurston County before Judge Munger.[148] Receiving a telegram from Omaha informing him of the judge's decision, Indian Commissioner Leupp instructed the attorney general to have the U.S. attorney appeal the ruling.[149] Six months later, with Sloan once more representing Thurston County, the court of appeals overturned Judge Munger's decision. Judge Walter H. Sanborn stated, "The lands and their proceeds, so long as they are held or controlled by the United States and the term of the trust has not expired . . . are not subject to taxation by any state or county."[150] Judge Sanborn's ruling was a rare—and temporary—Omaha victory. Meanwhile, the county continued to take advantage of any opportunity to produce revenue at Indian expense. Section Two of a reservation drainage act of February 18, 1909, provided that up to $240 could be demanded of each Omaha allottee to protect his or her land from flooding. County officials, of course, took full advantage of this "tax" windfall.[151]

The big blow fell in 1910, when Nebraska Senator Norris Brown introduced a bill in Congress to tax Omaha lands. Nebraska Third District Congressman James F. Latta, a member of the House Indian Affairs Committee, and South Dakota Representative Charles Burke shepherded Brown's bill through the House.[152] On April 27, congressmen nearly came to blows over Brown's tax proposal. Burke presented the case for Thurston County, arguing that despite President Taft's Omaha trust period extension in 1909, it was unfair for the Indians to remain tax-exempt, since they had paid no taxes for twenty-five years and owned nearly all the county land. Using county officials' standard argument, Burke claimed that taxation would benefit the Omahas, with improved roads and schools increasing their property values. Representative John J. Fitzgerald of New York had no real aversion to taxing Indians, but he was concerned that paying taxes to Thurston County would bankrupt the Omahas and that Congress would then have to support them. Oklahoma Congressman Charles D. Carter objected to Senator Brown's attempt to tax allotments still in trust and asked Burke, "Is not that a new departure in Indian legislation?"[153]

In a letter accompanying reports from both the Senate and House Indian Affairs Committees, Interior Secretary Richard A. Ballinger enumerated several reasons to tax Omaha property: (1) because of low revenues, Thurston County had no courthouse and could not afford to prosecute Indian crimes; (2) Indians paid no taxes while requiring high expenditures, especially in court costs; and (3) the county was in debt. The secretary agreed that the trust period had been a good idea, but he also believed that it was time for the Omahas to take on the responsibilities and privileges of citizenship. Omahas, he argued, could afford to pay taxes. Most leased their lands, and in February 1910, the Indian Office had been authorized to pay them the balance from their federal trust fund. Finally, echoing Burke, Ballinger claimed that the increase in the Omahas' property values over the next ten years would more than equal their tax bill.[154]

On May 6, 1910, Congress passed the Brown Act, which dictated that all Omaha lands allotted before 1885 would now be "subject to appraisement and assessment for the purposes of taxation and subject to taxation for local, school district, road district, county, and state purposes as provided by the laws of the State of Nebraska." The law included the following provisions: (1) lands could not be sold for unpaid taxes; (2) if taxes remained unpaid one year after they became due, the Thurston County treasurer could report delinquencies to the interior secretary, who was then authorized to pay the taxes from rent money on deposit; (3) however, if no funds were available, the taxes for that year would be excused.[155] The Brown Act effectively reversed Judge Sanborn's ruling in *United States v. Thurston County* and conflicted with Part Three, Section Four, of the Enabling Act of April 1864, which had admitted Nebraska to statehood and dictated, "No taxes shall be imposed by the State on lands or property therein belonging to or which may be purchased by the United States."[156]

At a meeting in Macy, Nebraska, in November 1910, attended by Congressman Latta and county officials, Senator Brown's private secretary began to explain the new taxation act to a large group of Omahas and soon found himself defending the legislation. Nearly all of the Indians objected to the Brown Act; Silas Wood blamed county officials for its passage, and Hiram Chase criticized Congress for passing the bill without Indian consent. Latta pointed out that an

Omaha delegation present in Washington while the bill was being debated had voiced no objections.[157] In 1915, Indian Commissioner Sells denied that the "taxation of the Omaha lands impose[d] any great hardship on the Indians."[158] But chief Indian Office Inspector E. B. Linnen disagreed. Omahas had complained to him that lessees were deducting their Indian landlords' taxes from their rent payments, thus depriving the Omahas of income. The provision of the Brown Act allowing those Omahas with no money in the bank to have their taxes excused was an open invitation for Indians to withdraw their deposits to avoid being taxed. It was especially unfair that some Omahas paid taxes while others did not. Ultimately, incompetent Indians with no control over their own funds bore the heaviest tax burden.[159]

President Taft's 1909 order had extended the trust period on "old" Omaha allotments to July 10, 1919. Nearly four years before the new expiration date, forces were at work to ensure that the first trust extension would be the last. On November 16, 1915, Walthill, Nebraska, citizens met to discuss the issue. A Pender banker, who could not be present, nevertheless expressed his views. George J. Adams, cashier of the Pender State Bank, adamantly opposed any further trust extensions. In the banker's opinion, the president had overstepped his authority in granting the first extension, and Adams was convinced that "if the Omahas [were] not now capable of manageing [*sic*] their own affairs they never [would] be." It was the duty of the United States, he insisted, to free up Omaha lands for taxation, since Thurston County had "incurred obligations" in anticipation of Omaha tax revenues.[160] Eighth Circuit Court Judge Guy T. Graves, who should not have become involved in the dispute, also opposed further trust extensions, citing the unfairness to both white and Indian Thurston County taxpayers. Graves emphasized that even with the Brown Act in effect, less than 50 percent of county lands were taxed, and he wanted to see all Indian allottees share the burden.[161]

Also in 1915, an Omaha "committee," whose members included attorneys Chase and Sloan, joined local whites in opposing further trust extensions. Both Chase and Sloan had been involved in shady land deals in the past, and their presence on the committee made it suspect. Their fellow Indians apparently did not trust the two Omaha attorneys. Early in 1916, the editors of *Indian School Journal* reprinted an Indian newspaper article whose author suspected that the committee leaders wanted their people's lands.[162] But at least one admirer considered the group to be public-spirited citizens with "absolutely no ulterior motives." This anonymous letter writer praised the committee's efforts to end the trust period, calling their campaign "a great cause" that would "benefit both . . . the much down trodden and abused Indian, and the taxpayers of Thurston County."[163]

Indian Office employees familiar with conditions on the Omaha Reservation unanimously supported a second trust extension. In 1915, Inspectors Linnen and Sweet reported that 87 percent of the Omahas who had been issued land patents had sold their property, and they strongly recommended that "in the best interests of these Indians . . . this trust period should be extended for another ten years." Linnen and Sweet also informed their superiors that Axel Johnson, because of his concerns, had recommended the issuance of only one fee-patent in his first seven months as Omaha superintendent.[164] Johnson, one of only a handful of white men to truly befriend the Omahas in the early twentieth century, urged the government to extend the trust period so that they could keep their lands.[165]

In 1916, the Omaha trust extension issue became moot as Thurston County and Congress found ways to tax the remaining Omaha lands. Section Twelve of the 1916 Indian Appropriation Act included an assessment against Omaha allottees' fee-patents in violation of the "letter and spirit" of both the 1882 Omaha Allotment Act and the Dawes Act of 1887, which promised that all allotments would be issued "free of all charges or incumbrance whatsoever."[166] Drainage ditches were to be constructed on certain Omaha allotments, and the offending appropriation act required that Indians owning these parcels be assessed up to $10 per acre for the cost of construction. When any Omaha received a patent to land within the drainage district before the assessment was paid, the unpaid drainage taxes would become a first lien against the property—an obvious encumbrance.[167]

To please their constituents, in 1916 both Nebraska Senator Norris Brown and Third District Representative Dan V. Stephens introduced bills to tax Omaha allotments issued in 1885 or later and therefore not covered by the 1910 Brown Act. In pushing his bill, Congressman Stephens claimed that there were "few, if any, either white or Indian who [were] opposed to its passage." Stephens was wrong; although a few Omahas backed the bill, believing that more lands to tax would reduce their own liabilities, most Omahas opposed the legislation.[168] Both Thurston County and the Nebraska lawmakers appeared anxious to rush the bill through Congress. Citing the heavy tax burden of the white minority of the county, the Senate hastily approved the legislation on May 27, 1916.[169]

To bolster their case on Capitol Hill, the Thurston County commissioners had hired noted Washington, D.C., Indian issues attorney Charles J. Kappler as their lobbyist. Early in August, both Kappler and Nebraska Senator Gilbert M. Hitchcock advised Stephens to save time by substituting the Senate version of the bill for his own, since the former had already cleared that chamber and therefore would not have to go back for reconsideration.[170] The Democrat-sponsored bill faced opposition from House Republicans, but Walthill Attorney Harry Keefe assured Representative Stephens that he would use his political influence to persuade House Minority Leader James R. Mann to drop his objections. The House approved the bill in December with just one insignificant word change.[171] No high-ranking Interior Department official raised a hand to stop this unfair legislation; Secretary Lane had no objections to taxing all Omaha lands as long as the lands could not be sold if taxes became delinquent.[172]

Probably because of his unflagging efforts to put Omaha lands on the Thurston County tax rolls, the *Walthill (Nebraska) Citizen* urged all Indians on the reservation to vote for Dan Stephens, "their truely [*sic*] good friend."[173] Stephens was no Indian's friend, as he proved in a December 18, 1916, letter to *Pender Republic* editor E. L. Barker: "It gives me pleasure to advise you that I have today secured the passage through the House of the bill taxing Indian lands. . . . I am very glad indeed to have been able to render this service to the people of your county."[174] On December 30, 1916, the disastrous Brown-Stephens Act became law. Under its Section Two, all allotments issued in 1885 or later, whether or not they were still in trust, would be taxed. As in the earlier Brown Act, taxes could be deducted from Indians' funds but would be excused if no money was available, and lands could not be forfeited for unpaid taxes.[175] Thurston County officials aggressively implemented the Brown-Stephens Act, taxing trust lands and, in some cases, violating the new law by selling the lands of penniless Indians who could not pay their taxes. For its part, the Interior Department abetted the taxation efforts of the county by arbitrarily designating July 10, 1919, as the expiration date for the trust periods of even the "new" 1893 allotments, which were scheduled to remain under government protection until 1925, 1926, or even 1929.[176]

With the aid of Congress, and at a tremendous cost to its Indian majority, Thurston County had largely solved its revenue problems by late 1916. But the Omahas' troubles had escalated. Local merchants continued to skirt the law by charging Indians usurious interest on loans and inflated prices for goods, and liquor remained a problem despite the best efforts of law enforcement officers. The tribe did receive another trust period extension, in 1919, but this made little difference, since "special legislation" had already taken away most government protection. Hundreds of unfortunate Omaha children born after 1893 had received little more than pocket change from the sale of their people's last unallotted lands, and many Indian adults were now both landless and poverty-stricken.

For decades, white and Indian land speculators and government officials had "used every method, fair and foul," to separate Omahas from their valuable lands.[177] By 1916, nearly 90 percent of Omaha allottees holding fee-patents had either sold their lands or taken mortgages they could not repay, and the property they had managed to keep could now be taxed. In an address before the Nebraska State Historical Society in 1928, Omaha tribal member William F. Springer traced his people's "greater hardships" to the 1906 Burke Act and the discretionary powers that it granted the secretary of the interior.[178] Springer was probably correct. As damaging as it was, the sale of heirship property, legalized in 1902, involved only a small percentage of reservation lands. But the Burke Act made possible the 1910 competency commission and its tragic consequences.

Except for isolated, minor victories, the years 1902–16 had been disastrous for the struggling Omahas. Because of their perceived high degree of acculturation, they had been forced to become "independent" much too soon. Now, surrounded by hostile whites, victimized by some of their own tribal members, and at the mercy of bureaucrats, they had become pawns in the struggle to control prime Nebraska lands. In 1896, anthropologist Alice Fletcher had marveled at the resilience of the allotted Indian: "That he stands at all under his burden is a wonder; that he staggers as he walks should not surprise us; that he falls often should not destroy our hope in him, or relax our efforts to help."[179] To face the future after decades of such "help," the Omahas would need all the strength they could muster.

Epilogue

The [Sacred] Pole stands for the authority of your ancestral ways. The spirit of these ways remains strong within you. That spirit does not depend upon particular material things from the past like hunting buffalo or living in earth lodges as your ancestors did. It lives on in the generosity with which you live your lives. It lives in the help and respect you give to one another. It lives in the blessings you pass on to those who come after you.

Robin Ridington, remarks to the Omaha people
at the 1989 powwow celebrating the return
of the Omahas' Sacred Pole to Nebraska

A study of the Omaha people during the nineteenth and early twentieth centuries represents a microcosm of the government's general policy-making toward Native Americans. Perhaps because the Omahas had always befriended Americans and cooperated with the government, federal program after federal program began on the Omaha Reservation. Nearly every program failed miserably, and government officials appeared to learn nothing from this experimentation. In their zeal to assimilate Indians, they ignored warnings from concerned agents and from the Omahas themselves and blindly applied the same disastrous policies to other unsuspecting tribes throughout the United States.

The government seldom honored its commitments to the Omahas. Repeated promises of protection from the Sioux never produced tangible results, and treaty obligations of mills, blacksmiths, and teachers were only slowly implemented. Likewise, the tribe often waited years for annuities, and proceeds from land sales met delay after delay. On the other hand, Congress acted quickly to accommodate Thurston County whites in their campaigns to tax Omaha lands and alienate Indian allotments. By late 1916, the Omahas' future was bleak. The newly enacted Brown-Stephens Act ensured that henceforth all allotments would be taxed, and tribal members saw their precious lands rapidly slipping away. Merchants who had systematically cheated the Indians conducted "business as usual," and alcohol remained a serious problem. These concerns, along with the violation of trust agreements, threatened the tribe's survival.

Many times in the past, explorers, reformers, and Indian agents had predicted the Omahas' demise. In 1800, travelers along the Missouri River believed smallpox had virtually ended the Omahas' existence as a tribe, and during the height of the Sioux attacks in the 1840s, Indian agents worried that the Omaha people would starve to death or be annihilated. In 1888, even the usually optimistic Alice Fletcher thought that the people's culture was dying and that the tribe might not endure. Fletcher and Francis La Flesche, fearing that the Omahas' Sacred Pole and its cultural secrets would be buried along with its last "keeper," Yellow Smoke, persuaded the elderly man to allow them to transfer the "Venerable Man" to the Peabody Museum at Harvard University for safekeeping.[1]

In her 1932 study of the Omahas (whom she called the "Antlers"), anthropologist Margaret Mead claimed that the tribe's culture had only "the shadow of [its former] rich complexity." Thirty-four years later, in a new introduction to her book, she was even more pessimistic, referring to the Omahas as a "culturally deprived" people.[2] True, the goal of many reformers, government officials, and missionaries had been to dilute Omaha culture and to assimilate the people into the white world. They had partially succeeded: traditional Omaha government had disintegrated with allotment, and many tribal customs had been temporarily abandoned. But in more recent times, anthropologist Robin Ridington and Nebraska folklorist Roger Welsch have vehemently denied that the Omahas are or ever were "culturally deprived." Even Mead, while announcing the end of the Omahas as a distinct culture, admitted that the tribe remained "emotionally bound" to an Indian identity.[3] Ridington argues that despite pressure to assimilate, the Omahas have remained determined to devise "some means by which the bands of the tribe might be kept together and the tribe itself saved from extinction."[4] Omaha culture has survived during the past century in music, oratory, games, and annual powwows held in Macy, Nebraska. Welsch, a student of the Omahas and an adopted member of the tribe, insists, "There is scarcely an Omaha occasion without opportunity for speech-making, gift-giving, and music—three pervasive characteristics of Omaha culture."[5]

The Omahas have kept their culture alive throughout the twentieth century, and recent events have contributed to a tribal cultural renaissance. In the 1980s, the Omahas reestablished the Hethu shka or Warrior Society, whose aim is to "keep alive the memory of historic and valorous acts" and to reacquaint the people with their ancestral customs.[6] The tribe also recently received remastered wax-cylinder recordings of their music that had originally been gathered by Francis La Flesche at the turn of the century. Likewise, many young Omahas are becoming vitally interested in learning and preserving tribal traditions. One teenager told the Peabody Museum curator: "Our young generations of Omahas do cherish the sacred ways. . . . Just as our elders have kept and are teaching us the ways now, we will teach the future Omahas."[7]

One event above all others defines the Omaha cultural renewal. In 1988, exactly one hundred years after Yellow Smoke surrendered the Sacred Pole, his great-great-grandson once more touched the tribe's most sacred object. In an emotional ceremony conducted in a courtyard outside the Peabody Museum, the Sacred Pole was officially returned to its rightful owners. On July 12, 1989, a Creek Indian artist associated with the museum accompanied the "Venerable Man" as he returned to Nebraska. Today, the Sacred Pole rests at the Center for Great Plains Studies in Lincoln, awaiting his final journey to a planned Omaha cultural center on the reservation.[8]

Although culturally rich, the Omahas have faced economic impoverishment during the last century. But in 1992, with the opening of Casino Omaha a few miles west of Onawa, Iowa, tribal financial fortunes began to improve. In 1992, each of the approximately five thousand tribal members received $1,000 from casino profits, and the following year, the casino management made a $500 per capita distribution.[9] Even more important, gambling revenues have made possible much-needed programs and improvements that will benefit all Omahas. The most visible improvement is the repair of reservation roads, but casino profits have also paid for renovation of the Macy, Nebraska, public school, scholarships for Indian students, expansion of health-care facilities and nutrition programs, reduction of tribal debt, and an emergency youth shelter.[10]

Casino Omaha is not a cure-all for the tribe's financial woes. Although it hires mostly Indian employees, the gambling establishment is neither a sure source of future tribal income nor a solid economic base on which to build a tribal future. Already, tribal gambling revenue is dwindling because of competition from riverboat casinos farther down the Missouri River in Council Bluffs, Iowa.

Despite the recent financial windfall, the Omaha people still face serious problems. Many Omahas lack higher education, and many are unemployed. As a result, a large percentage of families continue to live in poverty. Alcoholism, a legacy of the earliest contact with whites, continues to plague the tribe, and many babies are born with fetal alcohol syndrome. Nevertheless, tribal members express eternal hope. Seventy-nine-year-old former Omaha health director Pauline Tyndall sees better days ahead: "I think things are looking up for us. We've been so weary here—almost without a future."[11]

In the impassioned words of anthropologist Robin Ridington, Native Americans "survive as communities of relations. They survive in ceremonies and prayers. They survive in the gifts they give to honor one another. . . . They survive in cities and on reservations. They survive as nations."[12] The Omahas are survivors. They have weathered decades of exploitation by land-hungry whites. They have endured the well-intentioned but often misguided efforts of reformers. Their children reluctantly surrendered Indian names and the Omaha language to ethnocentric missionaries, and they survived the unfair laws designed to separate them from their lands. Many tribal members today remain on that tiny portion of the Omaha lands that became home to their ancestors in 1854. Through all of their trials, the people have retained their rich tribal culture and their distinct identity as the Omaha Nation. Today, tribal members struggle to maintain their Indian ways in a predominantly non-Indian society. In 1984, tribal historian Dennis Hastings addressed his people's challenge to survive in a bicultural world: "We have to take the good from our own Omaha ways and the good from non-Indian ways and try to go forward now."[13] Let us hope that with the Venerable Man once more among them, the Omaha people will go forward into a brighter future.

Notes

INTRODUCTION

1. By A.D. 1,000, buffalo were found not only on the Great Plains but also, in smaller numbers, in the Appalachian Mountains, where they were called Pennsylvania bison. As whites encroached on their territory, the buffalo moved farther west. By the 1760s, the eastern boundary of their range was the western Appalachian slopes. Settlers killed eastern buffalo for food, so it is reasonable to assume that Indians would have also. The Omahas probably moved west, following this important food source. Dary, *The Buffalo Book*, 7, 12–13.

2. McDonnell, "Land Policy on the Omaha Reservation," 400.

3. White, "The Winning of the West," 321, 322–23.

4. Kappler, *Indian Affairs*, 115, 260; "Treaty with the Mahas," *American State Papers* 2:226.

5. Kappler, *Indian Affairs*, 309, 479.

6. Ibid., 611.

7. See chapter 3 for a discussion of Omaha Agent J. B. Robertson, who illegally invested Indian funds and skimmed government money from a construction job on the Omaha Reservation. Also, in 1866, an investigation of Robertson's agency financial records showed irregularities.

8. Kappler, *Indian Affairs*, 872.

9. 22 *Statutes at Large* 341.

10. Green, *Iron Eye's Family*, 92, 94. Peebles and his associates also encouraged "squatters" to move onto Omaha lands. See chapter 5 for a detailed account of a legal battle involving the Omahas and members of the "Pender ring."

11. U.S. Congress, House, *Lands in Severalty to Indians*, 2–6.

12. 24 *Statutes at Large* 388.

13. U.S. Congress, House, *Disposal of Unallotted Land on the Omaha Indian Reservation*, 2.

14. 34 *Statutes at Large* 182.

CHAPTER 1

1. O'Shea and Ludwickson, *Archaeology and Ethnohistory of the Omaha Indians*, 16–17; Smith, *Omaha Indians*, 11.

2. Dorsey, "Migrations of Siouan Tribes," 213.

3. McGee, *The Siouan Indians*, 191.

4. Ibid., 193; Dorsey, "Migrations," 215; Fletcher and La Flesche, *The Omaha Tribe*, 70–72. Early sources do not call these people the "Omahas." Many early documents refer to them as the "Mahas," probably because whites misunderstood native speakers, who softly sounded the first letter of "Omaha" as "u" while placing the accent on the second syllable. They are also called

the "Makas" and the "Mahars" in some sources. For the purpose of this work, the modern "Omahas" will be used, except when quoting sources that use another form of the name.

5. McGee, *The Siouan Indians*, 193; Fletcher, "Tribal Life among the Omahas," 456.

6. Dorsey, "Migrations," 221–22.

7. Dorsey, *Omaha Sociology*, 212.

8. Ibid.; Fletcher and La Flesche, *The Omaha Tribe*, 73–74.

9. O'Shea and Ludwickson, *Archaeology and Ethnohistory of the Omaha Indians*, 17; Fletcher and La Flesche, *The Omaha Tribe*, 85.

10. O'Shea and Ludwickson, *Archaeology and Ethnohistory of the Omaha Indians*, 20–21; Fletcher and La Flesche, *The Omaha Tribe*, 85–86; Thorne, "Black Bird," 418.

11. "Truteau's Description of the Upper Missouri," in Nasatir, *Before Lewis and Clark* 2:378; "Table of Distances along the Missouri in Ascending from the Mouth up the White River, Taken by James Mackay, 1797," in ibid., 489.

12. "William Clark's Journal, September 18, 1804," in Moulton, *Lewis and Clark* 3:399; Fletcher and La Flesche, *The Omaha Tribe*, 86–87.

13. O'Shea and Ludwickson, *Archaeology and Ethnohistory of the Omaha Indians*, 37; Dorsey, *Omaha Sociology*, 213; Fletcher and La Flesche, *The Omaha Tribe*, 87–88.

14. Dorsey, *Omaha Sociology*, 213–14; J. L. Bean to Thomas H. Harvey, December 31, 1845, Letters Received by the Office of Indian Affairs (hereafter LROIA), Council Bluffs Agency, 1844–46, Reel (hereafter R) 216.

15. Fletcher and La Flesche, *The Omaha Tribe*, 81. According to Wedel, "The Ioway, Oto, and Omaha Indians in 1700," 9, the French explorer, trader, and prospector Pierre-Charles Le Sueur attracted bands of Sioux "as well as the Mahas" to his fort near the Big Sioux River in 1700. The Omahas probably hoped to receive trade items.

16. Smith, *Omaha Indians*, 13–14; Beers, *French and Spanish Records of Louisiana*, 15.

17. Nasatir, *Before Lewis and Clark* 1:98.

18. Fletcher and La Flesche, *The Omaha Tribe*, 78.

19. Francisco Cruzat, "Report of the Indian Tribes Who Received Presents at St. Louis, Dated November 15, 1777," in Houck, *The Spanish Regime* 1:144.

20. Will and Hyde, *Corn among the Indians*, 200, 204–5, 209; Schilz and Schilz, "Beads, Bangles, and Buffalo Robes," 6–7.

21. Sheldon, "Land Systems and Land Policies," 2; Fletcher and La Flesche, *The Omaha Tribe*, 88.

22. Farnham, *Farnham's Travels*, 146; Smith, *Omaha Indians*, 77–78.

23. Sheldon, "Land Systems and Land Policies," 5; Fletcher and La Flesche, *The Omaha Tribe*, 89–90.

24. Fletcher and La Flesche, *The Omaha Tribe*, 135, 196.

25. Will and Hyde, *Corn among the Indians*, 58; O'Shea and Ludwickson, *Archaeology and Ethnohistory of the Omaha Indians*, 7.

26. Fletcher and La Flesche, *The Omaha Tribe*, 271, 275, 693, 701–2.
27. Ibid., 217.
28. Ridington, "A Sacred Object as Text," 84.
29. Ibid., 83; Fletcher and La Flesche, *The Omaha Tribe*, 225, 229.
30. Fletcher and La Flesche, *The Omaha Tribe*, 597–98.
31. Ibid., 201. In this case, "old" pertains to wisdom, not necessarily age.
32. Ibid., 208–9; Mead, *Changing Culture* (1932), 61. It is generally agreed that in Mead's anthropological study, the mythical "Antlers" are the Omahas.
33. Fletcher, "Personal Studies of Indian Life," 443.
34. Barnes, *Two Crows Denies It*, 33; Fletcher and La Flesche, *The Omaha Tribe*, 208; Dorsey, *Omaha Sociology*, 362.
35. Dorsey, *Omaha Sociology*, 358–59; Fletcher, "Personal Studies of Indian Life," 441; Fletcher and La Flesche, *The Omaha Tribe*, 206.
36. Mead, *Changing Culture* (1932), 61; Thorne, "Black Bird," 412, 418.
37. Fletcher, "Personal Studies of Indian Life," 443.
38. Fortune, *Omaha Secret Societies*, 158.
39. Fletcher and La Flesche, *The Omaha Tribe*, 204.
40. Fortune, *Omaha Secret Societies*, 1, 156.
41. O'Shea and Ludwickson, "Omaha Chieftainship in the Nineteenth Century." In their discussion of the few exceptions to the treaty-signing order, O'Shea and Ludwickson, 327, explain that occasionally, chiefs who disagreed with treaty provisions refused to sign. Also, distance and danger sometimes became factors; for example, in 1830, Big Elk made the long, hazardous journey to sign the Prairie du Chien Treaty, but chiefs such as Little Cook and Hard Walker may have refused to cross hostile Sauk and Fox territory.
42. Barnes, *Two Crows Denies It*, 29; Houck, *The Spanish Regime* 1:144
43. O'Shea and Ludwickson, *Archaeology and Ethnohistory of the Omaha Indians*, 33.
44. Bradbury, *Travels in the Interior of America*, 89–90.
45. Irving, *Astoria*, 170–71.
46. O'Shea and Ludwickson, *Archaeology and Ethnohistory of the Omaha Indians*, 23.
47. Smith, *Omaha Indians*, 40–41, 51–52.
48. Ibid., 51–52. "Articles of Incorporation of the Missouri Company, St. Louis, May 1794," in Nasatir, *Before Lewis and Clark* 1:217–26.
49. "Journal of Truteau on the Missouri River, 1794–1795," in Nasatir, *Before Lewis and Clark* 1:285; John C. Ewers, "Symbols of Chiefly Authority in Spanish Louisiana," in McDermott, *The Spanish in the Mississippi Valley*, 275, states that Black Bird was the only Indian in Spanish Louisiana ever to be given a *gold* Spanish medal. Of course, in true Black Bird style, he demanded it.
50. Prucha, *Indian Peace Medals*, 16–17.
51. Hyde, *The Pawnee Indians*, 131–32; "Journal of Truteau," in Nasatir, *Before Lewis and Clark* 1:260.

52. "Journal of Truteau," in Nasatir, *Before Lewis and Clark* 1:302; Carondelet to Alcudia, January 8, 1796, in Nasatir, *Before Lewis and Clark* 2:389.

53. "Journal of Truteau," in Nasatir, *Before Lewis and Clark* 1:263.

54. Ibid., 280–81, 90.

55. "Petition of Clamorgan, January 15, 1800," in Nasatir, *Before Lewis and Clark* 2:608.

56. Schilz and Schilz, "Beads, Bangles, and Buffalo Robes," 12; Thorne, "Black Bird," 422–23; "Journal of Truteau," in Nasatir, *Before Lewis and Clark* 1:264.

57. Clamorgan to Salcedo, April 18, 1801, in Nasatir, *Before Lewis and Clark* 2:633–34.

58. Fletcher and La Flesche, *The Omaha Tribe*, 82; Fontenelle, "History of Omaha Indians," 78.

59. Thorne, "Black Bird," 427.

60. James, *Account of an Expedition*, 318; Irving, *Astoria*, 171–72; Fletcher and La Flesche, *The Omaha Tribe*, 82; Bradbury, *Travels in the Interior of America*, 85 n; "Journal of Truteau," in Nasatir, *Before Lewis and Clark* 1:283. Thorne, "Black Bird," 428, states that the use of poisons to strengthen chiefs' powers was neither original nor unique to Black Bird. In the early nineteenth century, Big Elk owned a poison pouch that had been in his family's possession for over one hundred years, and the tribal council also threatened to poison uncooperative tribespeople.

61. Brackenridge, *Journal of a Voyage*, 87–88.

62. James, *Account of an Expedition*, 318; "Journal of Truteau," in Nasatir, *Before Lewis and Clark* 1:287–88; Irving, *Astoria*, 171.

63. Bradbury, *Travels in the Interior of America*, 85 n.

64. "Journal of Truteau," in Nasatir, *Before Lewis and Clark* 1:293; Clamorgan to Carondelet, April 10, 1796, in Nasatir, *Before Lewis and Clark* 2:418.

65. "Mackay's Journal, Oct. 14, 1795–Jan. 18, 1796," in Nasatir, *Before Lewis and Clark* 1:359, 363.

66. Irving, *Astoria*, 175; James, *Account of an Expedition*, 317. Black Bird would not have been buried on horseback. In Omaha funeral customs, live horses were never interred with their owners but were sometimes killed at the gravesite.

67. Ronda, *Lewis and Clark among the Indians*, 14.

68. James, *Account of an Expedition*, 281, 320.

69. Big Elk quoted in Fletcher and La Flesche, *The Omaha Tribe*, 84.

70. Hyde, *The Pawnee Indians*, 133–34; O'Shea and Ludwickson, *Archaeology and Ethnohistory of the Omaha Indians*, 30.

71. O'Shea and Ludwickson, *Archaeology and Ethnohistory of the Omaha Indians*, 30; White, "The Winning of the West," 325.

72. Schilz and Schilz, "Beads, Bangles, and Buffalo Robes," 18, 21.

73. Delassus to Casa Calvo, St. Louis, April 13, 1801, in Nasatir, *Before Lewis and Clark* 2:631.

74. Bradbury, *Travels in the Interior of America*, 90; Irving, *Astoria*, 174–75; Farnham, *Farnham's Travels*, 146; "Clark's Journal, August 11, 1804 and August 14, 1804," in Moulton, *Lewis and Clark* 2:467, 478–79.

75. Irving, *Astoria*, 170.

76. O'Shea and Ludwickson, *Archaeology and Ethnohistory of the Omaha Indians*, 31; Barnes, *Two Crows Denies It*, 9.

77. Fletcher and La Flesche, *The Omaha Tribe*, 86–87; Farnham, *Farnham's Travels*, 146; "Clark's Journal, August 14, 1804," in Moulton, *Lewis and Clark* 2:478–79; Irving, *Astoria*, 174–75. In *The Effect of Smallpox on the Destiny of the Amerindian*, Stearn and Stearn use primary sources to explain the devastating effects of this disease on many Indian tribes, including the Omahas.

78. Hyde, *Red Cloud's Folk*, 9–10, 14.

79. Ibid., 14–15.

80. Beauharnais and Hacquart to the French minister, October 25, 1729, in Thwaites, *Collections of the State Historical Society of Wisconsin*, 77–78.

81. Hyde, *Red Cloud's Folk*, 15.

82. White, "The Winning of the West," 328–29.

83. "Clark's Journal, September 26, 1804," in Moulton, *Lewis and Clark* 3:119; "The Original Journal of Private Joseph Whitehouse," in Thwaites, *Original Journals of the Lewis and Clark Expedition* 7:64.

84. White, "The Winning of the West," 326.

85. Smith, *Omaha Indians*, 79, 129.

86. Schilz and Schilz, "Beads, Bangles, and Buffalo Robes," 24.

87. Johnson, "The Sixth's Elysian Fields," 24.

88. H. Atkinson and Benj. O'Fallon to Secretary of War James Barbour, November 8, 1825, *American State Papers* 2:606.

89. Smith, *Omaha Indians*, 129, 181; O'Shea and Ludwickson, *Archaeology and Ethnohistory of the Omaha Indians*, 39.

90. William Clark to John L. Bean, April 25, 1830, in U.S. Congress, Senate, *Correspondence on the Subject of the Emigration of Indians* 2:66–67; William Clark to the O'Maha Tribe, April 24, 1830, in ibid., 67; William Clark to Secretary of War John H. Eaton, November 1, 1830, in ibid., 182–83.

91. Fletcher and La Flesche, *The Omaha Tribe*, 85.

92. Ibid., 212.

93. Trudeau to Carondelet, May 30, 1795, in Nasatir, *Before Lewis and Clark* 1:326.

94. Fletcher and La Flesche, *The Omaha Tribe*, 82, 631.

95. Ewers, "The Influence of the Fur Trade," 17.

96. Ibid., 2–3.

97. Schilz and Schilz, "Beads, Bangles, and Buffalo Robes," 5–6.

98. Dippie, *The Vanishing American*, 43; Smith, *Omaha Indians*, 59–60.

99. Fletcher, "Hunting Customs of the Omahas," 693.

100. "The Big Elk, Chief of the Omahaws Nation of Indians, Cantonment Leavenworth, June 24, 1828, accompanying Dougherty to Clark, June 23 [*sic*], 1828," in LROIA, Upper Missouri Agency, 1824–35, R 883.

101.   Fletcher and La Flesche, *The Omaha Tribe*, 271, 614.

102.   Schilz and Schilz, "Beads, Bangles, and Buffalo Robes," 7–8. In *Keepers of the Game*, 19, 39, 61–62, 65, Martin argues that the religious significance of the hunt had been waning before the coming of the fur trade. Before white contact, there appear to have been limits placed on the number of animals a hunter could kill, since the hunter was required by tradition and spirituality to treat the remains of his prey with respect. Failure to do so would result in retaliation by animal spirits—poor hunting or tribal illness, for example. But European diseases and Christian interference with native beliefs changed the Indian worldview. Later, lured by European trade goods, armed with European weapons, and encouraged by European traders, Indians began to hunt indiscriminately; because they had begun to lose respect for both animals and the land, the slaughter of wildlife became acceptable. Christianity supported the fur trade by "elevating man above Nature" and secularizing the hunt. The cycle continued: participation in the trade increased Indian callousness toward nature as it whetted the desire for more durable goods. Although writing specifically about the Indians of subarctic Canada, Martin's observations could easily apply to the Omahas as well.

103.   Fletcher and La Flesche, *The Omaha Tribe*, 61; Schilz and Schilz, "Beads, Bangles, and Buffalo Robes," 8.

104.   Ewers, "The Influence of the Fur Trade," 11; La Flesche, *Omaha Bow and Arrow Makers*, 487–88.

105.   Fletcher and La Flesche, *The Omaha Tribe*, 618.

106.   Johnson, "The Sixth's Elysian Fields," 25.

107.   Ewers, "The Influence of the Fur Trade," 17.

108.   Schilz and Schilz, "Beads, Bangles, and Buffalo Robes," 6; Ewers, "The Influence of the Fur Trade," 20–21.

109.   Ewers, "The Influence of the Fur Trade," 20–21.

110.   Ibid., 1–2.

111.   Smith, *Omaha Indians*, 60–61.

112.   Ewers, "The Influence of the Fur Trade," 17.

113.   Sheldon, "Land Systems and Land Policies," 5.

114.   Fletcher and La Flesche, *The Omaha Tribe*, 269.

115.   McNickle, "Indian and European," 6–7.

116.   Sheldon, "Land Systems and Land Policies," 14–15; Royce, *Indian Land Cessions*, 527–28; *Johnson and Graham's Lessee v. McIntosh*, 8 U.S. (1 Wheat.) 543 (1923). See Royce's *Indian Land Cessions*, 528–33, for a thorough discussion of this precedent-setting Supreme Court decision.

117.   Royce, *Indian Land Cessions*, 16–17.

118.   Adams quoted in ibid., 536. In his study of the western Sioux, White argues convincingly that the Plains Indians did not range "accidentally" over the land. Although individuals may not have possessed private property, tribes recognized and enforced territoriality. Despite their fluidity, tribal boundaries did exist, and intertribal wars were frequently fought over rights to game and other natural resources. The politically astute Sioux declared that they held their lands in the same way Americans did—by "right of conquest." White, "The Winning of the West," 341.

119. Smith, *Omaha Indians*, 73–74.
120. Kappler, *Indian Affairs*, 115.
121. Ibid.
122. Ibid.; Fletcher and La Flesche, *The Omaha Tribe*, 622; Smith, *Omaha Indians*, 75.
123. *American State Papers* 2:226.
124. O'Shea and Ludwickson, *Archaeology and Ethnohistory of the Omaha Indians*, 38; Smith, *Omaha Indians*, 80–81.
125. Kappler, *Indian Affairs*, 260–62.
126. Ibid., 261–62.
127. Ibid., 261.
128. James, *Account of an Expedition*, 258, 260.

CHAPTER 2

1. Fletcher and La Flesche, *The Omaha Tribe*, 622; Kappler, *Indian Affairs*, 305–10.
2. Chapman, *The Otoes and Missourias*, 7–8.
3. Ibid., 8–10.
4. "Extract of the Minutes of the Council Held at Prairie du Chien, July 7 to 16, 1830," Office of Indian Affairs, Treaty File, July 15, 1830, Box 3, National Archives, cited in Chapman, *The Otoes and Missourias*, 10–11; Agent John Dougherty to Sub-agent J. L. Bean, May 14, 1830, in U.S. Congress, Senate, *Correspondence on the Subject of the Emigration of Indians* 2:93–94.
5. Chapman, *The Otoes and Missourias*, 13; Kappler, *Indian Affairs*, 309.
6. There was an additional, unstated reason for the treaty. Traders suffered as a result of Indian wars; warring Indians did not hunt, thus reducing traders' profits, and Indians who died in intertribal battles could not pay their debts. Chapman, *The Otoes and Missourias*, 8.
7. Kappler, *Indian Affairs*, 306.
8. Ibid., 306–7. According to Fletcher and La Flesche, *The Omaha Tribe*, 622, the promised farm equipment and the blacksmith did not reach the Omahas until years later. This was the first of many instances of treaty promises that were either ignored or delayed.
9. Kappler, *Indian Affairs*, 307–8; Fletcher and La Flesche, *The Omaha Tribe*, 622, reported that all qualified Omaha mixed-bloods received their allotted lands; some lived on their lands, whereas others sold theirs and remained with the tribe. For more thorough discussions of the "Half-Breed Tract," see Chapman, "The Nemaha Half-Breed Reservation," and Bohlken and Keck, "An Experience in Territorial Social Compensation."
10. Smith, *Omaha Indians*, 88.
11. O'Shea and Ludwickson, *Archaeology and Ethnohistory of the Omaha Indians*, 45; Babbitt, *Early Days at Council Bluffs*, 25–26, 30. In 1837, many of the Omahas were living temporarily at Big Village, north of Bellevue, but southwestern Iowa remained their most profitable hunting ground.

12.   O'Shea and Ludwickson, *Archaeology and Ethnohistory of the Omaha Indians*, 45–46; Dougherty to Carey A. Harris, December 6, 1837, LROIA, Council Bluffs Agency, 1836–43, R 215. The $5,000 per year referred to in Dougherty's letter was the combined annuity payment of the Omahas, Otoes, and Missourias. He was the agent for all three tribes.

13.   Chapman, *The Otoes and Missourias*, 20–21; O'Shea and Ludwickson, *Archaeology and Ethnohistory of the Omaha Indians*, 46.

14.   McKee, "The Platte Purchase," 129, 131–33.

15.   U.S. Congress, House, *Boundary Line*, 7–8.

16.   Ibid., 3–5.

17.   U.S. Congress, Senate, *Documents Relating to the Extension of the Northern Boundary of the State of Missouri*, 1–6; Henry F. Ellsworth to L. F. Linn, January 27, 1835, in ibid., 1–2; Pierre Menard and J. L. Bean to Linn, February 6, 1835, in ibid., 2–3; Dougherty to Linn, January 26, 1835, in ibid., 4–5.

18.   4 *Statutes at Large*, 729–30, 732; Trennert, *Alternative to Extinction*, 5–6. The 1834 Indian Trade and Intercourse Act was designed to keep the unorganized territory west of the Missouri exclusively Indian by barring white settlers, trappers, and whiskey sellers. In 1834, the government believed Indians could be "kept out of the way" and civilized with little expense or effort. For a careful discussion of the 1834 Indian Trade and Intercourse Act and the intercourse acts that preceded it, see Prucha, *American Indian Policy in the Formative Years*.

19.   U.S. Congress, Senate, *Thomas H. Benton, L. F. Linn, and Albert G. Harrison to Secretary of War Lewis Cass*, 5.

20.   U.S. Congress, Senate, *Report of the Committee on Indian Affairs*, 2.

21.   *Congressional Globe*, 24th Cong., 1st sess., 1836, 372, 421.

22.   Kappler, *Indian Affairs*, 479–80.

23.   Sunder, *Joshua Pilcher*, 120; Merrill, "Extracts from the Diary of Rev. Moses Merrill," 177.

24.   Smith, *Omaha Indians*, 93–94.

25.   Bean to Thomas H. Harvey, December 31, 1845, LROIA, Council Bluffs Agency, 1844–46, R 216.

26.   O'Shea and Ludwickson, *Archaeology and Ethnohistory of the Omaha Indians*, 45; "Report of Agent Daniel Miller, September 16, 1844," in U.S. Commissioner of Indian Affairs, *Annual Report of the Commissioner of Indian Affairs* (hereafter *ARCIA*), 140; "Report of Agent John Miller, September 10, 1847," in *ARCIA*, 139.

27.   Dougherty to Colonel T. L. McKenney, January 30, 1830, in John Dougherty Papers, Missouri Historical Society, cited in Mattison, "Indian Frontier," 248.

28.   Dougherty, "A Description of the Fur Trade," 114.

29.   Henry L. Ellsworth to Elbert Herring, October 4, 1833, and Omaha Indians to the President of the United States, October 3, 1833, in U.S. Congress, Senate, *Correspondence on the Subject of the Emigration of Indians* 4:595–96; "Articles of a Ft. Leavenworth Treaty, November 12, 1833," in ibid., 4:726–32.

30. O'Shea and Ludwickson, *Archaeology and Ethnohistory of the Omaha Indians*, 42; "Report of Agent Daniel Miller, September 3, 1842," in *ARCIA*, 432.

31. In 1840, Agent Joseph V. Hamilton of the Council Bluffs Agency reminded his superintendent that the Omahas had always been friendly to whites, and he recommended that the government continue to help them when their annuities from the Prairie du Chien Treaty expired in 1841. "Report of Agent Joseph V. Hamilton, September 30, 1840," in *ARCIA*, 319.

32. "Report of Agent Daniel Miller, September 16, 1844," in *ARCIA*, 139; Richard Elliott to T. Hartley Crawford, April 22, 1844, LROIA, Council Bluffs Agency, 1844–46, R 216.

33. J. L. Bean to Harvey, December 31, 1845, LROIA, Council Bluffs Agency, 1844–46, R 216.

34. Harvey to William Medill, February 6, 1846, LROIA, Council Bluffs Agency, 1844–46, R 216.

35. "Report of Superintendent Thomas H. Harvey, September 5, 1846," in *ARCIA*, 72.

36. Thomas L. Kane, "Winter Quarters among the Indians," in Mulder and Mortensen, *Among the Mormons*, 212; Aitchison, "The Mormon Settlements," 9.

37. Thomas L. Kane to Medill, April 21, 1847, Office of Indian Affairs, Letters Received, St. Louis Superintendency, cited in Trennert, "The Mormons and the Office of Indian Affairs," 393.

38. Pierre-Jean De Smet, letter to the Directors of the Association at Lyons, June 10, 1849, in Chittenden and Richardson, *Life, Letters, and Travels of Father Pierre-Jean De Smet*, 1188.

39. Edward McKinney to John Miller, September 16, 1847, LROIA, Council Bluffs Agency, 1847–51, R 217.

40. "Report of Agent John Dougherty, n.d. [1837]," in *ARCIA*, 26–27.

41. Extract from "Report of Agent John Dougherty, n.d. [1838]," *ARCIA*, 504.

42. Francis Paul Prucha, "American Indian Policy in the 1840s: Visions of Reform," in Clark, *The Frontier Challenge*, 93; "Report of Commissioner T. Hartley Crawford, November 25, 1841," in *ARCIA*, 238.

43. Trennert, *Alternative to Extinction*, 21.

44. "Report of Superintendent Joshua Pilcher, November 4, 1840," in *ARCIA*, 316–17; "Report of Superintendent David D. Mitchell, November 3, 1841," in *ARCIA*, 334; Smith, *Omaha Indians*, 101–2.

45. Trennert, *Alternative to Extinction*, 22, 149–50.

46. Mattison, "Indian Frontier," 251.

47. John E. Barrow to Luke Lea, April 25, 1850, LROIA, Council Bluffs Agency, 1847–51, R 217.

48. Trennert, *Alternative to Extinction*, 8.

49. Major Thomas Biddle to Colonel Henry Atkinson, October 29, 1819, *American State Papers* 2:357. In his letter (p. 358), Biddle recalled arriving at the Omaha camp and finding the otherwise responsible Big Elk too drunk to meet with him. When Biddle admonished him for his drunken

condition, the chief apologized and admitted that alcohol addiction had cost him much of his power.

50.   William Clark to Lewis Cass, November 10, 1831, LROIA, St. Louis Superintendency, cited in Unrau, *White Man's Wicked Water*, 35. Although not specifically concerned with the Omahas, Unrau's carefully researched book paints a disturbing portrait of the huge problems caused by alcohol in Indian country.

51.   William Clark to Herring, December 3, 1831, John L. Champe Papers, Folder 1831.

52.   Trennert, *Alternative to Extinction*, 7–8; "Report of Superintendent D. D. Mitchell, n.d. [1841]," cited in Trennert, *Alternative to Extinction*, 8.

53.   Bean quoted in Mattison, "Indian Frontier," 250.

54.   DeVoto, *Across the Wide Missouri*, 121; Clark to Herring, December 3, 1831, John L. Champe Papers, Folder 1831.

55.   "Report of Agent John Miller, September 15, 1848," in *ARCIA*, 465.

56.   "Report of Agent John Miller, September 10, 1847," in *ARCIA*, 141.

57.   Biddle to Atkinson, October 29, 1819, *American State Papers* 2:358.

58.   Daniel Miller to D. D. Mitchell, January 25, 1844, LROIA, Council Bluffs Agency, 1844–46, R 216.

59.   John Miller to Harvey, December 8, 1847, LROIA, Council Bluffs Agency, 1847–51, R 217.

60.   Trennert, *Alternative to Extinction*, 138.

61.   Mattison, "Indian Frontier," 262; Indian Claims Commission, *Omaha Tribe of Nebraska*, card 1 of 3, p. 4; "Report of Superintendent Thomas H. Harvey, September 5, 1846," in *ARCIA*, 75.

62.   Mattison, "Indian Frontier," 262.

63.   "Report of Superintendent Thomas H. Harvey, October 4, 1848," in *ARCIA*, 441; Manypenny, *Our Indian Wards*, 116; "Report of Superintendent Thomas H. Harvey, September 5, 1846," in *ARCIA*, 75.

64.   "Report of Superintendent Thomas H. Harvey, October 4, 1848," in *ARCIA*, 441–42.

65.   "Report of Superintendent D. D. Mitchell, October 8, 1849," in *ARCIA*, 133–34.

66.   "Report of Commissioner George W. Manypenny, November 26, 1853," in *ARCIA*, 11.

67.   "Report of Sub-agent John E. Barrow, October 20, 1850," in *ARCIA*, 40.

68.   F. J. Wheeling to Henry Warren, January 14, 1852, and A. C. Dodge, George W. Jones, and Bernhart Henn to Manypenny, January 10, 1854, LROIA, Council Bluffs Agency, 1852–57, R 218; Henn to Charles E. Mix, March 22, 1858, LROIA, Omaha Agency, 1856–63, R 604.

69.   Trennert, "The Mormons and the Office of Indian Affairs," 386.

70.   The Mormons were in violation of Section Eleven of the 1834 Indian Trade and Intercourse Act, which stipulated a $1,000 fine and possible forced removal of whites settling on Indian lands.

71.   Trennert, *Alternative to Extinction*, 145–46.

72.   Brooks, *On the Mormon Frontier: The Diary of Hosea Stout, 1844–1861* 1:188; Trennert, "The Mormons and the Office of Indian Affairs," 386–87.

73.   Brooks, *On the Mormon Frontier* 1:188; Bennett, *Mormons at the Missouri*, 70–71.

74.   Trading posts in Indian country violated Section Four of the 1834 Indian Trade and Intercourse Act.

75.   Brooks, *On the Mormon Frontier* 1:188–89; Bennett, *Mormons at the Missouri*, 72. Big Elk's request to use Mormon improvements contradicted a statement in Hosea Stout's diary. Stout quoted the chief as saying, "You may stay two years or until we sell as we mean to sell and go away" (see Brooks, *On the Mormon Frontier* 1:189).

76.   Brooks, *On the Mormon Frontier* 1:189–90.

77.   Bennett, *Mormons at the Missouri*, 96.

78.   Brooks, *On the Mormon Frontier* 1:205, 250–51; "Report of Agent John Miller, September 10, 1847," in *ARCIA*, 140.

79.   "Report of Agent Daniel Miller, September 3, 1842," in *ARCIA*, 432; Bennett, *Mormons at the Missouri*, 97–98.

80.   Harvey to Medill, May 17, 1847, LROIA, Council Bluffs Agency, 1847–51, R 217; Trennert, "The Mormons and the Office of Indian Affairs," 395.

81.   Trennert, *Alternative to Extinction*, 146–47; Thomas L. Kane, "Winter Quarters among the Indians," in Mulder and Mortensen, *Among the Mormons*, 212.

82.   Winter Quarters, High Council Minutes, April 19, 1847, cited in Bennett, *Mormons at the Missouri*, 98.

83.   John Miller to Harvey, August 9, 1847, LROIA, Council Bluffs Agency, 1847–51, R 217.

84.   John Miller to Brigham Young, April 14, 1847, LROIA, Council Bluffs Agency, 1847–51, R 217.

85.   *Journal History of the Church: A Chronological Collection of Newspapers and Other Items Related to the Church of Jesus Christ of Latter-Day Saints, as Compiled by Andrew Jensen*, LDS Church Archives, May 8, 1848, cited in Bennett, *Mormons at the Missouri*, 110. Young's rage against Miller may be understandable. Bennett (p. 100) discusses the possibility that the agent, under pressure from his superiors, incited the Omahas against the Mormons to ensure that the Mormons' stay in Indian country would be brief.

86.   Malin, "Thomas Jefferson Sutherland," 187–88; Thomas Jefferson Sutherland to Luke Lea, May 22, 1851, and Orson Hyde, "Indian Depredations Again," *Frontier Guardian* 3 (May 10, 1851), both in LROIA, Council Bluffs Agency, 1847–51, R 217

87.   "Report of Agent Daniel Miller, August 13, 1843," in *ARCIA*, 401–3.

88.   Daniel Miller to Mitchell, July 1, 1843, LROIA, Council Bluffs Agency, 1836–43, R 215; "Report of Superintendent Thomas H. Harvey, October 29, 1847," in *ARCIA*, 100–101.

89. Elliott to T. Hartley Crawford, April 22, 1844, LROIA, Council Bluffs Agency, 1844–46, R 216; John Miller to William L. Marcy, January 20, 1848, LROIA, Council Bluffs Agency, 1847–51, R 217; Bennett, *Mormons at the Missouri*, 93; Daniel Miller to Mitchell, July 1, 1843, LROIA, Council Bluffs Agency, 1837–43, R 215.

90. "Report of Agent Daniel Miller, August 13, 1843," in *ARCIA*, 401; "Report of Superintendent D. D. Mitchell, September 29, 1843," in *ARCIA*, 387; Harvey to Crawford, February 20, 1844, LROIA, Council Bluffs Agency, 1844–46, R 216; "Report of Agent John Miller, September 10, 1847," in *ARCIA*, 139–40; Harvey to Medill, April 22, 1847, John L. Champe Papers, Folder 1847; John Miller to Secretary of War William L. Marcy, January 20, 1848, LROIA, Council Bluffs Agency, 1847–51, R 217.

91. John Miller to Harvey, December 15, 1846, LROIA, Council Bluffs Agency, 1844–46, R 216; Brooks, *On the Mormon Frontier* 1:217.

92. *The Diary of Milo Appleton Harmon*, Winter 1846–1847, 10, cited in Bennett, *Mormons at the Missouri*, 96.

93. John Miller to Harvey, December 15, 1846, LROIA, Council Bluffs Agency, 1844–46, R 216; Brooks, *On the Mormon Frontier* 1:219.

94. O'Shea and Ludwickson, *Archaeology and Ethnohistory of the Omaha Indians*, 51.

95. Malin, "Indian Policy and Westward Expansion," 77.

96. Ibid.; "Report of Commissioner T. Hartley Crawford, November 25, 1841," in *ARCIA*, 231.

97. Malin, "Indian Policy and Westward Expansion," 80.

98. "Report of Superintendent Thomas H. Harvey, October 4, 1848," in *ARCIA*, 442.

99. Trennert, *Alternative to Extinction*, 152; "Report of Commissioner William Medill, November 30, 1848," in *ARCIA*, 388–89.

100. "Report of Commissioner William Medill, November 30, 1848," in *ARCIA*, 386; Trennert, *Alternative to Extinction*, 31–32.

101. "Report of Commissioner Orlando Brown, November 30, 1849," in *ARCIA*, 12; "Report of Commissioner Luke Lea, November 27, 1850," in *ARCIA*, 7; "Report of Commissioner Luke Lea, November 27, 1851," in *ARCIA*, 6–7.

102. "Report of Superintendent D. D. Mitchell, October 25, 1851," in *ARCIA*, 61.

103. Thomas Jefferson Sutherland to the editors of the *Cincinnati Daily Nonpareil*, May 29, 1851, cited in Malin, "Thomas Jefferson Sutherland," 189; Thomas Jefferson Sutherland, "Nebraska—A Glympse of It—A Peep into Its Unwritten History—Together with a Few Facts for a Future Historian," *Putnam's Monthly* (May 1854), cited in ibid. 185. See also ibid., 181.

104. Peters, *A Comprehensive Program for Historic Preservation in Omaha*, 12.

105. Manypenny, *Our Indian Wards*, 116; Malin, *The Nebraska Question*, 179.

106. U.S. Congress, Senate, *Report of the Secretary of War, November 30, 1844*, 124–25; *Congressional Globe*, 28th Cong., 2d sess., 1844, 41.

107. Stephen A. Douglas to J. H. Crane, D. M. Johnson, and L. J. Eastin, December 17, 1853, in Johannsen, *The Letters of Stephen A. Douglas*, 270; *Congressional Globe*, 30th Cong., 1st sess., 1848, 467; Malin, "Indian Policy and Western Expansion," 52.

108. *Congressional Globe*, 32d Cong., 1st sess., 1851, pt. 1, 80, and 32d Cong., 2d sess., 1852, 47.

109. *Congressional Globe*, 32d Cong., 2d sess., 1852, 475, and 32d Cong., 2d sess., 1853, 557–58; Hoopes, *Indian Affairs and Their Administration*, 217–20; Malin, *The Nebraska Question*, 105.

110. *Congressional Globe*, 32d Cong., 2d sess., 1853, 561, and 32d Cong., 2d sess., 1853, 560.

111. *Congressional Globe*, 30th Cong., 1st sess., 1848, 56, and 32d Cong., 1st sess., 1852, 1666; Malin, "The Nebraska Question," 9; Ray, *The Repeal of the Missouri Compromise*, 81–82, 82–83 n; *Congressional Globe*, 32d Cong., 1st sess., 1852, 1760–61. Atchison's silence was probably due to his early opposition to the organization of Nebraska. He later changed his mind.

112. Olson, *History of Nebraska*, 74.

113. *Congressional Globe*, 32d Cong., 1st sess., 1853, 1116; Manypenny, *Our Indian Wards*, 117; 10 *Statutes at Large* 238–39.

114. "Report of Commissioner George W. Manypenny, November 26, 1853," in *ARCIA*, 9; Smith, *Omaha Indians*, 108.

115. "Report of George W. Manypenny, November 26, 1853," in *ARCIA*, 9; Manypenny, *Our Indian Wards*, 117; Benton quoted in Malin, *The Nebraska Question*, 132.

116. Malin, *The Nebraska Question*, 133.

117. Ibid., 133–34.

118. "Report of George W. Manypenny, November 26, 1853," in *ARCIA*, 8–10; Hoopes, *Indian Affairs and Their Administration*, 220–21.

119. "Report of George W. Manypenny, November 26, 1853," in *ARCIA*, 10–11.

120. U.S. Congress, Senate, *Message from the President of the United States to the Two Houses of Congress*, 275.

121. Olson, *History of Nebraska*, 71.

122. "De Smet, Extract from a Letter in French, Dated on Board the Steamer *Ontario*, Fort Benton, Montana, June 10, 1866," in Chittenden and Richardson, *Life, Letters, and Travels of Father Pierre-Jean De Smet*, 1200.

123. Trennert, *Alternative to Extinction*, 158.

CHAPTER 3

1. Alfred Cumming to George Manypenny, January 4, 1854, LROIA, Council Bluffs Agency, 1852–57, R 218; Indian Claims Commission, *Omaha Tribe of Nebraska*, card 1 of 3, p. 4. The Indian Claims Commission brief dates Gatewood's orders on December 15, 1853, but Superintendent Cumming's letter states that they were issued on October 19. The December date probably denotes when Gatewood actually received them.

2. Cumming to Manypenny, January 4, 1854, LROIA, Council Bluffs Agency, 1852–57, R 218; Smith, *Omaha Indians*, 111; Preamble to the "Gatewood Treaty," January 27, 1854, LROIA, Council Bluffs Agency, 1852–57, R 218.

3. Indian Claims Commission, *Omaha Tribe of Nebraska*, card 1 of 3, p. 4.

4. Smith, *Omaha Indians*, 110–12; Text of the Gatewood Treaty, January 27, 1854, LROIA, Council Bluffs Agency, 1852–57, R 218. All sixty men present at the council signed the treaty.

5. Text of the Gatewood Treaty, January 27, 1854, LROIA, Council Bluffs Agency, 1852–57, R 218.

6. Ibid.

7. Cumming to Manypenny, Letter and Telegram, February 20, 1854, LROIA, Council Bluffs Agency, 1852–57, R 218.

8. Manypenny to Interior Secretary Robert McClelland, March 1, 1854, LROIA, Council Bluffs Agency, 1852–57, R 218. Manypenny's use of the plural "treaties" refers to the Omaha agreement plus a similar treaty negotiated by Gatewood with the Otoes. Even if everything else about the Omaha treaty had been acceptable, the proposed long-term annuities would have defeated it. But in writing the installment payments into the agreement, Gatewood obeyed the wishes of the Omahas. Smith, *Omaha Indians*, 113.

9. Manypenny to McClelland, March 1, 1854, LROIA, Council Bluffs Agency, 1852–57, R 218.

10. Ibid. Missionary William Hamilton admitted that Peter Sarpy was a major player in the Gatewood Treaty, but Hamilton defended the trader, calling him a friend to the Omahas. Hamilton, "Autobiography of Rev. William Hamilton," 65.

11. "Vive La Bagatelle!" *St. Louis Republican*, February 20, 1854, LROIA, Council Bluffs Agency, 1852–57, R 218.

12. Cumming to Manypenny, June 16, 1853, December 27, 1853, and February 20, 1854, LROIA, Council Bluffs Agency, 1852–57, R 218.

13. "Report of Agent Daniel Miller, September 3, 1842," in *ARCIA*, 432; Kappler, *Indian Affairs*, 611. Although Omaha tribal boundaries had shifted on occasion before the 1854 treaty, the leaders accepted the boundaries claimed by federal negotiators. Smith, *Omaha Indians*, 123. From the time the Omahas signed this treaty, the Poncas alleged that part of the Omaha cession was their land. Acting Commissioner of Indian Affairs Charles E. Mix agreed with the Poncas, citing an 1825 peace treaty signed at Ponca Village, which appeared to be on lands sold by the Omahas. Memo from Charles E. Mix to the Secretary of the Interior, January 11, 1855, John L. Champe Papers, Folder 1858.

14. Kappler, *Indian Affairs*, 611.

15. Ibid., 611–13. William Hamilton claimed that the $1,000 payment to Lewis Saunsoci was to be divided with Logan Fontenelle. The two had apparently escorted a touring "dancing party." William Hamilton to Walter Lowrie, December 9, 1856, *American Indian Correspondence: The Presbyterian Historical Society Collection of Missionary Letters, 1833–1893*

(hereafter *PHS*), R 4, Volume 2, Letter 33. The provision for fairly large annuity payments for a relatively short time reflected Manypenny's personal reservations about annuities, which he felt had a detrimental effect on Indians. He believed annuities were counterproductive because "nothing but necessity [would] draw them to work." Interview with the Mississippi Bands of Chippewa, February 17, 1855, in Documents Relating to the Negotiations of Ratified and Unratified Treaties with Various Indian Tribes, Treaty File 287, Frame (hereafter F) 349.

16. Kappler, *Indian Affairs*, 613–14. All of the 1853–54 treaties that created reservations contained clauses providing for rights-of-way through the reserves. This meant that even though Indian title had not been extinguished, railroad development could proceed. This was the first group of treaties in which these concessions were clearly defined. Malin, "Indian Policy and Westward Expansion," 102–3.

17. Kappler, *Indian Affairs*, 612–13. The concept of allotment in severalty to Indians was not new; Indian lands had been allotted during the colonial period, and the practice became increasingly common in the early 1800s. In 1854 and 1855, after the passage of the Kansas-Nebraska Act, allotment in severalty became a regular provision of treaties with tribes such as the Omahas, who lived in the two new territories and whose lands were coveted by whites. But in 1854, there was no national movement to assimilate Indians, and despite the provisions so carefully spelled out in the treaty, no Omaha lands were allotted at that time. For a discussion of early allotment, see Paul W. Gates, "Indian Allotments Preceding the Dawes Act," in Clark, *The Frontier Challenge*, 141–70.

18. Manypenny, *Our Indian Wards*, 119.

19. Bernhart Henn, George W. Jones, and A. C. Dodge to Manypenny, March 1, 1854, LROIA, Council Bluffs Agency, 1852–57, R 218.

20. Hamilton to Walter Lowrie, January 26, 1854, *PHS*, R 5, Volume 1, Letter 60.

21. Father Pierre-Jean De Smet to the Editor of *Precis Historiques*, December 30, 1854, in Chittenden and Richardson, *Life, Letters, and Travels of Father Pierre-Jean De Smet*, 1207.

22. 10 *Statutes at Large*, 1046–47.

23. Cumming to Manypenny, January 9, 1855, LROIA, Council Bluffs Agency, 1852–57, R 218.

24. George Hepner to Cumming, December 27, 1854, LROIA, Council Bluffs Agency, 1852–57, R 218. When Hepner spoke with the chiefs, their hereditary leader was eight-year-old Cross Elk, who was under the guardianship of Joseph La Flesche. At that time the tribal council said the Omahas had no active principal chief.

25. Barnes, *Two Crows Denies It*, 38–39.

26. Gilmore, "The True Logan Fontenelle," 66. Fontenelle's presence in Washington was not required; Lewis Saunsoci accompanied the group as its official interpreter.

27. Fontenelle may have been the initial signer of the treaty because he was the only member of the delegation who could read or write. Therefore

only he knew how and where to sign. Manypenny and the other white negotiators knew nothing of Omaha protocol, nor did they care. Their concern was only for the treaty. Gilmore, "The True Logan Fontenelle," 68–69.

28.   Gilmore, "The True Logan Fontenelle," 65; Notes to "Two Crows' War Party in 1854," in Dorsey, *The Ǫegiha Language*, 458; "Battle between the Omahas and Dakotas in 1855," in Dorsey, *The Ǫegiha Language*, 464. According to Gilmore, "The True Logan Fontenelle," 65, Omahas often derisively referred to mixed-bloods as "white men." At least one white man did not consider Fontenelle a chief. Hiring Fontenelle as official interpreter in 1852, Agent J. E. Barrow referred to him simply as an "Omaha half-breed." J. E. Barrow to D. D. Mitchell, April 8, 1852, LROIA, Council Bluffs Agency, 1852–57, R 218.

29.   Fontenelle, "History of Omaha Indians," 81; Giffen, *Oo-Mah-Ha Ta-Wa-Tha*, 24.

30.   Gilmore, "The True Logan Fontenelle," 67–68; "Speeches of the Chiefs of the Omaha Tribe of Indians upon the Subject of Their Situation, Recorded by L. B. Kinney," September 12, 1855, LROIA, Council Bluffs Agency, 1852–57, R 218; Hepner to Cumming, August 4, 1855, LROIA, Council Bluffs Agency, 1852–57, R 218.

31.   "Report of Commissioner George Manypenny, November 25, 1854," in *ARCIA*, 7–8.

32.   Hepner to Cumming, November 12, 1854, and John Haverty to Manypenny, December 1, 1854, LROIA, Council Bluffs Agency, 1852–57, R 218.

33.   "Deposition of Thomas L. Griffy before Thomas B. Cuming, Nebraska Territorial Secretary," December 27, 1855, LROIA, Council Bluffs Agency, 1852–57, R 218. According to Griffy, Fontenelle also boasted that the Omahas had sold land, north of Ayoway Creek, that did not belong to them. This may have been true, since the Poncas repeatedly accused the Omahas of selling part of their lands.

34.   Hamilton to Walter Lowrie, November 2, 1854, *PHS*, R 5, Volume 1, Letter 88; A. C. Dodge to Walter Lowrie, January 25, 1855, *PHS*, R 5, Volume 1, Letter 110.

35.   A. C. Dodge and Bernhart Henn to McClelland, January 2, 1854, LROIA, Council Bluffs Agency, 1852–57, R 218.

36.   Henn to Manypenny, January 31, 1854, and Iowa Congressional Delegations to Manypenny, March 1, 1854, LROIA, Council Bluffs Agency, 1852–57, R 218.

37.   Addison Cochran to C. J. Faulkner, November 24, 1854, LROIA, Council Bluffs Agency, 1852–57, R 218.

38.   Enos Lowe to the Iowa Congressional Delegation, November 27, 1854, LROIA, Council Bluffs Agency, 1852–57, R 218.

39.   George W. Jones, A. C. Dodge, and Bernhart Henn to Manypenny, December 11, 1854, LROIA, Council Bluffs Agency, 1852–57, R 218.

40.   Hadley E. Johnson to Manypenny, April 17, 1855, LROIA, Council Bluffs Agency, 1852–57, R 218.

41. McClelland to Manypenny, January 12, 1855, LROIA, Council Bluffs Agency, 1852–57, R 218.
42. Hepner to Cumming, February 8, 1855, LROIA, Council Bluffs Agency, 1852–57, R 218.
43. Ibid.
44. Ibid. Fear of the Sioux may not have been the only reason Logan Fontenelle alone accompanied Hepner. If Griffy's statement was correct, Fontenelle wanted to discuss a private deal with the agent.
45. McClelland to Manypenny, March 28, 1855, LROIA, Council Bluffs Agency, 1852–57, R 218.
46. Hepner to Cumming, April 1, 1855, and April 18, 1855, LROIA, Council Bluffs Agency, 1852–57, R 218.
47. McClelland to Manypenny, May 11, 1855, LOIA, Council Bluffs Agency, 1852–57, R 218.
48. Hepner to Cumming, June 4, 1855, LROIA, Council Bluffs Agency, 1852–57, R 218.
49. B. Y. Shelley and Other Nebraska Citizens to McClelland, June 16, 1855, LROIA, Council Bluffs Agency, 1852–57, R 218. Shelley and the other Nebraskans sent their letter directly to Secretary McClelland because they considered Commissioner Manypenny biased toward Indians. For a discussion of Shelley's claims, see U.S. Congress, House, *B. Y. Shelley*, H. Rept. 592, and U.S. Congress, House, *B. Y. Shelley*, H. Rept. 26.
50. Petition from Citizens of Nebraska Territory and Iowa, n.d., LROIA, Council Bluffs Agency, 1852–57, R 218.
51. Hepner to Cumming, July 2, 1855, LROIA, Council Bluffs Agency, 1852–57, R 218.
52. Hepner to Cumming, August 4, 1855, LROIA, Council Bluffs Agency, 1852–57, R 218; Fletcher and La Flesche, *The Omaha Tribe*, 100–101.
53. "Battle between the Omahas and Dakotas in 1855," in Dorsey, *The Ȼegiha Language*, 464; Fontenelle, "History of Omaha Indians," 81; Fletcher and La Flesche, *The Omaha Tribe*, 100–101; Hamilton to Walter Lowrie, July 28, 1855, *PHS*, R 5, Volume 1, Letter 137.
54. "Report of Agent George Hepner, November 1, 1855," in *ARCIA*, 86–87; "Report of John Haverty, in the Absence of Superintendent Alfred Cumming, October 19, 1855," in *ARCIA*, 69–70; Hamilton to Walter Lowrie, July 28, 1855, *PHS*, R 5, Volume 1, Letter 134.
55. Hepner to Cumming, September 1, 1855, LROIA, Council Bluffs Agency, 1852–57, R 218; "Report of Commissioner George W. Manypenny, November 26, 1855," in *ARCIA*, 7; Hamilton to Walter Lowrie, July 28, 1855, *PHS*, R 5, Volume 1, Letter 134.
56. Hepner to Cumming, August 9, 1855, LROIA, Council Bluffs Agency, 1852–57, R 218. The settlers were not afraid of the Omahas. What they did fear was that the Omahas' presence would attract hostile Sioux.
57. J. B. Robertson to Manypenny, October 1, 1855, and Hepner to Cumming, October 13, 1855, LROIA, Council Bluffs Agency, 1852–57, R 218.

58.   Hepner to Cumming, August 15, 1855, and "Speeches of the Chiefs of the Omaha Tribe," September 12, 1855, LROIA, Council Bluffs Agency, 1852–57, R 218. Either out of genuine hatred for the Omahas or from sheer frustration, George Hepner allegedly wished all the Omahas dead and in hell.

59.   Peter A. Sarpy to Manypenny, November 26, 1855, LROIA, Council Bluffs Agency, 1852–57, R 218.

60.   Hamilton to Walter Lowrie, December 9, 1856, *PHS*, R 4, Volume 2, Letter 33.

61.   William E. Moore to A. M. Robinson, January 12, 1860, and William F. Wilson to Robinson, August 12, 1859, LROIA, Omaha Agency, 1856–63, R 604; "Report of Superintendent A. M. Robinson, October 8, 1859," in *ARCIA*, 113; Hyde, *Spotted Tail's Folk*, 80–81; Hyde, *The Pawnee Indians*, 248.

62.   R. J. Burtt to Walter Lowrie, September 27, 1860, *PHS*, R 4, Volume 1, Letter 84; George B. Graff to Robinson, October 3, 1860, and Graff to Robinson, December 13, 1860, LROIA, Omaha Agency, 1856–63, R 604.

63.   "Proceedings of a Council Held at Joseph La Flesche's House," January 20, 1860, and Graff to Robinson, October 3, 1860, LROIA, Omaha Agency, 1856–63, R 604.

64.   M. C. Wilbur to Graff, September 28, 1860, LROIA, Omaha Agency, 1856–63, R 604; Furnas to Albin, August 23, 1864, LROIA, Omaha Agency, 1864–70, R 605; Burtt to Walter Lowrie, August 30, 1864, *PHS*, R 4, Volume 1, Letter 208; "Report of Agent Robert W. Furnas, September 10, 1864," in *ARCIA*, 352; Burtt to John C. Lowrie, September 30, 1862, *PHS*, R 4, Volume 1, Letter 131; O. H. Irish to H. B. Branch, September 3, 1862, and Irish to Branch, September 29, 1862, LROIA, Omaha Agency, 1856–63, R 604.

65.   R. B. Van Valkenburgh to E. B. Taylor, September 5, 1865, *ARCIA*, 402; Furnas to Taylor, October 24, 1865, LROIA, Omaha Agency, 1864–70, R 605. According to correspondence among Indian agents, superintendents, and the Office of the Commissioner of Indian Affairs, R. B. Van Valkenburgh was acting commissioner for part of August and September 1865, during Dennis N. Cooley's term of office. No reason for Cooley's absence is given in any of the correspondence. J. H. Leavenworth to Van Valkenburgh, September 19, 1865, *ARCIA*, 396–97; Taylor to Van Valkenburgh, September 15, 1865, *ARCIA*, 397; Taylor to Van Valkenburgh, September 15, 1865, *ARCIA*, 397–400; Taylor to Van Valkenburgh, August 24, 1865, *ARCIA*, 401–2; Van Valkenburgh to Taylor, September 5, 1865, *ARCIA*, 402.

66.   T. T. Gillingham to Edward P. Smith, August 9, 1875, LROIA, Omaha Agency, 1871–76, R 606.

67.   Hepner to Cumming, December 30, 1854, LROIA, Council Bluffs Agency, 1852–57, R 218.

68.   Irish to Branch, September 7, 1861, LROIA, Omaha Agency, 1856–63, R 604.

69.   W. P. Callon to Denman, September 2, 1867, and Denman to N. G. Taylor, August 11, 1868, LROIA, Omaha Agency, 1864–70, R 605; Jacob Vore to John Q. Smith, November 22, 1876, LROIA, Nebraska Agencies, 1876, R 519.

70. Burtt to Walter Lowrie, December 22, 1862, *PHS*, R 4, Volume 1, Letter 149; Furnas to Albin, August 3, 1864, LROIA, Omaha Agency, 1864–70, R 605; William P. Dole to Furnas, August 19, 1864, Robert W. Furnas Papers, 1844–1905 (hereafter RFP), R 1, F 480–81.

71. Omaha Chiefs and Head Men to the Commissioner of Indian Affairs, August 28, 1866, Letters Received, Northern Superintendency, 1861–1866, R 134.

72. Indian Claims Commission, *Omaha Tribe of Nebraska*, card 1 of 3, p. 7.

73. "Report of Commissioner George W. Manypenny, November 26, 1855," in *ARCIA*, 7; "Report of Agent J. B. Robertson, October 10, 1856," in *ARCIA*, 104; "Report of Agent J. B. Robertson, October 17, 1857," in *ARCIA*, 149–50.

74. Charles Sturges to Walter Lowrie, March 2, 1857, *PHS*, R 4, Volume 2, Letter 50.

75. "Report of Agent W. E. Wilson, August 29, 1858," in *ARCIA*, 101; Furnas to Taylor, July 20, 1865, LROIA, Omaha Agency, 1864–70, R 605.

76. "Report of Agent Robert W. Furnas, September 10, 1864," in *ARCIA*, 352; Furnas to Irish, April 5, 1865, RFP, R 12, F 12910; Irish to Furnas, May 12, 1865, RFP, R 1, F 578–79; Furnas to Taylor, July 24, 1865, RFP, R 12, F 12930–31; "Report of Robert W. Furnas, August 15, 1865," in *ARCIA*, 405; Callon to Denman, June 3, 1867, Letters Received, Northern Superintendency, 1867, R 135; Vore to Commissioner of Indian Affairs, August 13, 1877, LROIA, Nebraska Agencies, 1877, R 521.

77. La Flesche, *The Middle Five*, xix–xx; Milner, *With Good Intentions*, 154, 156; Green, "The Make-Believe White Man's Village," 243, 245; Fletcher and La Flesche, *The Omaha Tribe*, 629–30, 633; Fletcher, *Historical Sketch of the Omaha Tribe*, 6–7.

78. The tribal affiliation of Iron Eye's mother became a source of controversy among the Omahas' most prominent ethnographers. Fletcher and La Flesche, *The Omaha Tribe*, 631, insisted that she was an Omaha, but Dorsey, *Omaha Sociology*, 215, stated that she was definitely a Ponca. However, the problem of her son's fitness to be an Omaha chief was solved at his formal adoption by the Omaha chief Big Elk.

79. Fletcher and La Flesche, *The Omaha Tribe*, 632–33; Graff to Robinson, December 13, 1860, LROIA, Omaha Agency, 1856–63, R 604; Furnas to John C. Lowrie, July 29, 1866, *PHS*, R 17, Volume 1, Letter 403.

80. Fletcher and La Flesche, *The Omaha Tribe*, 618–19; Gilmore, "First Prohibition Law in America," 397; Burtt to Walter Lowrie, June 6, 1869, *PHS*, R 4, Volume 1, Letter 76.

81. Barnes, *Two Crows Denies It*, 25; Hamilton to Walter Lowrie, September 8, 1856, *PHS*, R 4, Volume 2, Letter 22.

82. "Report of Agent O. H. Irish, October 29, 1861," in *ARCIA*, 63; Walter Lowrie to William P. Dole, May 7, 1861, LROIA, Omaha Agency, 1856–63, R 604; Sturges to Walter Lowrie, n.d., *PHS*, R 4, Volume 2, Letter 67. It is understandable that the Presbyterians lavished praise on La Flesche,

since he and his band were their school's chief supporters. "Report of William Hamilton, August 28, 1868," in *ARCIA*, 241–42.

83.   Farb, "Robert W. Furnas as Omaha Indian Agent," 186–95; Barnes, *Two Crows Denies It*, 25–26; Samuel G. Daily to Furnas, March 19, 1864, RFP, R 1, F 428–29; Daily to Furnas, March 31, 1864, RFP, R 1, F 432. Chaput, "Generals, Indians, Agents, Politicians," 270.

84.   Farb, "Robert W. Furnas as Omaha Indian Agent," 196; Dole to Furnas, June 18, 1864, RFP, R 1, F 462. Dole reminded Furnas that since Fontenelle and La Flesche were not U.S. citizens, they could not legally trade.

85.   Furnas to Taylor, February 28, 1866, and Furnas to Taylor, December 30, 1865, LROIA, Omaha Agency, 1864–70, R 605; Furnas to Walter Lowrie, May 5, 1866, *PHS*, R 17, Volume 1, Letter 371.

86.   Taylor to Dennis N. Cooley, March 27, 1866, LROIA, Omaha Agency, 1864–70, R 605; Cooley to Taylor, April 4, 1866, RFP, R 1, F 667–68; S. Orlando Lee to Walter Lowrie, April 18, 1866, *PHS*, R 17, Volume 1, Letter 364. When La Flesche fled the reservation, he took with him the Omaha tribal records. No Knife, leader of the tribal police, followed him and forced him to turn over the archives. Barnes, *Two Crows Denies It*, 39; Furnas to John C. Lowrie, July 29, 1866, *PHS*, R 17, Volume 1, Letter 403.

87.   Furnas to John C. Lowrie, July 29, 1866, *PHS*, R 17, Volume 1, Letter 403.

88.   Green, *Iron Eye's Family*, 36; Milner, *With Good Intentions*, 159.

89.   Burtt to Walter Lowrie, March 22, 1861, *PHS*, R 4, Volume 1, Letter 93.

90.   Keller, *American Protestantism and United States Indian Policy*, 10.

91.   Hamilton to Walter Lowrie, April 16, 1855, *PHS*, R 5, Volume 1, Letter 123; Samuel S. Bayliss to Manypenny, February 12, 1856, and T. B. Cuming to Manypenny, April 4, 1856, LROIA, Council Bluffs Agency, 1852–57, R 218.

92.   "Statement of John Hileman," April 21, 1856, "Statement of Robert Shields," February 5, 1856, W. R. English to Manypenny, February 8, 1856, and "Lo, the Poor Indian," *The Nebraskian*, February 6, 1856, all in LROIA, Council Bluffs Agency, 1852–57, R 218.

93.   R. W. McClelland to Manypenny, February 29, 1856, "Report of Agent Daniel Vanderslice, June 7, 1856," Vanderslice to Cumming, June 10, 1856, and Vanderslice to J. B. Robertson, May 19, 1856, all in LROIA, Council Bluffs Agency, 1852–57, R 218. George Hepner testified that he had solicited bids from several contractors to provide the provisions in question. It was very cold on the day the provisions arrived in Omaha; Hepner waited, but the Indians never came to receive their goods. He said the flour appeared to be fine but because of the bitter cold, he did not conduct a thorough inspection. When the Omahas refused to accept the flour, Hepner had it inspected. Hepner to Vanderslice, May 27, 1856, LROIA, Council Bluffs Agency, 1852–57, R 218.

94.   Sturges to Walter Lowrie, November 14, 1857, *PHS*, R 4, Volume 2, Letter 57; Sturges to Walter Lowrie, December 11, 1857, *PHS*, R 4, Volume 2, Letter 60.

95.   Hamilton to Walter Lowrie, September 2, 1856, *PHS*, R 4, Volume 2, Letter 21; Hamilton to Walter Lowrie, December 9, 1856, *PHS*, R 4, Volume 2, Letter 33. The interpreter in question was Lewis Saunsoci, whom Hamilton believed could be "bought for a trifle."

96.   John A. Parker to Ferris Ferguson, March 12, 1858, LROIA, Omaha Agency, 1856–63, R 604. The insurance company returned Robertson's deposit.

97.   Ferguson to Interior Secretary J. Thompson, March 12, 1858, and Ferguson to Thompson, July 21, 1858, LROIA, Omaha Agency, 1856–63, R 604; Furnas to Taylor, October 24, 1865, LROIA, Omaha Agency, 1864–70, R 605; "Report of Agent Robert Furnas, August 1, 1866," in *ARCIA*, 216; U.S. Congress, Senate, *Memorial of Omaha Indians*, 2.

98.   Omaha Chiefs and Head Men to the Commissioner of Indian Affairs, June 11, 1859, "Statement of Lewis Saunsoci," September 4, 1859, William F. Wilson to Robinson, September 4, 1859, and Thomas K. Whitacre and F. Charles Goodell to the Commissioner of Indian Affairs, August 29, 1859, all in LROIA, Omaha Agency, 1856–63, R 604.

99.   "Mr. Patrick" was probably the same John Patrick who later surfaced as a purveyor of provisions to the Winnebagoes temporarily on the Omaha Reservation. The association of Patrick, West, and Black may have been a new "Indian ring" in the making.

100.   Council of Omaha Chiefs, August 28, 1859, "Notarized Statement of Hiram Chase," October 15, 1859, "Statement of David Jones," n.d., and Wilson to Robinson, August 30, 1859, all in LROIA, Omaha Agency, 1856–63, R 604. A strange addendum to the "petition" hints that someone other than Indians was involved in its writing. The Omahas swore that they were not urged by any white man to write the petition. Omaha Chiefs and Head Men to the Commissioner of Indian Affairs, June 11, 1859, LROIA, Omaha Agency, 1856–63, R 604.

101.   Sturges to Wilson, August 11, 1859, "Statement of Citizens of Burt County, Territory of Nebraska," August 29, 1859, Wilson to John Litcher, September 26, 1859, Wilson to A. B. Greenwood, October 17, 1859, and Robinson to Wilson, October 17, 1859, all in LROIA, Omaha Agency, 1856–63, R 604.

102.   Sturges to Serena Munson, n.d., *PHS*, R 4, Volume 2, Letter 52; Sturges to Walter Lowrie, July 1, 1857, *PHS*, R 4, Volume 2, Letter 106.

103.   Sturges to Walter Lowrie, November 14, 1857, *PHS*, R 4, Volume 2, Letter 57; Burtt to Walter Lowrie, November 21, 1865, *PHS*, R 17, Volume 1, Letter 289; Sturges to Walter Lowrie, July 1, 1858, *PHS*, R 4, Volume 1, Letter 64.

104.   Irish to Walter Lowrie, July 29, 1862, *PHS*, R 4, Volume 1, Letter 119; Hamilton to [Walter Lowrie], August 25, 1862, *PHS*, R 4, Volume 1, Letter 124.

105.   Joseph La Flesche to Wilson, n.d., LROIA, Omaha Agency, 1856–63, R 604; Burtt to an unnamed correspondent, May 12, 1863, *PHS*, R 4, Volume 1, Letter 167; William F. Wilbur to Charles E. Mix, January 19, 1859,

LROIA, Omaha Agency, 1856–63, R 604; Sturges to Walter Lowrie, n.d., *PHS*, R 4, Volume 2, Letter 67.

106. "Report of Agent O. H. Irish, September 4, 1863," in *ARCIA*, 242; Sturges to Walter Lowrie, March 2, 1857, *PHS*, R 4, Volume 2, Letter 50; William E. Moore to Robinson, January 12, 1860, LROIA, Omaha Agency, 1856–63, R 604; "Report of Agent Robert Furnas, September 10, 1864," in *ARCIA*, 350; "Report of Agent T. T. Gillingham, September 1, 1874," in *ARCIA*, 203.

107. Sturges to Walter Lowrie, February 19, 1858, *PHS*, R 4, Volume 2, Letter 72; Furnas to Burtt, December 18, 1865, *PHS*, R 18, Volume 1, Letter 478.5; Furnas to Walter Lowrie, December 20, 1865, *PHS*, R 17, Volume 1, Letter 298.

108. La Flesche, *The Middle Five*, xvii, 26–28, 112; "Report of R. J. Burtt, October 29, 1861," in *ARCIA*, 58. In Burtt's defense, he understood the difficulties the children had in learning a new language. "The *words* are in *English*, while they do their *thinking* in *Omaha*." R. J. Burtt, "Annual Report of the Omaha Mission, October 29, 1861," *PHS*, R 4, Volume 1, Letter 112.

109. Coleman, *Presbyterian Missionary Attitudes*, 42; Walter Lowrie to R. J. Burtt, February 14, [1866], cited in ibid., 98.

110. Milner, *With Good Intentions*, 21, 25–26. Hicksite (liberal) Quakers manned the Otoe, Missouria, Winnebago, Pawnee, Sauk and Fox, Great Nemaha, Santee Sioux, and Omaha Agencies of the Northern Superintendency of Nebraska.

111. Hamilton to Edward Painter, September 7, 1869, *PHS*, R 19, Volume 1, Letter 175; "Quaker Report on Indian Agencies in Nebraska," 182–83.

112. "Report of Agent W. P. Callon, July 1, 1868," in *ARCIA*, 241; "Report of Superintendent H. B. Denman, November 6, 1868," in *ARCIA*, 228; Omaha Chiefs and Head Men to Denman, June 29, 1868, *PHS*, R 17, Volume 1, Letter 533; W. P. Callon to Denman, June 30, 1868, *PHS*, R 18, Volume 1, Letter 533; Ely S. Parker to John C. Lowrie, July 31, 1869, *PHS*, R 19, Volume 1, Letter 141. The day-school experiment was short-lived, however. In 1879, the boarding school reopened.

113. "Plain Talk by the Omahas"; Milroy, "To A. B. Meacham, October 13, 1879"; "In Self-Defence"; "Report of William Hamilton, September 7, 1869," in *ARCIA*, 346; Dorsey, "To A. B. Meacham, January 19, 1880," 43.

114. Milner, *With Good Intentions*, 165–66. General Philip Sheridan to General William T. Sherman, February 23, 1877, "List of Supplies and Costs," LROIA, Nebraska Agencies, 1877–78, R 522.

115. Illick, "Some of Our Best Indians," 292–93; Fritz, *The Movement for Indian Assimilation*, 156. Another reason for the reduction in Quaker agents was that appointments as Indian agents were political plums that politicians could not afford to give to "do-gooders." Illick, "Some of Our Best Indians," 293.

116. Joseph La Flesche to A. B. Meacham, December 20, 1878, in Dorsey, *The Ǫegiha Language*, 682; Hu-pe-dha[n], "To A. B. Meacham, December 20, 1878"; Hupeca to A. B. Meacham, n.d., in Dorsey, *The Ǫegiha Language*, 734–36.

117.   Farb, "Robert W. Furnas as Omaha Indian Agent," 278; Painter to Barclay White, July 7, 1873, LROIA, Omaha Agency, 1871–76, R 606; Hamilton to John C. Lowrie, July 3, 1869, *PHS*, R 19, Volume 1, Letter 193; Callon to Denman, December 18, 1867, Letters Received, Northern Superintendency, 1867, R 135; Hamilton to Painter, September 6, 1869, *PHS*, R 19, Volume 1, Letter 208; Hamilton to John C. Lowrie, July 3, 1869, *PHS*, R 19, Volume 1, Letter 193.

118.   Irish to Branch, September 24, 1863, September 28, 1863, LROIA, Omaha Agency, 1856–63, R 604; Furnas to Albin, January 15, 1865, LROIA, Omaha Agency, 1864–70, R 605.

119.   La Flesche quoted in Giffen, *Oo-Mah-Ha Ta-Wa-Tha*, 34.

120.   Fletcher and La Flesche, *The Omaha Tribe*, 635; Milner, *With Good Intentions*, 158–59; "Report of Agent Jacob Vore, August 1877," in *ARCIA*, 144–45; Jacob Vore to Commissioner of Indian Affairs, August 30, 1877, LROIA, Nebraska Agencies, 1877, R 521; "Report of Agent Jacob Vore, July 29, 1878," in *ARCIA*, 95; "Statement of the Omaha People," August 16, 1877, LROIA, Nebraska Agencies, 1877, R 521; Barnes, *Two Crows Denies It*, 39; Dorsey, *Omaha Sociology*, 357–58.

121.   Irish to Branch, October 16, 1863, LROIA, Omaha Agency, 1856–63, R 604; Furnas to Dole, May 3, 1864, Letters Received, Northern Superintendency, 1861–66, R 134; Joseph La Flesche to Graff, April 30, 1864, RFP, R 1, F 435.

122.   Kappler, *Indian Affairs*, 345–46, 498; U.S. Congress, House, *Removal of the Winnebago Indians*, 1; U.S. Congress, House, *Winnebago Indians*, 1–10; McGee, *The Siouan Indians*, 196.

123.   U.S. Congress, House, *Memorial of the Legislature of Minnesota*, 1–2; Brigadier General Alfred Sulley to J. P. Usher, July 16, 1863, *ARCIA*, 322–23; Charles E. Mix to C. W. Thompson, October 31, 1863, *ARCIA*, 324; Branch to Dole, October 22, 1863, *ARCIA*, 325; McGee, *The Siouan Indians*, 196.

124.   "Council Held May 3, 1864," RFP, R 1, F 436–39; Furnas to Dole, December 19, 1864, RFP, R 11, F 11346–47; Furnas to Albin, June 8, 1864, Letters Received, Northern Superintendency, 1861–66, R 134; Farb, "Robert W. Furnas as Omaha Indian Agent," 269–70; Dole to Furnas, December 28, 1864, RFP, R 1, F 544.

125.   Green, *Iron Eye's Family*, 32; "Statement of Omaha Chiefs and Head Men," February 6, 1865, LROIA, Omaha Agency, 1864–70, R 605; Kappler, *Indian Affairs*, 872. Although only five men were originally chosen to negotiate in Washington, the treaty contains the signatures of five more: Village Maker, Yellow Smoke, Hard Walker, Fire Chief, and White Cow. Joseph La Flesche's influence on his people was so great that when treaty negotiations took place in March 1865, Agent Furnas offered him $2,500 to throw his support behind the controversial treaty. The treaty itself does not mention this verbal promise, which amounted to a bribe. George W. Doane to Lewis V. Bogy, November 19, 1866, LROIA, Omaha Agency, 1864–70, R 605.

126.   Kappler, *Indian Affairs*, 872–73. The prospect of the Omahas buying back their land was dim, since they had no cash. The final allotments did include unmarried women over eighteen, although they were few.

127.   Omaha Chiefs and Head Men to the President of the United States, February 8, 1868, and Denman to N. G. Taylor, February 8, 1868, LROIA, Omaha Agency, 1864–70, R 605; "Report of Superintendent H. B. Denman, November 6, 1868," in *ARCIA*, 227; Omaha Chiefs and Head Men to the Commissioner of Indian Affairs, June 3, 1869, LROIA, Omaha Agency, 1864–70, R 605; "Report of Samuel M. Janney, September 25, 1869," in *ARCIA*, 334.

128.   Omaha Chiefs and Head Men to the Commissioner of Indian Affairs, February 5, 1866, LROIA, Omaha Agency, 1864–70, R 605; Furnas to [E. B. Taylor], February 25, 1866, RFP, R 12, F 12971–72; U.S. Land Commissioner (signature illegible) to Louis V. Bogy, February 22, 1867, and U.S. Land Commissioner (signature illegible) to N. G. Taylor, August 8, 1867, LROIA, Omaha Agency, 1864–70, R 605.

129.   Callon to Denman, August 16, 1867, LROIA, Omaha Agency, 1864–70, R 605.

130.   "Quaker Report on Indian Agencies in Nebraska," 181; "Report of Agent Edward Painter, September 21, 1869," in *ARCIA*, 344; Painter to Janney, July 18, 1871, LROIA, Omaha Agency, 1871–76, R 606; "Report of Superintendent Samuel M. Janney, September 26, 1871," in *ARCIA*, 436. The rules for allotting Omaha lands are found in LROIA, Omaha Agency, 1864–70, R 605. For the complete list of Omaha allottees in 1871, see LROIA, Omaha Agency, 1871–76, R 606.

131.   Gillingham to White, May 4, 1874, LROIA, Omaha Agency, 1871–76, R 606; Vore to the Commissioner of Indian Affairs, May 4, 1877, LROIA, Nebraska Agencies, 1877, R 521; Gillingham to Edward P. Smith, June 4, 1875, LROIA, Omaha Agency, 1871–76, R 606; Barnes, *Two Crows Denies It*, 14–15.

132.   Elam Clark to Schuyler Colfax, October 20, 1870, LROIA, Omaha Agency, 1864–70, R 605; "Report of Agent Edward Painter, August 25, 1870," *ARCIA*, 250–51; Omaha Chiefs and Head Men to the President, Secretary of the Interior, and Commissioner of Indian Affairs, n.d., LROIA, Omaha Agency, 1864–70, R 605; "Report of Agent Edward Painter, August 21, 1871," in *ARCIA*, 446.

133.   U.S. Congress, Senate, *A Paper Relative to the Desire of Certain Indian Tribes*, 1–3; "Report of Edward Painter, August 21, 1871," in *ARCIA*, 445–46.

134.   U.S. Congress, House, *Letter from the Secretary of the Interior*, 1–6. See also U.S. Congress, Senate, *Letter from the Secretary of the Interior*, S. Misc. Doc. 41, 1–4.

135.   17 *Statutes at Large* 391–93.

136.   Milner, *With Good Intentions*, 162; "Report of Superintendent Barclay White, September 27, 1873," in *ARCIA*, 185; "Report of Agent Edward Painter, August 29, 1873," in *ARCIA*, 191.

137.   "Report of Agent Edward Painter, August 29, 1873," in *ARCIA*, 191–92; U.S. Congress, Senate, *Memorial of Omaha Indians*, 2–3; U.S. Congress, House, *Omaha Indian Lands in Nebraska*, 2–3; Gillingham to White, December 13, 1873, LROIA, Omaha Agency, 1871–76, R 606.

138.   "Deed of Conveyance from Omahas to Winnebagoes," July 31, 1874, LROIA, Omaha Agency, 1871–76, R 606.

139.   "Report of Agent Howard White, August 30, 1879," in *ARCIA*, 108; "The Omaha Chiefs to the Commissioner of Indian Affairs, March 18, 1880," in Dorsey, *Omaha and Ponka Letters*, 82–85; Wishart, *An Unspeakable Sadness*, 234–35.

140.   U.S. Congress, Senate, *Memorial of Omaha Indians*, 2–4.

141.   Fletcher and La Flesche, *The Omaha Tribe*, 635–36; "Letter from the Omahas, February 5, 1878"; Joseph La Flesche to Meacham, December 20, 1878, in Dorsey, *The Ǫegiha Language*, 681.

142.   "Report of Agent George W. Wilkenson, September 29, 1882," in *ARCIA*, 113.

CHAPTER 4

1.   Fritz, *The Movement for Indian Assimilation*, 168–75. Extermination was not the policy of the more humane Generals George Crook and William T. Sherman. As commander of the Military Division of the Mississippi after the Civil War, General Sherman was charged with protecting western settlers and westbound emigrants. Although he reacted strongly to Indian depredations such as the December 1866 Fetterman Massacre and the 1873 Modoc War, Sherman never advocated killing women and children. Athearn, *William Tecumseh Sherman*, 71, 99. On the other hand, in the *New York Times* on October 6, 1876, Custer was quoted as saying that there "ought to be one Indian war, and then no more Indians."

2.   Mardock, *The Reformers and the American Indian*, 146–49; Fritz, *The Movement for Indian Assimilation*, 185.

3.   Fritz, *The Movement for Indian Assimilation*, 185, 190–91. For a complete official discussion of the Ponca controversy, see U.S. Congress, Senate, *Removal of the Ponca Indians*, i–xxvii, 1–520. The Ponca removal is also well covered in Mardock, *The Reformers and the American Indian*, 168–91.

4.   Hoxie, "Beyond Savagery," 21–23. Thomas H. Tibbles gave a personal, and somewhat self-serving, account of the trial of Standing Bear and the eastern lecture tour in *Buckskin and Blanket Days*, 193–221.

5.   Fritz, *The Movement for Indian Assimilation*, 197. New Indian reform organizations gained prominence in the 1880s. For thorough discussions of the Women's National Indian Association, the Indian Rights Association, and the National Indian Defense Association, plus the Indian advocacy monthly *Council Fire*, see Wanken, "'Women's Sphere' and Indian Reform," Hagan, *The Indian Rights Association*, and Behrens, "In Defense of `Poor Lo.'"

6.   Tibbles, *Buckskin and Blanket Days*, 236–37; Mark, *A Stranger in Her Native Land*, 38–42; Alice Fletcher to L. Carr, August 3, 1881, Peabody Museum Papers, Harvard University Archives, Cambridge, Massachusetts, cited in Mark, *A Stranger in Her Native Land*, 42.

7.   Tibbles, *Buckskin and Blanket Days*, 237.

8.   Mark, *A Stranger in Her Native Land*, 53–63.

9.   Dorsey, *Omaha and Ponka Letters*, 29–33, 553–54; Dorsey, *The Çegiha Language*, 677, 717; Mark, *A Stranger in Her Native Land*, 68–69. Without the Omahas' permission, 238 such letters were published, with English translations. In 1894, Francis La Flesche expressed his displeasure at the publication of these and other letters. "Too much of the private affairs of many of the Omahas has been published by the Bureau of Ethnology without their consent." Francis La Flesche, quoted in Judd, *The Bureau of American Ethnology*, 52.

10.   La Flesche, "Alice C. Fletcher."

11.   Fletcher, "Personal Studies of Indian Life," 454; U.S. Board of Indian Commissioners, *Annual Report* (hereafter *BIC Report*) *1885*, 128.

12.   Lurie, "The Lady from Boston," 80–81.

13.   Mark, *A Stranger in Her Native Land*, 70; U.S. Congress, Senate, *Memorial of the Members of the Omaha Tribe*, 1–14. (This document is also included in U.S. Congress, House, *Sale of a Part of Omaha Indian Reservation in Nebraska*.)

14.   Alice C. Fletcher and Francis La Flesche Papers, National Anthropological Archives, Smithsonian Institution, Washington, D.C. (hereafter Fletcher Papers), cited in Mark, *A Stranger in Her Native Land*, 70.

15.   Alice C. Fletcher to Henry L. Dawes, February 1882, and Fletcher to Samuel J. Kirkwood, February 8, 1882, Fletcher Papers, cited in Mark, *A Stranger in Her Native Land*, 71.

16.   Mark, *A Stranger in Her Native Land*, 71–72; Welch, "Alice Cunningham Fletcher," 53; Fletcher to Mrs. Dawes, January 25, 1883, Henry L. Dawes Papers, Library of Congress, Washington, D.C., cited in Mark, *A Stranger in Her Native Land*, 76. Senator Dawes' wife and daughter were especially helpful to Fletcher.

17.   Fletcher and La Flesche, *The Omaha Tribe*, 639; Mark, *A Stranger in Her Native Land*, 74–75.

18.   *Congressional Record*, 47th Cong, 1st sess., 1882, pt. 4:3027–28, 3032.

19.   U.S. Congress, House, *Sale of a Part of Omaha Indian Reservation*, 1.

20.   Mark, *A Stranger in Her Native Land*, 76; Fletcher to Commissioner T. J. Morgan, February 4, 1882, Fletcher Papers, cited in Mark, *A Stranger in Her Native Land*, 76.

21.   22 *Statutes at Large* 341–43.

22.   Ibid., 342.

23.   Ibid., 342–43.

24.   "Report of Commissioner Hiram Price, October 10, 1883," in *ARCIA*, lxiii; Mark, *A Stranger in Her Native Land*, 88–89, 93. The allottees in 1871 represented about 25 percent of the Omahas. A handwritten list of the Omahas allotted as a result of the 1865 treaty shows a total of 331, but there are numbering errors; the actual figure is 316. LROIA, Omaha Agency, 1871–76, R 606.

25.   Mark, *A Stranger in Her Native Land*, 89; Welch, "Alice Cunningham Fletcher," 117; Fletcher, "Lands in Severalty to Indians," 660; *BIC Report, 1884*, 55.

26. "Report of Agent George Wilkinson, August 27, 1883," in *ARCIA*, 105.

27. Mark, *A Stranger in Her Native Land*, 89; Fletcher, "Lands in Severalty to Indians," 660; *BIC Report, 1889*, 150. Fletcher deliberately allotted land so that Indians and whites would be thrown together, since in her opinion, "the salvation of the Indians [was] to get them out among the whites." *BIC Report, 1884*, 55.

28. Mark, *A Stranger in Her Native Land*, 90–92.

29. Ibid., 92–93. According to Mark, Wilkinson had several ways to make recalcitrant Indians obey: he could refuse them permission to leave the reservation, remove them from tribal offices, or generally harass them.

30. "Report of Commissioner Hiram Price, October 15, 1884," in *ARCIA*, xlix; Mark, *A Stranger in Her Native Land*, 93–94; Fletcher, "Lands in Severalty to Indians," 661–62. The tribal census listed 1,194 Omahas, but since wives were not given allotments, only 954 persons actually received lands in severalty.

31. Mark, *A Stranger in Her Native Land*, 93; "Proceedings of the Second Annual Meeting of the Lake Mohonk Conference of Friends of the Indian" (hereafter "Annual LMC") (1884), 26.

32. *BIC Report, 1889*, 150.

33. Francis La Flesche to Rosalie Farley, n.d., La Flesche Family Papers (hereafter LFP); "Remarks of Susette Tibbles," in *BIC Report, 1886*, 121; "Report of Agent Jesse F. Warner, September 10, 1888," in *ARCIA*, 170; Otis, *The Dawes Act*, 105–6; Henry L. Dawes, "Comment," in "Proceedings of the Fifth Annual LMC" (1887), 69. Although Francis La Flesche used the name "Frank" in correspondence with his family, for the sake of clarity he will always be referred to here as Francis. During the postallotment period, La Flesche was employed by the Bureau of Indian Affairs in Washington, D.C., and became a rich source of information and advice for his family in Nebraska. The correspondence between La Flesche and his sister Rosalie reflects the controversies in which the Omahas were embroiled during the 1880s and 1890s.

34. Fletcher to Henry M. Teller, October 8, 1882, *Records of the Bureau of Indian Affairs*, cited in Mark, *A Stranger in Her Native Land*, 122; "An Omaha Speech in 1884"; Mark, *A Stranger in Her Native Land*, 122–23; Welch, "Alice Cunningham Fletcher," 126; Green, *Iron Eye's Family*, 78.

35. "Report of Agent George W. Wilkinson, September 18, 1885," in *ARCIA*, 135; "Report of Commissioner Hiram Price, October 15, 1884," in *ARCIA*, l.

36. Welch, "Alice Cunningham Fletcher," 134; Mark, *A Stranger in Her Native Land*, 131; Sindahaha to Fletcher, May 25, 1886, Fletcher Papers, and Wahininga to Commissioner of Indian Affairs, July 22, 1886, *Records of the Bureau of Indian Affairs*, cited in Mark, *A Stranger in Her Native Land*, 131. Commissioner J. D. C. Atkins had no objection to Omaha self-government, but he could not approve it because the Omahas were under Nebraska jurisdiction and an Indian government would create a "state within a state."

37. "Report of William H. Waldby," in *BIC Report, 1887*, 25; "Report of Agent Robert H. Ashley, August 26, 1890," in *ARCIA*, 189; "Report of Agent Jesse F. Warner, September 11, 1889," in *ARCIA*, 238.

38. Joseph La Flesche to Fletcher, February 23, 1886, Fletcher Papers, cited in Welch, "Alice Cunningham Fletcher," 133; Inshta Theamba ("Bright Eyes"), introduction to Tibbles, *Ploughed Under*, 4; Susette Tibbles, "Testimony," in *BIC Report, 1886*, 120. The basic argument over citizenship was that Susette Tibbles wanted her people, whether they were prepared or not, to have all the rights and responsibilities that full citizenship entailed, whereas many other Omahas simply wanted tribal autonomy.

39. Green, *Iron Eye's Family*, 87–88.

40. Mark, *A Stranger in Her Native Land*, 128–29; Susette Tibbles, "Testimony," in *BIC Report, 1886*, 122–23, 135; Green, *Iron Eye's Family*, 80.

41. Mark, *A Stranger in Her Native Land*, 128–30; Ed Farley to Fletcher, February 23, 1886, cited in Green, *Iron Eye's Family*, 79; Joseph La Flesche to Fletcher, March 13, 1886, Alice Fletcher Papers, cited in Clark and Webb, "Susette and Susan La Flesche," 143; Joseph La Flesche to Fletcher, May 14, 1885, Martha LeB. Goddard to Fletcher, May 23, 1885, and Joseph La Flesche to Fletcher, March 13, 1996, all in Fletcher Papers, cited in Mark, *A Stranger in Her Native Land*, 129–30. Tibbles' efforts on behalf of the Omahas were not entirely unselfish, since he had strong support among local whites eager to lease Indian lands and perhaps to pay him for the privilege. His questionable tactics led Prucha, in *American Indian Policy in Crisis*, 115, to call Tibbles "one of the strangest characters in the history of Indian reform."

42. Francis La Flesche to Rosalie Farley, June 6, 1887, LFP.

43. Ibid., December 16, 1886, LFP.

44. "Report of Commissioner Hiram Price, October 15, 1884," in *ARCIA*, xlviii.

45. 22 *Statutes at Large* 341.

46. 23 *Statutes at Large* 370; 24 *Statutes at Large* 214.

47. Francis La Flesche to Rosalie and Ed Farley, September 16, 1886, LFP. La Flesche's letter to his half-sister and her husband gives the impression that the tribe as a whole voted to grant the 1885 and 1886 payment extensions.

48. 25 *Statutes at Large* 150.

49. U.S. Congress, Senate, In *Response to Senate Resolution of January 31, 1888*, 1–2; Sheldon, "Land Systems and Land Policies," 209.

50. 26 *Statutes at Large* 329.

51. U.S. Congress, House, *Time of Payment for Lands*, 1–3.

52. U.S. Congress, Senate, *A Communication from the Secretary of the Interior*, 2–4; Francis La Flesche to Rosalie Farley, n.d., LFP.

53. U.S. Congress, Senate, *Petition of Members of the Omaha Tribe*, 3–4. According to this petition, the Omahas wanted their $70,000 in two large payments because their $10,000 annuity was usually taken by traders for debts, leaving the Indians with nothing.

54. Two Crows, Sindahaha, Chazuninga, and John Pilcher to George W. E. Dorsey, n.d., LFP.

55. "Report of Acting Commissioner E. M. Marble, November 1, 1880," in *ARCIA*, xvii.

56. U.S. Congress, House, *Lands in Severalty to Indians*, 2–6.

57. Henry E. Fritz, "The Board of Indian Commissioners and Ethnocentric Reform," in Smith and Kvasnicka, *Indian-White Relations*, 72. Gates' entire pamphlet, entitled "Land and Law as Agents in Educating Indians," is included in *BIC Report, 1885*, 13–35.

58. Fritz, "The Board of Indian Commissioners and Ethnocentric Reform," in Smith and Kvasnicka, *Indian-White Relations*, 71–73.

59. Lyman Abbott to Dawes, July 20, 1885, Dawes Papers, Box 27, Library of Congress, cited in Prucha, *American Indian Policy in Crisis*, 245.

60. Morgan, *Houses and House-Life of the American Aborigines*, 80–81.

61. General Porter, "Remarks," in *BIC Report, 1886*, 134–35.

62. *Congressional Record*, 46th Cong., 3d sess., 1881, 781, 783. Despite his highly emotional oratory during the congressional debate, Henry Teller was not a defender of the Indian status quo. He believed that whites should "manage" Indians, but in his opinion, land in severalty was not the solution.

63. U.S. Congress, House, *Lands in Severalty to Indians*, 7–10.

64. Dawes to Teller, September 19, 1882, Dawes Papers, Library of Congress, cited in Washburn, *The Assault on Indian Tribalism*, 47–48.

65. Washburn, *The Assault on Indian Tribalism*, 12; Priest, *Uncle Sam's Stepchildren*, 194–95.

66. "Proceedings of the Second Annual LMC" (1884), 26; Mark, *A Stranger in Her Native Land*, 117; Fritz, "The Board of Indian Commissioners and Ethnocentric Reform," in Smith and Kvasnicka, *Indian-White Relations*, 70–71.

67. 24 *Statutes at Large* 390.

68. Henry L. Dawes, "Comment," in "Proceedings of the Tenth Annual LMC" (1892), 126.

69. Alice C. Fletcher, "The Crowning Act," *Morning Star*, cited in Mark, *A Stranger in Her Native Land*, 118.

70. Thayer, "The Dawes Bill and the Indians," 320–21; "Seventh Annual Report of the Indian Rights Association, 1889," in *Indian Rights Association Papers* (hereafter *IRAP*), R 103.

71. Washburn, *The Assault on Indian Tribalism*, 29–30.

72. "Report of Agent George Wilkinson, August 27, 1883," in *ARCIA*, 105. Otis, *The Dawes Act*, 49; "Report of Agent George Wilkinson, September 6, 1884," in *ARCIA*, 118; "Report of Agent George Wilkinson, September 18, 1885," in *ARCIA*, 135.

73. *BIC Report, 1884*, 5–6; *BIC Report, 1885*, 112.

74. Samuel B. Capen, "Testimony," in "Proceedings of the Fifth Annual LMC" (1887), 40.

75. "The Omahas: An Unhopeful Outlook," 181.

76. Ibid., 181–82.

77. *BIC Report, 1886*, 122; "Miss Fletcher Sadly Disappointed."

78. "Report of Agent Charles H. Potter, September 1, 1886," in *ARCIA*, 186–88.
79. Ibid., 187–88.
80. Otis, *The Dawes Act*, 49; "Report of Commissioner J. D. C. Atkins, September 28, 1886," in *ARCIA*, xx. Atkins' reaction to Potter's and other negative reports was a masterpiece of understatement: "All transition periods have their peculiar difficulties and discouragements."
81. Fletcher to Mrs. Dawes, August 13, 1886, Dawes Papers, cited in Mark, *A Stranger in Her Native Land*, 132–33; *BIC Report, 1886*, 118.
82. Fletcher, "The Problem of the Omahas."
83. Welch, "Alice Cunningham Fletcher," 136.
84. "The Omaha Experiment a Failure."
85. "Report of Agent Jesse F. Warner, September 19, 1887," in *ARCIA*, 152–53.
86. Goddard to Herbert Welsh, August 2, 1886, IRAP, Series I-A, R 2.
87. Mark, *A Stranger in Her Native Land*, 106–7; Goddard to Welsh, August 2, 1886, *IRAP*, Series I-A, R 2.
88. Goddard to Welsh, August 2, 1886, *IRAP*, Series I-A, R 2.
89. Lurie, "The Lady from Boston," 80, 83.
90. Ibid., 84.
91. Manypenny, "Shall We Persist in a Policy That Has Failed?" 156.

CHAPTER 5
1. Fletcher, "The Allotted Indians' Difficulties."
2. Henry L. Dawes to Eliphalet Whittlesey, April 24, 1887, in Board of Indian Commissioners, Letters Received, cited in Fritz, *The Movement for Indian Assimilation*, 213.
3. *Council Fire* 12 (June 1889): 70; U.S. Congress, Senate, *Petition of Members of the Omaha Tribe*, 1–2.
4. "Letter from Dr. La Flesche"; La Flesche, "The Omahas and Citizenship."
5. Tibbles, "Perils and Promises of Indian Citizenship," 461–62. Ironically, many Omahas overestimated their property's value, and their assessments were later lowered.
6. "Report of Agent Robert H. Ashley, August 17, 1892," in appendix to *ARCIA*, 186–87; Ebenezer Kingsley, "Statement," in "Proceedings of the Twelfth Annual LMC" (1894), 36. Kingsley, a Hampton Institute–educated Winnebago, charged that his people and the Omahas sold their votes for as little as fifty cents each.
7. Tibbles, "Perils and Promises of Indian Citizenship," 461; La Flesche, "The Omahas and Citizenship"; "Letter from Dr. La Flesche."
8. "Proclamation of the Organization of Thurston County," March 29, 1889, in Thurston County (Series 4), County Board of Superintendents Records, preceding vol. 1.
9. Henry L. Dawes, "The Severalty Law," in "Proceedings of the Thirteenth Annual LMC" (1895), 51; Frissell, "A Visit to the Omahas."
10. *Council Fire* 12 (June 1889): 70.

11. Dawes, "The Severalty Law," 51.

12. Ward Shepard, "Land Problems of an Expanding Indian Population," in La Farge, *The Changing Indian*, 78.

13. "Report of Commissioner John H. Oberly, December 3, 1888," in *ARCIA*, XL.

14. "Proceedings of the Seventh Annual LMC" (1889), 84–89, 94–97.

15. Otis, *The Dawes Act*, 110, 113.

16. "Proceedings of the Eighth Annual LMC" (1890), 82–83; "Proceedings of the Ninth Annual LMC" (1891), 87; *Congressional Record*, 51st Cong., 1st sess., March 10, 1890, 2068.

17. "Proceedings of the Ninth Annual LMC" (1891), 87; *BIC Report, 1891*, 99.

18. U.S. Congress, Senate, *Letter from the Secretary of the Interior*, S. Exec. Doc. 73 (hereafter *Leases in Severalty on the Omaha and Winnebago Reservations*), 6. During this period, the Omahas and Winnebagoes were united as one agency. Every effort has been made, where possible, to separate data and reports on the two tribes.

19. Ibid., 4–5.

20. Ibid., 1–2, 4. The Winnebagoes had leased huge amounts of their lands. The Thurston County clerk reported 22,134 acres of their reservation under lease in 1891.

21. "Report of Agent Robert H. Ashley, August 26, 1890," in *ARCIA*, 187.

22. *Leases in Severalty on the Omaha and Winnebago Reservations*, 1–2, 4. For a complete 1890 list of Omaha and Winnebago allottees and their leased lands, see Exhibit A, "Abstract of Leased Lands," in ibid., 8–10.

23. 26 *Statutes at Large* 795.

24. 28 *Statutes at Large* 305.

25. C. C. Painter to Herbert Welsh, October 5, 1894, *IRAP*, Series I-A, R 11.

26. *BIC Report, 1895*, 7; 30 *Statutes at Large* 85.

27. Kinney, *A Continent Lost*, 222; 31 *Statutes at Large* 229.

28. C. C. Painter, "The Indian and His Property," in "Proceedings of the Seventh Annual LMC" (1889), 86–87; Francis La Flesche to Rosalie Farley, n.d., LFP.

29. Kinney, *A Continent Lost*, 221–22; Francis La Flesche, "An Indian Allotment," in "Proceedings of the Eighteenth Annual LMC" (1900), 77.

30. Appendix to "Report of Commissioner T. J. Morgan, August 27," 1892, in *ARCIA*, 186–87.

31. "Twelfth Annual Report, 1894," in *IRAP*, R 103; C. C. Painter, "Remarks," in "Proceedings of the Twelfth Annual LMC" (1894), 86–87; C. C. Painter to Herbert Welsh, October 5, 1894, *IRAP*, Series I-A, R 11; "Report of Agent William H. Beck, August 20, 1896," in *ARCIA*, 197. In 1894, Dr. Susan La Flesche told C. C. Painter that 80 percent of Omaha men and 50 percent of Omaha women drank whenever they had the opportunity. Painter suspected a white plot to keep the Omahas drunk and therefore unfit to farm their own lands. "Proceedings of the Twelfth Annual LMC" (1894), 87.

32. "Report of Acting Commissioner Frank C. Armstrong, September 14, 1894," in *ARCIA*, 35; "Report of Commissioner Daniel M. Browning, September 15, 1896," in *ARCIA*, 40; "Report of Commissioner William A. Jones, September 10, 1897," in *ARCIA*, 42; "Report of Commissioner William A. Jones, October 1, 1900," in *ARCIA*, 76; "Report of Commissioner William A. Jones, October 15, 1901," in *ARCIA*, 73; "Report of Commissioner William A. Jones, October 15, 1903," in *ARCIA*, 57; "Report of Commissioner William A. Jones, October 17, 1904," in *ARCIA*, 76; "Report of Commissioner Francis E. Leupp, September 30, 1905," in *ARCIA*, 83; "Report of Superintendent John F. MacKey, August 15, 1904," in *ARCIA*, 235. Not all commissioners during this period reported leasing figures, and no separate Omaha and Winnebago leasing data was given for 1894.

33. "Report of Acting Agent W. A. Mercer, November 12, 1898," in *ARCIA*, 329; "Report of Agent Charles P. Mathewson, August 31, 1899," in *ARCIA*, 234.

34. "Report of Acting Agent W. A. Mercer, November 16, 1898," in *BIC Report, 1898*, 24–25.

35. "Platform," in "Proceedings of the Eighteenth Annual LMC" (1900), 7–8.

36. "Eighteenth Annual Report, 1900," in *IRAP*, Series II, R 103.

37. William A. Jones, "Testimony," in "Proceedings of the Eighteenth Annual LMC" (1900), 78.

38. Francis La Flesche, "An Indian Allotment," in "Proceedings of the Eighteenth Annual LMC" (1900), 78.

39. "Report of Agent Charles P. Mathewson, August 24, 1901," in *ARCIA*, 270; "Report of Agent Charles P. Mathewson, August 26, 1902," in *ARCIA*, 240; "Report of Agent Charles P. Mathewson, August 24, 1903," in *ARCIA*, 201.

40. "Report of Superintendent John F. MacKey, August 15, 1904," in *ARCIA*, 235.

41. "Report of Commissioner William A. Jones, October 1, 1900," in *ARCIA*, 18. Despite his obvious dissatisfaction with leasing, Commissioner Jones played a role in its growth by curtailing rations to able-bodied Indians in 1901, in many cases leaving rentals as their sole source of support. W. David Baird, "William A. Jones: 1897–1904," in Kvasnicka and Viola, *The Commissioners of Indian Affairs*, 215.

42. "Report of Commissioner Robert G. Valentine, September 12, 1912," in *ARCIA*, 5.

43. Green, *Iron Eye's Family*, 92.

44. The Omaha People to T. J. Morgan, December 22, 1890, William E. Peebles to Thomas McCauley, December 25, 1890, and "Credentials," n.d., all in LFP; Green, *Iron Eye's Family*, 92–93.

45. Rosalie Farley to Francis La Flesche, May 14, 1893, and Lease, December 31, 1890, LFP.

46. Green, *Iron Eye's Family*, 93; Rosalie Farley to Francis La Flesche, May 14, 1893, LFP.

47. Rosalie Farley to Francis La Flesche, May 14, 1893, LFP; Green, *Iron Eye's Family*, 94–95.

48. Rosalie Farley to Francis La Flesche, May 14, 1893, LFP; "Records of the U.S. Circuit Court, District of Nebraska, Number 18, Docket Q2," cited in Green, *Iron Eye's Family*, 94.

49. Rosalie Farley to Francis La Flesche, May 14, 1893, LFP.

50. Ibid., May 25, 1893, LFP.

51. Rosalie Farley to Francis La Flesche, May 14, 1893, May 25, 1893, May 28, 1893, and September 11, 1893, all in LFP. In April 1894, William Peebles was still trying to exact payment from the Omahas for legal fees. When they received their annuity, he sent a message threatening to prosecute them if they refused to pay. Ibid., April 8, 1894, LFP.

52. Rosalie Farley to Francis La Flesche, November 20, 1893, LFP.

53. Ibid., January 2, 1894, LFP.

54. Ibid.

55. Green, *Iron Eye's Family*, 95.

56. Breckenridge and Breckenridge to Rosalie Farley, December 26, 1893, LFP.

57. *Farley v. Peebles et al.*, 70 N.W. 232 (1897). The events surrounding the leasing controversy in 1890–94 are cited from Rosalie Farley's letters to her half-brother Francis La Flesche. As a participant in the controversy, Rosalie could not, of course, have been completely objective, but her letters were written after the events occurred, and she did not appear to be campaigning on her own behalf. Most important, her version of the mismanaged trial at West Point is fully supported by the lengthy opinion of the Nebraska Supreme Court given when it overturned Judge Norris' ruling in 1897.

58. Rosalie Farley to Francis La Flesche, June 7, 1896, LFP.

59. "Leasing the Indian Lands," *Thurston Republic*, May 29, 1896, 1, reprinted from the *Lyons (Nebraska) Mirror*.

60. Alice Fletcher to Rosalie Farley, June 20, 1896, LFP.

61. Rosalie Farley to Francis La Flesche, August 17, 1893, LFP; C. C. Painter to Herbert Welsh, October 4, 1894, *IRAP*, Series I-A, R 11.

62. "Report of Commissioner Daniel M. Browning, September 14, 1895," in *ARCIA*, 37–38.

63. Ibid., 38; Rosalie Farley to Francis La Flesche, November 20, 1893, LFP.

64. Painter to Welsh, October 5, 1894, IRAP, Series I-A, R 11; *Beck v. Fluornoy Live-Stock and Real Estate Co.*, 65 F. 30, (1894), 37–38.

65 "Report of Commissioner Daniel M. Browning, September 14, 1895," in *ARCIA*, 38–39.

66. Ibid., 40. At the time Commissioner Browning submitted his annual report, the U.S. district attorney was trying to have the state-ordered injunction transferred to the federal courts, and Beck had suspended his evictions.

67. Ibid., 41.

68. Green, *Iron Eye's Family*, 95–96; Rosalie Farley to Francis La Flesche, July 29, 1895, LFP; "Settlers Tell the Story," *Omaha Morning World-*

Herald, July 24, 1895, 1; "Big Pow Wow at Pender," *Omaha Daily Bee,* July 24, 1895, 1; "Report of Commissioner Daniel M. Browning, September 14, 1895," in *ARCIA,* 37–41. The congressional delegation consisted of Senators John M. Thurston and William V. Allen and Representatives George D. Meiklejohn, W. E. Andrews, and Jesse B. Strode.

69. "Big Pow Wow at Pender," *Omaha Daily Bee,* July 24, 1895, 1.

70. U.S. Congress, Senate, *Transcript of the Proceedings,* 56–148.

71. "Settlers Tell the Story," *Omaha Morning World-Herald,* July 24, 1895, 1.

72. Rosalie Farley to Francis La Flesche, July 29, 1895, LFP.

73. Ibid.

74. U.S. Congress, Senate, *Transcript of the Proceedings,* 7–8.

75. Ibid., 10–11.

76. Ibid., 5–6. The painfully honest Charles Robinson gave perhaps the most direct indictment of allotment when he said he had an allotment but had done nothing with it; if he had more land, he said, he would do even less. Ibid., 9–10.

77. Ibid., 6.

78. Ibid., 4.

79. Ibid., 9.

80. S. A. Combs to William Allen, July 26, 1895, Exhibit I, ibid., 167.

81. U.S. Congress, Senate, *Transcript of the Proceedings,* 12.

82. Ibid., 7.

83. Ibid., 18–19. An April 1893 letter from Rosalie Farley to her half-brother Francis supported Beck's charges against Wheeler and Chittenden. Rosalie Farley to Francis La Flesche, April 5, 1893, LFP.

84. "Report of Commissioner Daniel M. Browning, September 14, 1895," in *ARCIA,* 40; U.S. Congress, Senate, *Transcript of the Proceedings,* 148–49.

85. John M. Thurston to John M. Reynolds, July 27, 1895, Exhibit N, U.S. Congress, Senate, *Transcript of the Proceedings,* 169–71; W. E. Andrews to Reynolds, July 31, 1895, Exhibit O, U.S. Congress, Senate, *Transcript of the Proceedings,* 171–72; Allen to Reynolds, July 29, 1895, Exhibit K, U.S. Congress, Senate, *Transcript of the Proceedings,* 167–68.

86. "Making Trouble for Beck," *Thurston Republic,* March 19, 1897, 5, reprinted from the *Omaha Daily Bee,* March 19, 1897.

87. "Captain Wm. H. Beck Removed," *Thurston Republic,* May 21, 1897, 1.

88. Hagan, "Kiowas, Comanches, and Cattlemen."

89. Berthrong, "Cattlemen on the Cheyenne-Arapaho Reservation." The most militant of the Cheyenne warrior societies were the "Dog Soldiers," who destroyed fences, set fire to pastures, and killed cattle grazing on the reservation. Ibid., 21.

90. "The Indian Agency," *Thurston Republic,* February 26, 1897, 4.

91. "Peebles Would Succeed Beck," *Thurston Republic,* March 5, 1897, 1, reprinted from the *Omaha Daily Bee,* March 2, 1897.

92. "Relieves Captain Beck," *Thurston Republic,* June 11, 1897, 2.

93. Rosalie Farley to Francis La Flesche, August 6, 1898, LFP.

94. Fletcher and La Flesche, *The Omaha Tribe*, 640; 27 *Statutes at Large* 630–31.

95. 26 *Statutes at Large* 794.

96. Through his position as agency clerk, Thomas Sloan more than once became involved in shady land transactions. He had also been the front man for Agent William Beck's alleged land-leasing scheme. Only one-sixteenth Omaha, the activist and "progressive" Thomas Sloan is an enigmatic figure in tribal history. After graduating from Hampton Institute in 1899, he returned to the reservation and studied law under his friend and fellow Omaha Hiram Chase. Following his employment at the Omaha Agency, he entered private law practice and served for a time as a tribal delegate to Washington. As an attorney, he specialized in Indian cases, but it is evident from his land dealings that his people's welfare was not his top priority. Hertzberg, *The Search for an American Indian Identity*, 46.

97. Rosalie Farley to Francis La Flesche, April 5, 1893, LFP.

98. Ibid., September 11, 1893, and Ed Farley to Francis La Flesche, April 2, 1895, LFP.

99. Francis La Flesche to Rosalie Farley, January 23, 1898, LFP.

100. "Report of Agent Charles P. Mathewson, August 31, 1899," in *ARCIA*, 233; "Report of Agent Charles P. Mathewson, August 20, 1900," in *ARCIA*, 275; "Report of Agent Charles P. Mathewson, August 24, 1903," in *ARCIA*, 202.

101. "Report of Agent Charles P. Mathewson, August 20, 1900," in *ARCIA*, 273.

102. "Report of Agent Charles P. Mathewson, August 24, 1903," in *ARCIA*, 202; "Report of Superintendent John F. MacKey, August 15, 1904," in *ARCIA*, 236; 37 *Statutes at Large* 111.

103. Sara T. Kinney, "Letter," in "Proceedings of the Ninth Annual LMC" (1891), 81.

104. C. C. Painter, "Some Dangers Which Now Threaten the Interests of the Indians," in "Proceedings of the Tenth Annual LMC" (1892), 71–72; Painter to Welsh, October 5, 1894, *IRAP*, Series I-A, R 11; "Twelfth Annual Report, 1894," in *IRAP*, Series II, R 103.

105. "Report of Acting Agent William H. Beck, August 25, 1893," in *ARCIA*, 195.

106. Henry L. Dawes, "The Severalty Law," in "Proceedings of the Thirteenth Annual LMC" (1895), 50–51.

107. Ebenezer Kingsley, "Statement," in "Proceedings of the Twelfth Annual LMC" (1894), 80. One Omaha told C. C. Painter that there was really no increase in alcohol consumption in the early 1890s; alcohol consumption was just more out in the open because no one worried about punishment. C. C. Painter, "Some Dangers Which Now Threaten the Interests of the Indians," in "Proceedings of the Tenth Annual LMC" (1892), 73–74.

108. "Report of Agent Robert H. Ashley, September 1, 1892," in *ARCIA*, 306.

109. "The Indian Temperance Question," 5.

110. H. B. Frissell, "Land in Severalty," in "Proceedings of the Twelfth Annual LMC" (1894), 47; "Twelfth Annual Report, 1894," in *IRAP*, Series II, R 103.

111. *Revised Statutes of the United States, Passed at the First Session of the Forty-Third Congress, 1873–74*, 375, cited in Unrau, *White Man's Wicked Water*, 109.

112. *United States v. Downing*, 25 F. Cas. 906 (D. Ct. Kan. 1876) (No. 14,991); Unrau, *White Man's Wicked Water*, 110–11.

113. *United States v. Downing*, 908; Unrau, *White Man's Wicked Water*, 111–12.

114. *Bates v. Clark*, 95 U.S. 204 (1877).

115. "Report of Commissioner William A. Jones, October 15, 1901," in *ARCIA*, 51; "Report of Commissioner William A. Jones, October 16, 1902," in *ARCIA*, 52.

116. "Report of Commissioner William A. Jones, October 15, 1901," in *ARCIA*, 51; "Report of Commissioner William A. Jones, October 16, 1902," in *ARCIA*, 52; "Report of Commissioner William A. Jones, October 17, 1904," in *ARIA*, 56.

117. "Report of Acting Agent William H. Beck, August 25, 1894," in *ARCIA*, 189; "Report of Acting Agent William H. Beck, August 20, 1895," in *ARCIA*, 200; "Report of Acting Agent William H. Beck, August 20, 1896," in *ARCIA*, 197; "Report of Superintendent John F. MacKey, August 15, 1904," in *ARCIA*, 235–36.

118. U.S. Congress, Senate, *Sale of Intoxicating Liquors to Indians*, 1–13. This report contains a complete discussion of the Meiklejohn Bill and documents supporting its passage.

119. Ibid., 13.

120. 29 *Statutes at Large* 506.

121. "Report of Agent Charles P. Mathewson, July 20, 1900," in *ARCIA*, 277; Picotte, "Another Appeal," 8.

122. "Report of Agent Charles P. Mathewson, August 24, 1903," in *ARCIA*, 203.

123. A. O. Wright to the Commissioner of Indian Affairs, November 16, 1904, Winnebago Agency Subject Files (hereafter WASF), Box A-106.

124. A. O. Wright to the Commissioner of Indian Affairs, November 16, 1904, WASF, Box A-106.

125. "E. J. Smith's Testimony," October 12, 1904, WASF, Box A-106; Thomas L. Sloan to A. O. Wright, October 20, 1904, Omaha Agency Subject Files (hereafter OASF), Box A-105. John Ashford must have had a change of heart, since he allegedly had been convicted of liquor trafficking in 1895. Combs to Allen, July 26, 1895, Exhibit I, U.S. Congress, Senate, *Transcript of the Proceedings*, 167.

126. A. O. Wright to the Commissioner of Indian Affairs, November 16, 1904, WASF, Box A-106.

127. *In the Matter of Heff*, 25 S. Ct. 506 (1905). Albert Heff had been sentenced to four months in the Shawnee County, Kansas, jail and fined $200 plus court costs.

128. "Report of Superintendent John F. MacKey, August 24, 1905," in *ARCIA*, 249. Flinn, "Firewater and the Indians," 25–26.

129. "The Whiskey Decision a Bad Thing for the Allotted Indian."

130. "Leupp Is Coming," *Pender (Nebraska) Times*, December 23, 1904, 1.

131. "Decision Received," *Pender (Nebraska) Times*, April 28, 1905, 1. The *Heff* decision created a curious situation; the state of Nebraska now had to deal with the expected increase in liquor traffic due to a federal court ruling.

132. J. A. Tracy to John F. MacKey, July 30, 1905, OASF, Box A-97. Unallotted Indians were not covered by the *Heff* decision; liquor sales to them were still illegal.

133. "Affidavit of Jack Fremont," July 25, 1905, "Affidavit of Thomas Treads On Toe," July 25, 1905, and "Affidavit of Grover Story Teller," July 25, 1905, all in OASF, Box A-96.

134. "Affidavit of Walter Adair," August 3, 1905, OASF, Box A-96.

135. "Affidavit of Little Rabbit," August 8, 1905, OASF, Box A-96.

136. "Affidavit of Arthur Mitchell," August 7, 1905, and "Affidavit of George Ramsey," August 8, 1905, OASF, Box A-96.

137. "Affidavit of Jeremiah Parker," August 8, 1905, "Affidavit of James Wood," August 8, 1905, and "Affidavit of John Wood," August 8, 1905, all in OASF, Box A-96.

138. "Affidavit of Charles Funkhouser," August 22, 1905, OASF, Box A-96.

139. J. A. Singhaus to MacKey, July 29, 1905, August 17, 1905, OASF, Box A-97.

140. Tracy to MacKey, August 18, 1905, August 22, 1905, OASF, Box A-97. It is unclear what grounds Iowa authorities used for the arrests of Wise and Allen. Since Wise had an Iowa liquor license and the *Heff* decision removed obstacles to liquor sales to allotted Indians, it is possible that Superintendent MacKey was able to provide Marshal Tracy with names of unallotted Indians.

141. Singhaus to MacKey, August 26, 1905, OASF, Box A-97.

142. Ibid.

143. "Report of Superintendent John M. Commons, August 18, 1906," in *ARCIA*, 265.

144. "Against Mathewson," *Pender (Nebraska) Times*, February 28, 1902, 1; "Playing a Dangerous Game," *Omaha Daily Bee*, July 24, 1902, 1. The original handwritten lease ledger for this period, which includes names of lessees, names of Indian allottees, descriptions of leased lands, dates, and in many cases, annual rental rates, is located in the Winnebago Agency Lease Ledger, 1895–1902, Container #516503.

145. "Against Mathewson," *Pender (Nebraska) Times*, February 28, 1902, 1. Besides the leasing fraud charges, Agent Mathewson also was accused of keeping alcohol in his house at the agency—a violation of federal law. An Indian working in the agent's home allegedly found bottled beer in the cellar. "Inspector Is Here," *Pender (Nebraska) Times*, June 6, 1902, 1.

146. "Charges against Agency," *Omaha Daily Bee*, February 25, 1902, 1. It is unclear what action, if any, Commissioner Jones took on Rosewater's charges, since the same reporter sent conflicting stories to the *Omaha World-Herald* and the *Sioux City Journal*. See *Pender (Nebraska) Times*, March 7, 1902, 1.

147. "Ball Still Arollin', " *Pender (Nebraska) Times*, March 7, 1902, 1.

148. "Trouble at Agency," *Pender (Nebraska) Times*, February 7, 1902, 1.

149. "Gone to Washington," *Pender (Nebraska) Times*, February 21, 1902, 1; "Omaha Report Is Ready," *Omaha Daily Bee*, February 28, 1902, 1. By May 30, 1902, Commissioner Jones and Interior Secretary Ethan A. Hitchcock still had not reviewed Agent McComas' report. "The Investigation," *Pender (Nebraska) Times*, May 30, 1902, 1.

150. "Gone to Washington," *Pender (Nebraska) Times*, February 21, 1902, 1.

151. "The Investigation," *Pender (Nebraska) Times*, May 30, 1902, 1; "Inspector Is Here," *Pender (Nebraska) Times*, June 6, 1902, 1. An investigative reporter assigned by Rosewater to the Omaha Agency was arrested and charged with impersonating a federal official. This, of course, only stiffened the editor's resolve to get at the truth. "Inspector Is Here," *Pender (Nebraska) Times*, June 6, 1902, 1.

152. "His Salary Clipped," *Pender (Nebraska) Times*, January 30, 1903, 1; *Pender (Nebraska) Times*, February 20, 1902, 1.

153. "Mathewson Gets It," *Pender (Nebraska) Times*, July 3, 1903, 1.

154. "Nothing New," *Pender (Nebraska) Times*, March 14, 1902, 1; "The Leases," *Pender (Nebraska) Times*, October 24, 1902, 1.

155. *BIC Report, 1894,* 7–8.

CHAPTER 6

1. "Affairs at Omaha Agency," *Omaha Daily Bee*, March 4, 1902, 10; "Inspector McComas Again," *Pender (Nebraska) Times*, March 7, 1902, 1.

2. A. O. Wright to the Commissioner of Indian Affairs, November 16, 1904, WASF, Box A-106.

3. "Relating to Usurious Practices," n.d., and "Relating to Monopolization of Trade and Consequently High Prices Charged," n.d., WASF, Box A-106.

4. Wright to the Commissioner of Indian Affairs, November 16, 1904, WASF, Box A-106.

5. Ibid.; "Testimony of C. J. O'Connor, Regarding Monopolization of Trade," n.d., and "William O'Dell's Testimony," n.d., WASF, Box A-106. The Bureau of Catholic Missions was unfamiliar with Father Joseph Schell, and he had never been assigned to the Winnebago Agency. O'Dell was not intimidated and refused to incriminate his fellow merchants.

6. "Statement of C. J. O'Connor," n.d., and "Testimony of C. J. O'Connor Relative to Snapping of Checks," n.d., WASF, Box A-106.

7. "Testimony of C. J. O'Connor Regarding Usurious Practices," n.d., and "Testimony of Thomas Ashford, Jr.," October 12, 1904, WASF, Box A-106.

8. "Testimony of C. J. O'Connor Regarding Monopolization of Trade," n.d., WASF, Box A-106; "G. C. Maryott's Statement," n.d., WASF, Box A-105; A. O. Wright to the Commissioner of Indian Affairs, November 16, 1904, WASF, Box A-106.

9. Wright to the Commissioner of Indian Affairs, November 16, 1904, WASF, Box A-106.

10. 34 *Statutes at Large* 328, 1017, 72; 35 *Statutes at Large* 782; 39 *Statutes at Large* 124.

11. Kneale, *Indian Agent*, 207–8. Although Kneale did not identify the mixed-blood Thurston County attorney, it was quite likely Omaha lawyer Hiram Chase.

12. Ibid., 208–9.

13. "Report of Axel Johnson, January 1, 1915," James McLaughlin Papers (hereafter MP), R 5, F 26; Henry A. Larson to Albert H. Kneale, May 10, 1913, and A. E. Hess to W. A. Martindale, May 13, 1913, OASF, Box A-97.

14. Assistant U.S. Attorney (signature illegible) to Axel Johnson, July 5, 1915, OASF, Box A-97.

15. Will Estill to Charles Smith, December 14, 1914, Estill to Johnson, December 16, 1914, and Estill to S. A. M. Young, December 16, 1914, all in OASF, Box A-97.

16. "Report of E. B. Linnen, Chief Inspector, and E. M. Sweet, Jr., Inspector on the Omaha Reservation, Nebraska, March 13, 1915," File #993655-14-150, Bureau of Indian Affairs (hereafter BIA). This material is from Richmond R. Clow, Research File for the Study of Omaha and Winnebago Trust Lands (hereafter cited as Richmond Clow Research File). Will Estill may have been conspired against in this instance, but he was not "an honest and upright man." Always lurking on the fringes of the reservation, Estill became involved in numerous cases of land fraud.

17. Larson to Johnson, October 14, 1914, November 24, 1915, OASF, Box A-97.

18. Larson to Johnson, April 17, 1916, OASF, Box A-97. It is possible that further "budget constraints" had resulted in the removal of a regular officer, since Johnson was appointed only for the remainder of the fiscal year. Chief Special Officer Larson was able to supply Johnson with a badge (#87) but no weapon. Larson to Johnson, April 25, 1916, OASF, Box A-97.

19. W. H. Lamar to Bo Sweeney, April 9, 1915, Larson to All Officers, May 4, 1915, Larson to Johnson, December 10, 1915, and E. B. Meritt to Larson, December 30, 1915, all in OASF, Box A-97.

20. Special Officer (signature illegible) to Johnson, June 15, 1916, and Special Officer (no signature) to Larson, June 15, 1916, OASF, Box A-97. In his temporary status as a special deputy, Axel Johnson assisted in the Rosalie arrests.

21. *United States v. Celestine*, 30 S. Ct. 93 (1909); *United States v. Sutton*, 30 S. Ct. 116 (1909); *Hallowell v. United States*, 31 S. Ct. 587 (1911).

22. *United States v. Fred Nice*, 36 S. Ct. 696 (1916).

23.   Larson to All Superintendents and Officers, June 30, 1916, Special Officer (signature illegible) to Johnson, July 26, 1916, OASF, Box A-97.

24.   F. L. Gallagher to Johnson, August 31, 1916, OASF, Box A-97.

25.   "Dan's Confession," *Walthill (Nebraska) Times*, September 29, 1916, in Dan V. Stephens Papers (hereafter SP), Series 7, Box 42, Folder 239.

26.   32 *Statutes at Large* 275.

27.   Holford, "The Subversion of the Indian Land Allotment System," 13–14.

28.   Ibid., 14.

29.   "Report of Commissioner William A. Jones, October 16, 1902," in *ARCIA*, 65–66.

30.   "Report of Agent Charles P. Mathewson, August 26, 1902," in *ARCIA*, 239.

31.   "To Sell Certain Lands," *Pender (Nebraska) Times*, April 11, 1902, 1.

32.   "The Heirship Lands," *Pender (Nebraska) Times*, July 11, 1902, 1; "Indian Heirship Lands," *Bancroft (Nebraska) Blade*, July 18, 1902, 1.

33.   "Don't Want to Sell," *Pender (Nebraska) Times*, July 25, 1902, 1; "Indians Make a Protest," *Omaha Daily Bee*, July 26, 1902, 1; *Bancroft (Nebraska) Blade*, August 1, 1902, 2. Of the 150 Omahas attending the council, only Silas Wood voted to sell his lands. Despite the general opposition to land sales, the *Pender (Nebraska) Times* reported that some land deals had already been made. "Don't Want to Sell," *Pender (Nebraska) Times*, July 25, 1902, 1.

34.   *Omaha Daily Bee*, July 24, 1902, 1, reprinted in *Pender (Nebraska) Times*, July 25, 1902, 1.

35.   "Robinson's Letter," *Pender (Nebraska) Times*, August 1, 1902, 2. In addition to helping settlers buy land, Robinson saw the extended payment period as a way to ensure that all heirs would receive their fair share of the proceeds.

36.   "New Rules Out," *Pender (Nebraska) Times*, October 24, 1902, 1; "All Deeds Are Void," *Pender (Nebraska) Times*, October 3, 1902, 1; "Knocks Out Speculators," *Omaha Daily Bee*, September 30, 1902, 1.

37.   "Department Won't Change," *Pender (Nebraska) Times*, December 12, 1902, 1; "Will Stand Pat," *Pender (Nebraska) Times*, February 13, 1903, 1; "Land Sales Held Up," *Pender (Nebraska) Times*, September 11, 1903, 1.

38.   "Inspector Is Here," *Pender (Nebraska) Times*, September 25, 1903, 1.

39.   "Mathewson Resigns," *Pender (Nebraska) Times*, October 2, 1903, 1. Mathewson's replacement at the Omaha Agency was John MacKey. The Omahas and the Winnebagoes once more had separate agencies.

40.   "New Land Rules," *Pender (Nebraska) Times*, October 9, 1903, 1; "Thurston County Map," *Pender (Nebraska) Times*, April 29, 1904, 1.

41.   "Report of Commissioner William A. Jones, October 17, 1904," in *ARCIA*, 64–65; "Report of Commissioner Francis E. Leupp, September 30, 1905," in *ARCIA*, 32. By June 30, 1906, $158,639.34 had been deposited for Omahas. Only the Yankton Sioux in South Dakota had realized more from

heirship land sales. "Report of Commissioner Francis E. Leupp, September 30, 1906," in *ARCIA*, 97.

42. "Report of Commissioner Robert G. Valentine, September 15, 1909," in *ARCIA*, 67.

43. "Report of Commissioner Francis E. Leupp, September 30, 1906," in *ARCIA*, 96, 99–103; "A New Wrinkle," *Pender (Nebraska) Times*, November 10, 1905, 1.

44. "Report of Commissioner William A. Jones, October 17, 1904," in *ARCIA*, 62, 66.

45. "Report of Superintendent John F. MacKey, August 24, 1905," in *ARCIA*, 249; "Report of Superintendent John M. Commons, August 18, 1906," in *ARCIA*, 264.

46. "Report of Commissioner William A. Jones, October 17, 1904," in *ARCIA*, 63.

47. "Report of Superintendent John M. Commons, August 18, 1906," in *ARCIA*, 264–65.

48. "Report of Superintendent Axel Johnson, January 1, 1915," MP, R 5, F 12–13.

49. "Report of Commissioner Francis E. Leupp, September 30, 1906," in *ARCIA*, 28; Hoxie, *A Final Promise*, 220; U.S. Congress, House, *Allotment of Lands in Severalty*, 1–2. See also U.S. Congress, Senate, *Allotment of Lands in Severalty*.

50. 34 *Statutes at Large* 182.

51. "Report of Commissioner Francis E. Leupp, September 30, 1906," in *ARCIA*, 30. For a discussion of the workings of the Burke Act and his role in its passage, see Leupp, *The Indian and His Problem*, 61–78.

52. U.S. Congress, House, *Allotment of Lands in Severalty*, 2.

53. *BIC Report, 1906*, 17–19.

54. Samuel M. Brosius to Merrill M. Gates, October 30, 1908, *IRAP*, R 20.

55. "Report of Commissioner Francis E. Leupp, September 30, 1906," in *ARCIA*, 31.

56. Francis E. Leupp to the Secretary of the Interior, February 8, 1906, U.S. Congress, House, *Allotment of Lands in Severalty*, 3–4.

57. "Report of Commissioner Francis E. Leupp, September 30, 1907," in *ARCIA*, 64.

58. John M. Commons to the Commissioner of Indian Affairs, December 2, 1908, OASF, Box A-102.

59. "Petition to Extend the Omaha Trust Period," n.d., WASF, Box A-105; "Want an Extension," *Pender (Nebraska) Times*, January 22, 1904, 1. The 1893 allotments, assigned by Rankin in 1899–1900, are referred to as the "new" allotments and had a later trust expiration date.

60. "Chase Admits Incompetency," *Pender (Nebraska) Times*, October 29, 1909, 1.

61. "Twenty-Five Year Extension Period Extended," *Pender (Nebraska) Times*, August 10, 1906, 1.

62. "Against Extension," *Pender (Nebraska) Times*, February 5, 1904, 1.

63. "Leupp Is Coming," *Pender (Nebraska) Times*, December 23, 1904, 1; "Report of Superintendent John F. MacKey, August 24, 1905," in *ARCIA*, 249.

64. Commons to the Commissioner of Indian Affairs, December 2, 1908, OASF, Box A-102; "Report of Superintendent John M. Commons, August 18, 1906," in *ARCIA*, 265.

65. Robert G. Valentine to Commons, February 19, 1909, March 15, 1909, OASF, Box A-102.

66. C. F. Hauke to Commons, May 1, 1909, and Commons to the Commissioner of Indian Affairs, May 20, 1909, OASF, Box A-102. On June 2, Commons added one more name to the list of persons aged twenty-one to twenty-five. Commons to the Commissioner of Indian Affairs, June 2, 1909, OASF, Box A-102.

67. Commons to the Commissioner of Indian Affairs, May 20, 1909, OASF, Box A-102.

68. Ibid.; Commons to the Commissioner of Indian Affairs, June 1, 1909, OASF, Box A-102.

69. Commons to the Commissioner of Indian Affairs, June 1, 1909, June 19, 1909, OASF, Box A-102.

70. "Reservation Matters," *Pender (Nebraska) Times*, June 11, 1909, 1.

71. Susan La Flesche Picotte to Valentine, July 13, 1909, BIA, Omaha, File #55028-09-150.

72. Picotte to Valentine, July 13, 1909, and Picotte to the Secretary of the Interior, June 28, 1909, BIA, Omaha, File #55028-09-150, cited in McDonnell, "Land Policy on the Omaha Reservation," 402.

73. "Annual Report, Omaha and Winnebago Agency, July 1, 1910," Richmond Clow Research File.

74. "Report of Commissioner Robert G. Valentine, November 1, 1910," in *ARCIA*, 48; Commons to Valentine, July 16, 1909, BIA, Omaha, File #55028-09-150.

75. "Not So Bad," *Pender (Nebraska) Times*, August 13, 1909, 1.

76. Memorandum by F. H. Abbott, "Problem of the Omahas," July 29, 1909, BIA, Omaha, File #61671-09-127, cited in McDonnell, "Land Policy on the Omaha Reservation," 402; "Not So Bad," *Pender (Nebraska) Times*, August 13, 1909, 1; "Abbott Talks," *Pender (Nebraska) Times*, October 15, 1909, 1.

77. Valentine, "Making Good Indians," 611, 601; McDonnell, "Land Policy on the Omaha Reservation," 401.

78. Valentine, "Making Good Indians," 600; Kneale, *Indian Agent*, 223–24; McDonnell, "Land Policy on the Omaha Reservation," 404.

79. William McConihe and H. P. Marble to the Commissioner of Indian Affairs, February 18, 1910, and McConihe to Marble, February 10, 1910, BIA, Omaha, File #61671-09-127, cited in McDonnell, "Land Policy on the Omaha Reservation," 404; U.S. Congress, Senate, *Taxation of Lands of Omaha Indians in Nebraska*, 2.

80. "Report of Commissioner Robert G. Valentine, November 1, 1910," in *ARCIA*, 48. Dividing the Omahas into three competency classes also

affected leasing rules. Class One and Class Two Indians could continue to initiate their own leases following established rules, but Class Three leases would be controlled by the agency superintendent. Despite strict rules, some whites continued to lease Class Three lands without going through the agency. "Late Agency News," *Winnebago (Nebraska) Chieftain*, July 15, 1910, 8; "Late Agency News," *Winnebago (Nebraska) Chieftain*, August 20, 1910, 1.

81.   "Omaha Indians to Be Free," *Omaha Daily Bee*, February 28, 1910, 1–2; McConihe to F. H. Abbott, March 6, 1910, BIA, Omaha, File #114127-14-127.

82.   McConihe to Abbott, March 10, 1910, BIA, Omaha, File #114127-14-127, cited in McDonnell, "Land Policy on the Omaha Reservation," 404; "20,000 Acres," *Pender (Nebraska) Times*, March 4, 1910, 1. Janet McDonnell obtained her fee-patent figures from the Omaha Tract Book in the Bureau of Indian Affairs area office in Aberdeen, South Dakota, and from Competency Commission examination forms at the Winnebago Agency. A handwritten land sale and fee-patent ledger at the Federal Records Center in Kansas City lists allottees by name and allotment number and includes the tract book page on which each land transaction can be found. This ledger includes the names of approximately 175 of the Omahas whose fee-patents were issued on March 10, 1910. Winnebago Agency Land Sale and Fee-Patent Book #30, Container #516423.

83.   "Competent Omahas," *Pender (Nebraska) Times*, March 25, 1910, 1; "Late Agency News," *Winnebago (Nebraska) Chieftain*, April 8, 1910, 8.

84.   McDonnell, "Land Policy on the Omaha Reservation," 404–5, citing the following: "Allotment and Estate Files at the Omaha Agency" and McConihe and Marble to the Commissioner of Indian Affairs, January 15, 1910, BIA, Omaha, File #61671-09-127; E. B. Linnen, "Report on the Omaha Agency, October 24, 1916," BIA, Omaha, File #150.

85.   *1910 Omaha Reservation Methodology*, 3–4, Richmond Clow Research File.

86.   Ibid., 3; McDonnell, "Land Policy on the Omaha Reservation," 405.

87.   "Agency Matters," *Pender (Nebraska) Times*, March 11, 1910, 1; "Object," *Pender (Nebraska) Times*, March 18, 1910, 1; McConihe to Abbott, March 6, 1910, BIA, Omaha, File #114127-14-127.

88.   "Deeds Coming," *Pender (Nebraska) Times*, April 1, 1910, 1; "To Indict," *Pender (Nebraska) Times*, April 8, 1910, 1.

89.   "Deeds Coming," *Pender (Nebraska) Times*, April 1, 1910, 1; "Eight Indicted," *Pender (Nebraska) Times*, April 22, 1910, 1, reprinted from *Omaha Daily Bee*, April 20, 1910.

90.   "Eight Indicted," *Pender (Nebraska) Times*, April 22, 1910, 1, reprinted from the *Omaha Daily Bee*, April 20, 1910; "Men Fined in Indian Land Cases"; "Agency Matters," *Pender (Nebraska) Times*, March 11, 1910, 1.

91.   All information on the disposition of fee-patented Omaha lands is taken from the Richmond Clow Research File. Clow obtained this material from the "Omaha and Winnebago Competency Report" and from the Thurston County Courthouse in Pender, Nebraska, where his researchers

conducted title searches. The patentees mentioned are representative of the tragic land loss on the Omaha Reservation as a result of the work of the competency commission.

92.   Richmond Clow Research File.

93.   McDonnell, "Land Policy on the Omaha Reservation," 406–7, citing the following: Marble, Andrew Pollack, and Frank McIntyre to the Commissioner of Indian Affairs, September 30, 1910, BIA, Omaha, File #70731-10-127; Valentine to E. P. Holcombe, November 30, 1910, BIA, Omaha, File #34939-11-127; Hauke to Marble, McIntyre, and Pollack, March 23, 1911, and Hauke to McIntyre, June 20, 1911, BIA, Santee, File #24448-11-127; Abbott to H. G. Wilson, January 13, 1911, BIA, General Services File, File #70942-10-312.

94.   Circular 619, "Valentine to All Superintendents," April 8, 1912, BIA, Numbered Circulars.

95.   S. A. M. Young, "Report on the Omaha Agency," November 25–26, 29–30, 1912, BIA, Omaha, File #126946-12-150, cited in McDonnell, "Land Policy on the Omaha Reservation," 407.

96.   "Proceedings of the Thirtieth Annual LMC" (1912), 81–82; Diane T. Putney, "Robert Grosvenor Valentine, 1909–12," in Kvasnicka and Viola, *The Commissioners of Indian Affairs*, 241.

97.   Edgar Meritt, "Memorandum for the Commissioner," December 1, 1913, BIA, General Services, File #152446-13-312, cited in McDonnell, "Land Policy on the Omaha Reservation," 407; "Report of Commissioner Cato Sells, October 15, 1917," in *ARCIA*, 3–4; "Report of Commissioner Cato Sells, September 30, 1920," in *ARCIA*, 48–49.

98.   Cato Sells to Johnson, December 4, 1914, MP, R 5, F 714–15; Sells to S. A. M. Young, December 4, 1914, MP, R 5, F 716–17.

99.   Sells to Charles E. Burton, December 4, 1914, MP, R 5, F 710; Sells to E. D. Mossman, December 4, 1914, MP, R 5, F 711; Sells to A. W. Leech, December 4, 1914, MP, R 5, F 712; Sells to Arvel R. Snyder, December 4, 1914, MP, R 5, F 713.

100.   "Report of Axel Johnson: Social and Economic Effects of a Liberal Policy of Granting Patents in Fee on the Omaha Reservation," January 1, 1915, MP, R 6, F 18–27 (hereafter "Report of Axel Johnson").

101.   Ibid., F 28–31.

102.   "Report of E. B. Linnen, Chief Inspector, and E. M. Sweet, Jr., Inspector on the Omaha Reservation, Nebraska," March 31, 1915, BIA, File #993655-14-150, Richmond Clow Research File.

103.   "Report of S. A. M. Young," December 19, 1914, MP, R 5, F 738–54.

104.   E. D. Mossman to the Commissioner of Indian Affairs, December 28, 1914, MP, R 7, F 745–53.

105.   "From the War-Path to the Plow," 80. Indian Rights Association, "Thirty-Second Annual Report, 1914," in *IRAP*, R 102.

106.   Henry C. Lafferty to Franklin K. Lane, January 7, 1915, MP, R 6, F 36; Lane to Lafferty, January 12, 1915, MP, R 6, F 37; Lafferty to Lane, March 31, 1915, MP, R 6, F 65–66; "Petition of the Cheyenne River Sioux," March 1915, MP, R 6, F 68.

107. Franklin K. Lane, "Circular," April 8, 1915, MP, R 6, F 71.

108. Frank A. Thackery to Matthew K. Sniffen, May 25, 1915, *IRAP*, R 30.

109. Leech to an unidentified correspondent, June 20, 1916, MP, R 7, F 154–57.

110. James McLaughlin to O. M. McPherson, June 9, 1916, MP, R 7, F 78–80.

111. McDonnell, "Land Policy on the Omaha Reservation," 408, citing the following: Arthur Mullen to the Commissioner of Indian Affairs, August 14, 1919, BIA, General Services, File #85492-19-312; H. S. Traylor to Sells, April 8, 1919, BIA, Omaha, File #31768-19-150; John F. Farley to Sells, March 26, 1919, BIA, Omaha, File #27231-19-127.

112. Leech to an unidentified correspondent, June 20, 1916, MP, R 7, F 156.

113. Commons to the Commissioner of Indian Affairs, December 2, 1908, OASF, Box A-102; U.S. Congress, House, *Disposal of Unallotted Land on the Omaha Indian Reservation*, 1–4; U.S. Congress, House, *Survey of Tribal Lands on Omaha Indian Reservation*, 1–4; U.S. Congress, House, *Disposal of Unallotted Land, Omaha Indian Reservation, Nebr.*, 1–5; 22 *Statutes at Large* 341; 27 *Statutes at Large* 612, 630.

114. Commons to the Commissioner of Indian Affairs, December 2, 1908, OASF, Box A-102.

115. U.S. Congress, House, *Disposal of Unallotted Land on the Omaha Indian Reservation*, 3.

116. Ibid., 4.

117. Ibid., 2; U.S. Congress, House, *Survey of Tribal Lands on Omaha Indian Reservation*, 3.

118. 37 *Statutes at Large* 111; Commons to the Commissioner of Indian Affairs, December 2, 1908, OASF, Box A-102.

119. Jones to the Commissioner of Indian Affairs, July 1, 1913, and Hauke to John S. Spear, July 23, 1913, OASF, Box A-96.

120. Hauke to Spear, March 14, 1914, and Hauke to Dan V. Stephens, September 8, 1914, OASF, Box A-96.

121. Hauke to Johnson, January 16, 1915, OASF, Box A-96.

122. Hauke to Stephens, September 8, 1914, and Assistant Attorney General to the Secretary of the Interior, March 3, 1915, OASF, Box A-96.

123. *Chase v. United States*, 222 F. 594 (1915).

124. Ibid., 598.

125. Assistant Attorney General to the Secretary of the Interior, May 21, 1915, Richmond Clow Research File; Assistant Attorney General to the Secretary of the Interior, June 10, 1915, and Meritt to the Secretary of the Interior, July 20, 1915, OASF, Box A-96.

126. Meritt to the Secretary of the Interior, July 20, 1915, OASF, Box A-96; *Chase v. United States*, 222 F. 593 (1915). The Interior Department had denied Thomas Sloan an allotment he claimed he was entitled to because his mother was an Omaha. But in *Sloan v. United States* in October 1902, a district court judge ruled that Margaret Sloan, mother of Thomas Sloan, had

previously been granted a 320-acre allotment on the Nemaha "half-breed" tract in southeastern Nebraska and was ineligible for an allotment on the Omaha Reservation. The judge ruled that because Margaret Sloan held no land titles on the reservation, she could not pass along any land to her son. Sloan's case was dismissed, and he was ordered to pay court costs. 95 F. 193 (1899); 118 F. 283 (1902).

127.   Jones to the Attorney General, July 21, 1915, OASF, Box A-96; *United States as Trustee v. Hiram Chase*, 36 S. Ct. 553 (1916).

128.   *United States v. Chase*, 38 S. Ct. 24 (1917).

129.   Harry L. Keefe to B. A. Martindale, August 29, 1913, OASF, Box A-96.

130.   Sells to Francis La Flesche, November 24, 1913, and Sells to Spear, November 25, 1913, OASF, Box A-96.

131.   Keefe to the Commissioner of Indian Affairs, November 26, 1913, OASF, Box A-96.

132.   Sells to Spear, November 26, 1913, OASF, Box A-96.

133.   Sells to Johnson, December 30, 1914, OASF, Box A-96.

134.   Keefe to Johnson, January 5, 1915, OASF, Box A-96. Unfortunately, letters at the Federal Records Center in Kansas City do not indicate whether Keefe succeeded in "jumping the gun" on his purchase for the historical society.

135.   U.S. Congress, House, *Disposal of Unallotted Land, Omaha Indian Reservation, Nebr.*, 2. See also U.S. Congress, Senate, *Sale and Designation of Lands in Omaha Indian Reservation*, 2.

136.   Preston C. West to the Secretary of the Interior, January 26, 1915, and Meritt to Johnson, January 4, 1915, February 13, 1916, OASF, Box A-96.

137.   Meritt to Johnson, April 24, 1915, OASF, Box A-96.

138.   Meritt to Johnson, September 10, 1915, OASF, Box A-96. The assistant commissioner wanted assurances that when the larger areas were set aside, the Indians would disinter their people who were buried on allotments and rebury them in one of the tribal cemeteries.

139.   U.S. Congress, House, *Setting Apart of Tribal Lands for Cemetery Purposes*, 1–2. See also U.S. Congress, Senate, *The Omaha Indians*, 1–2.

140.   Thurston County (Series 4), County Board of Superintendents Records, vol. 1 (1889–1903), 155, 292.

141.   *Congressional Record*, 53d Cong., 1st sess., 1893, 25, pt. 1:1274; Clow, "Taxing the Omaha and Winnebago Trust Lands," 4.

142.   Clow, "Taxing the Omaha and Winnebago Trust Lands," 4; Daniel M. Browning to William Beck, October 31, 1893, Letters Sent, BIA, cited in Clow, "Taxing the Omaha and Winnebago Trust Lands," 4.

143.   "Thurston County, Nebraska, Some Facts and Figures Showing the Inequalities of the Burden of Taxation on Different Parts of the County," *Pender (Nebraska) Times*, supplement, March 2, 1900.

144.   "Ball Still Arollin'," *Pender (Nebraska) Times*, March 4, 1902, 1.

145.   *United States v. James A. Rickert*, 23 S. Ct. 478 (1903); "Little Left to Tax," *Pender (Nebraska) Times*, February 27, 1903, 1; Cohen, *Handbook of Federal Indian Law*, 254–55.

146. "Increases Evaluation," *Pender (Nebraska) Times*, May 26, 1905, 1; Thurston County (Series 4), County Board of Superintendents Records, vol. 2, 42–45.

147. "Enjoins County," *Pender (Nebraska) Times*, July 28, 1905, 1. This was the first lawsuit of this type ever brought in federal court, and the government contended that the money on deposit was a trust fund, in lieu of Indian lands, and so should remain tax-exempt until the trust period elapsed. Indians' deposits ranged from $60 to $2,516, and the tax that Thurston County hoped to extract would have been 20 percent of those amounts.

148. *United States v. Thurston County et al.*, 140 F. 456 (1905); "Report of Commissioner Francis E. Leupp, September 30, 1906," in *ARCIA*, 95.

149. "Report of Commissioner Francis E. Leupp, September 30, 1905," in *ARCIA*, 34.

150. *United States v. Thurston County, Neb., et al.*, 143 F. 287, 292 (1906). These proceedings further demonstrated Sloan's lack of concern for his people's welfare. He appeared to be pro-Indian when his personal welfare was at stake, but at other times he was simply a "lawyer for hire."

151. 35 *Statutes at Large* 628–29.

152. "All Omaha Lands Are Taxable," *Pender (Nebraska) Times*, May 13, 1910, 1.

153. *Congressional Record*, 61st Cong., 2d sess., April 27, 1910, 45, pt. 5:5449–51.

154. U.S. Congress, House, *Taxation of Lands of Omaha Indians in Nebraska*, 1–3. Also see Senator Norris Brown's report in U.S. Congress, Senate, *Taxation of Lands of Omaha Indians in Nebraska*, 1–3.

155. 36 *Statutes at Large* 348. In December 1914, an assistant interior secretary informed the treasurer for Cuming County, Nebraska, that there were no funds available to pay the land taxes in 1912 for twenty-eight parcels of Indian land. Five of these parcels were listed as belonging to Joseph La Flesche, who had died years before, and five belonged to Rosalie La Flesche Farley. La Flesche's tax bill amounted to $60.32, and Rosalie Farley owed $127.26. There is an error on the list, which includes the lands of "Susan La Flesche Tibbles." This should either be Susan La Flesche Picotte or Susette La Flesche Tibbles. The amount due was $113.40. Bo Sweeney to Herman Zeplin, December 16, 1914, OASF, Box A-96.

156. Field Solicitor, Aberdeen, South Dakota, "Taxation of Omaha-Winnebago Trust Lands," 6, Richmond Clow Research File; *United States v. Thurston County, Neb., et al.*, 143 F. 287 (1906); 13 *Statutes at Large* 407.

157. "Indian Meeting," *Pender (Nebraska) Times*, November 8, 1910, 1.

158. Sells to Johnson, February 15, 1915, Letters Sent, BIA, cited in Clow, "Taxing the Omaha and Winnebago Trust Lands," 10.

159. "Report of E. B. Linnen, Chief Inspector, and E. M. Sweet, Jr., Inspector on the Omaha Reservation, Nebraska," March 31, 1915, BIA, File #993655-14-150, Richmond Clow Research File. In 1913, H. D. Hancock, the First National Bank of Pender assistant cashier, had expressed delight that in the future, taxes on Indian lands would be taken from the Omahas' rent receipts, since "the tax problem [was] the one drawback to [the] county." At

that time Hancock wanted to know if lessees could pay their landlords' taxes and deduct those sums from their rents. H. D. Hancock to Spear, July 8, 1913, WASF, Box A-108.

160. George J. Adams to L. C. Brownrigg, November 16, 1915, WASF, Box A-105.

161. Guy T. Graves to the Committee Opposing a Trust Extension, November 23, 1915, WASF, Box A-105.

162. "The Omaha and His Land."

163. Letter to Hiram Chase, November 27, 1915, WASF, Box A-105.

164. "Report of E. B. Linnen, Chief Inspector, and E. M. Sweet, Jr., Inspector on the Omaha Reservation, Nebraska, March 31, 1915," File #993655-14-150, BIA, Richmond Clow Research File.

165. "Report of Axel Johnson," January 1, 1915, MP, R 6, F 31–32.

166. 24 *Statutes at Large* 389.

167. 39 *Statutes at Large* 142–43.

168. Stephens to Gilbert M. Hitchcock, May 17, 1916, SP, Series 1, Box 19, Folder 152; Clow, "Taxing the Omaha and Winnebago Trust Lands," 12.

169. U.S. Congress, Senate, *Taxation of Winnebago and Omaha Indian Lands*, 1.

170. Clow, "Taxing the Omaha and Winnebago Trust Lands," 12; Hitchcock to Stephens, August 7, 1916, SP, Series 1, Box 20, Folder 153; Charles J. Kappler to Stephens, August 8, 1916, SP, Series 1, Box 20, Folder 159.

171. Keefe to Stephens, August 28, 1916, SP, Series 1, Box 20, Folder 159; U.S. Congress, House, *Taxation of Winnebago and Omaha Indian Lands*, 1–3.

172. U.S. Congress, House, *Lands of Winnebago and Omaha Indians*, 2. See also U.S. Congress, House, *Taxation of Winnebago and Omaha Indian Lands*, 1–3, and U.S. Congress, Senate, *Taxation of Winnebago and Omaha Indian Lands*, 1–2.

173. *Walthill (Nebraska) Citizen*, October 26, 1916, from a newspaper clipping in SP, Series 7, Box 42, Folder 238.

174. "Bill to Tax Indians Lands," *Pender (Nebraska) Republic*, December 29, 1916, 4.

175. 39 *Statutes at Large* 866.

176. Field Solicitor, Aberdeen, South Dakota, "Taxation of Omaha-Winnebago Trust Lands," 9–10, Richmond Clow Research File.

177. Mead, *Changing Culture* (1932), 30.

178. Springer, "The Omaha Indians," 32.

179. Fletcher, "The Allotted Indian's Difficulties," 661.

EPILOGUE

1. Fletcher and La Flesche, *The Omaha Tribe*, 248–49.

2. Mead, *Changing Culture* (1932), 29; Mead, *Changing Culture* (1966), xi.

3. Mead, *Changing Culture* (1966), xvi.

4. Ridington, "Omaha Survival," 46.

5. Roger Welsch, "Omaha Song Today," in Lee and La Vigna, *Omaha Indian Music*, 5.

6. Ridington, "Omaha Survival," 47.

7. Cary Alice Wolf, cited in Ridington, "A Sacred Object as Text," 88.

8. Ridington, "A Sacred Object as Text," 84–85.

9. Julie Anderson, "Two Tribes Distribute Casino Cash," *Omaha World-Herald*, December 23, 1994, 18.

10. Michael Kelly, "Hope, Problems Combine in Reservation Life," *Omaha World-Herald*, November 24, 1994, 12.

11. Cited in Kelly, "Hope, Problems Combine in Reservation Life," 13.

12. Ridington, "A Sacred Object as Text," 86.

13. Dennis Hastings, in Lee and La Vigna, *Omaha Indian Music*, 3. These words were part of Hastings' remarks in 1984 at the Library of Congress when he discussed the return of the cylinder recordings of Omaha music made by ethnographers Alice Fletcher and Francis La Flesche between 1880 and 1910.

Bibliography

MANUSCRIPTS
National Archives, Washington, D.C.
Bureau of Indian Affairs. Central Classified Files. Record Group 75.
————. Circular #619. Numbered Circulars. Record Group 75.
Documents Relating to the Negotiations of Ratified and Unratified Treaties with Various Indian Tribes. National Archives Microfilm Publications. Record Group 75. Series T494. Reel 5.
Letters Received by the Office of Indian Affairs, Council Bluffs Agency, 1836–43, 1844–46, 1847–51, 1852–57. National Archives Microfilm Publications. Record Group 75. Series M234. Reels 215–18.
Letters Received by the Office of Indian Affairs, Nebraska Agencies, 1876–78. National Archives Microfilm Publications. Record Group 75. Series M234. Reels 519, 521–22.
Letters Received by the Office of Indian Affairs, Omaha Agency, 1856–63, 1864–70, 1871–76. National Archives Microfilm Publications. Record Group 75. Series M234. Reels 604–6.
Letters Received by the Office of Indian Affairs, Upper Missouri Agency, 1824–35. National Archives Microfilm Publications. Record Group 75. Series M234. Reel 883.

Nebraska State Historical Society, Lincoln
John L. Champe Papers. Manuscript 31. Box 2.
Robert W. Furnas Papers. 1844–1905. Manuscript 2642. Microfilm. Reels 1, 11–12.
La Flesche Family Papers. Manuscript 2026. Microfilm. Reel 1.
Letters Received, Northern Superintendency, 1861–66, 1867. Microfilm. Record Group 508. Box 8. Reels 134–35.
Dan V. Stephens Papers. Manuscript 3643.
Thurston County (Series 4). County Board of Superintendents Records. Microfilm. Record Group 237. Reel 1.

Miscellaneous
Clow, Richmond R. Research File for the Study of Omaha and Winnebago Trust Lands. Office of Professor Michael L. Tate, History Department, University of Nebraska at Omaha. Eight boxes.
James McLaughlin Papers. Assumption Abbey Archives. Richardton, North Dakota. Microfilm Reels 5–7.
Omaha Agency Subject Files. Federal Records Center. Kansas City, Missouri.

"Proceedings of the Annual Meetings of the Lake Mohonk Conference of Friends of the Indian." 1884, 1887, 1889–94, 1900, 1912. Microfiche, University of Nebraska at Omaha Library.

Winnebago Agency Lease Ledger, 1895–1902, Book #89. Federal Records Center. Kansas City, Missouri.

Winnebago Agency Subject Files. Federal Records Center. Kansas City, Missouri.

Winnebago Agency Land Sale and Fee-Patent Book #30. Federal Records Center. Kansas City, Missouri.

GOVERNMENT DOCUMENTS

American State Papers: Indian Affairs. Vol. 2.

Dorsey, James Owen. *The Ǧegiha Language*. Department of the Interior, United States Geographical and Geological Survey of the Rocky Mountain Region. Contributions to American Ethnology, vol. 6. Washington, D.C.: Government Printing Office, 1890.

————. *Omaha and Ponka Letters*. Smithsonian Institution. Bureau of American Ethnology Bulletin Number 11. Washington, D.C.: Government Printing Office, 1891.

————. *Omaha Sociology*. Third Annual Report of the Bureau of American Ethnology. Washington, D.C.: Government Printing Office, 1884.

Fletcher, Alice C., and Francis La Flesche. *The Omaha Tribe*. Twenty-Seventh Annual Report of the Bureau of American Ethnology. Washington, D.C.: Government Printing Office, 1911.

Kappler, Charles J., comp. and ed. *Indian Affairs: Laws and Treaties*. Vol. 2. Washington, D.C.: Government Printing Office, 1904.

La Flesche, Francis. *Omaha Bow and Arrow Makers*. Annual Report of the Smithsonian Institution. Washington, D.C.: Government Printing Office, 1927.

McGee, W. J. *The Siouan Indians: A Preliminary Sketch*. Fifteenth Annual Report of the Bureau of American Ethnology. Washington, D.C.: Government Printing Office, 1897.

Morgan, Lewis Henry. *Houses and House-Life of the American Aborigines*. Contributions to North American Ethnology, vol. 4. Washington, D.C.: Government Printing Office, 1881.

Royce, Charles C., comp. *Indian Land Cessions in the United States*. Eighteenth Annual Report of the Bureau of American Ethnology, part 2. Washington, D.C.: Government Printing Office, 1899.

U.S. Board of Indian Commissioners. *Annual Report*. 1884–87, 1889, 1891, 1894, 1895, 1898, 1906. University of Nebraska at Omaha Microfilm Collection, Call #I20.5.

U.S. Commissioner of Indian Affairs. *Annual Report of the Commissioner of Indian Affairs to the Secretary of the Interior*. 1837–38, 1840–44, 1846–51, 1853–58, 1861, 1863–66, 1868–71, 1873–74, 1877, 1880, 1882–90, 1892–1907, 1909–10, 1912, 1917, 1920.

U.S. Congress. *Congressional Globe*. 1836, 1845, 1848, 1851–53.

U.S. Congress. *Congressional Record*. 1881–82, 1890, 1893, 1910.

U.S. Congress. House. *Allotment of Lands in Severalty to Certain Indians.* 59th Cong., 1st sess., 1906. H. Rept. 1558. Serial set 4906.

————. *Boundary Line between Land of the United States and Missouri.* 23d Cong., 2d sess., 1835. H. Doc. 107. Serial set 273.

————. *B. Y. Shelley.* 36th Cong., 1st sess., 1860. H. Rept. 592. Serial set 1070.

————. *B. Y. Shelley.* 37th Cong., 2d sess., 1862. H. Rept. 26. Serial set 1144.

————. *Colonel Dodge's Journal.* 24th Cong., 1st sess., 1836. H. Doc. 181. Serial set 289.

————. *Disposal of Unallotted Land, Omaha Indian Reservation, Nebr.* 62d Cong., 2d sess., 1912. H. Rept. 571. Serial set 6131.

————. *Disposal of Unallotted Land on the Omaha Indian Reservation.* 60th Cong., 2d sess., 1909. H. Doc. 1431. Serial set 5557.

————. *Lands in Severalty to Indians.* 46th Cong., 2d sess., 1880. H. Rept. 1576. Serial set 1938.

————. *Lands of Winnebago and Omaha Indians, Nebraska.* 64th Cong., 1st sess., 1916. H. Rept. 994. Serial set 6903.

————. *Letter from the Secretary of the Interior Relative to the Disposition of Portions of Indian Reservations in the Northern Superintendency.* 42d Cong., 2d sess., 1872. H. Exec. Doc. 84. Serial set 1510.

————. *Memorial of the Legislature of Minnesota for the Removal of the Winnebago Indians, and the Indemnification of the Early Settlers upon Their Reservation.* 36th Cong., 1st sess., 1860. H. Misc. Doc. 68. Serial set 1065.

————. *Message from the President of the United States Transmitting Copies of Treaties Which Have Lately Been Ratified between the United States and the Choctaw Indians and between the United States and the Confederated Tribes of the Sacs and Foxes, and Other Tribes.* 21st Cong., 2d sess., 1831. H. Doc. 123. Serial set 209.

————. *Omaha Indian Lands in Nebraska.* 43d Cong., 1st sess., 1874. H. Exec. Doc. 109. Serial set 1607.

————. *Removal of the Winnebago Indians.* 27th Cong., 2d sess., 1842. H. Rept. 680. Serial set 409.

————. *Sale of a Part of Omaha Indian Reservation in Nebraska.* 47th Cong., 1st sess., 1882. H. Rept. 1530. Serial set 2069.

————. *Setting Apart of Tribal Lands for Cemetery Purposes for the Omaha Indians.* 64th Cong., 1st sess., 1916. H. Rept. 210. Serial set 6903.

————. *Survey of Tribal Lands on Omaha Indian Reservation.* 61st Cong., 2d sess., 1910. H. Doc. 630. Serial set 5836.

————. *Taxation of Lands of Omaha Indians in Nebraska.* 61st Cong., 2d sess., 1910. H. Rept. 1042. Serial set 5592.

————. *Taxation of Winnebago and Omaha Indian Lands, Nebraska.* 64th Cong., 1st sess., 1916. H. Rept. 1098. Serial set 6905.

————. *Time of Payment for Lands of Omaha Indians in Nebraska.* 53d Cong., 2d sess., 1894. H. Rept. 958. Serial set 3271.

————. *Winnebago Indians.* 28th Cong., 1st sess., 1844. H. Rept. 363. Serial set 446.

U.S. Congress. Senate. *Allotment of Lands in Severalty to Certain Indians.* 59th Cong., 1st sess., 1906. S. Rept. 1998. Serial set 4904.

————. *A Communication from the Secretary of the Interior Relative to Proposed Legislation for the Relief of the Omaha Indians.* 49th Cong., 1st sess., 1886. S. Exec. Doc. 90. Serial set 2339.

————. *Correspondence on the Subject of the Emigration of Indians between the 30th November, 1831, and 27th December, 1833.* 23d Cong., 1st sess., 1835. S. Doc. 512, vols. 2 and 4. Serial set 245.

————. *Documents Relating to the Extension of the Northern Boundary of the State of Missouri.* 24th Cong., 1st sess., 1836. S. Doc. 206. Serial set 281.

————. *In Response to Senate Resolution of January 31, 1888, Information Relative to Sale of Lands in the Omaha Reservation.* 50th Cong., 1st sess., 1888. S. Exec. Doc. 77. Serial set 2510.

————. *Letter from the Secretary of the Interior.* 42d Cong., 2d sess., 1872. S. Misc. Doc. 41. Serial set 1481.

————. *Letter from the Secretary of the Interior, Transmitting in Response to a Resolution, a Copy of a Communication from the Commissioner of Indian Affairs, with Accompanying Papers, in Regard to Leases in Severalty on the Omaha and Winnebago Reservations.* 51st Cong., 2d sess., 1891. S. Exec. Doc. 73. Serial set 2818.

————. *Memorial of Omaha Indians in Relation to Lands Sold by the United States to the Winnebagoes, and to Certain Accounts with the Government.* 47th Cong., 1st sess., 1882. S. Misc. Doc. 78. Serial set 1993.

————. *Memorial of the Members of the Omaha Tribe of Indians for a Grant of Land in Severalty.* 47th Cong., 1st sess., 1882. S. Misc. Doc. 31. Serial set 1993.

————. *Message from the President of the United States to the Two Houses of Congress at the Commencement of the First Session of the Thirty-Third Congress, December 6, 1853.* 33d Cong., 1st sess., 1853. S. Exec. Doc. 1. Serial set 690.

————. *The Omaha Indians.* 64th Cong., 1st sess., 1916. S. Rept. 710. Serial set 6899.

————. *A Paper Relative to the Desire of Certain Indian Tribes in the Northern Superintendency to Sell a Portion of Their Lands with a View to the Purchase of Other Lands.* 41st Cong., 3d sess., 1871. S. Exec. Doc. 35. Serial set 1440.

————. *Petition of Members of the Omaha Tribe of Indians in Regard to Citizenship and Taxation, and Praying for the Payment of Their Annuities.* 50th Cong., 1st sess., 1888. S. Misc. Doc. 26. Serial set 2516.

————. *Removal of the Ponca Indians.* 46th Cong., 2d sess., 1880. S. Rept. 670. Serial set 1898.

————. *Report of the Committee on Indian Affairs, March 16, 1836.* 24th Cong., 1st sess., 1836. S. Doc. 251. Serial set 281.

————. *Report of the Secretary of War, November 30, 1844.* 28th Cong., 2d sess., 1844. S. Doc. 2. Serial set 449.

————. *Sale and Designation of Lands in Omaha Indian Reservation in Nebraska.* 62d Cong., 2d sess., 1912. S. Rept. 459. Serial set 6120.

————. *Sale of Intoxicating Liquors to Indians.* 54th Cong., 2d sess., 1897. S. Rept. 1294. Serial set 3474.

————. *Taxation of Lands of Omaha Indians in Nebraska.* 61st Cong., 2d sess., 1910. S. Rept. 397. Serial set 5583.

————. *Taxation of Winnebago and Omaha Indian Lands, Nebraska.* 64th Cong., 1st sess., 1916. S. Rept. 491. Serial set 6899.

————. *Thomas H. Benton, L. F. Linn, and Albert G. Harrison to Secretary of War Lewis Cass, February 8, 1836.* 24th Cong., 1st sess., 1836. S. Doc. 251. Serial set 281.

————. *Transcript of the Proceedings Had before Senators William V. Allen and John M. Thurston and Congressmen George D. Meiklejohn, W. E. Andrews, and Jesse B. Strode, Members of the Nebraska Delegation in the Fifty-Fourth Congress of the United States, Sitting as a Body at the Omaha and Winnebago Reservations and at Pender, Thurston County, Nebr., on the 24th and 25th Days of July, A. D. 1895, for the Purpose of Inquiring into the Condition of Affairs on Said Reservations.* 54th Cong., 1st sess., 1896. S. Doc. 79. Serial set 3349.

U.S. *Statutes at Large* 4 (1824–35), 10 (1851–55), 13 (1863–65), 17 (1871–73), 22–32 (1881–1903), 34–37 (1905–13), 39 (1915–17).

COURT CASES

Bates v. Clark. 95 U.S. 204 (1877).
Beck v. Fluornoy Live-Stock and Real Estate Co. 65 F. 30 (1894).
Chase v. United States. 222 F. 593 (1915).
Farley v. Peebles et al. 70 N.W. 231 (1897).
Hallowell v. United States. 31 S. Ct. 587 (1911).
In the Matter of Heff. 25 S. Ct. 506 (1905).
Johnson and Graham's Lessee v. McIntosh. 8 U.S. (1 Wheat.) 543 (1923).
Sloan v. United States. 95 F. 193 (1899).
Sloan v. United States. 118 F. 283 (1902).
United States v. Celestine. 30 S. Ct. 93 (1909).
United States v. Chase. 38 S. Ct. 24 (1917).
United States v. Downing. 25 F. Cas. 906 (D. Ct. Kan. 1876) (No. 14,991).
United States v. Fred Nice. 36 S. Ct. 696 (1916).
United States v. James A. Rickert. 23 S. Ct. 478 (1903).
United States v. Sutton. 30 S. Ct. 116 (1909).
United States v. Thurston County et al. 140 F. 456 (1905).
United States v. Thurston County, Neb., et al. 143 F. 287 (1906).
United States as Trustee v. Hiram Chase. 36 S. Ct. 553 (1916).

NEWSPAPERS

Bancroft (Nebraska) Blade, July-August 1902.
New York Times, October 1876.
Omaha Daily Bee, July 1895, March 1897, February-September 1902, February, April 1910.
Omaha Morning World-Herald, July 1895.
Omaha World-Herald, November-December 1994.

Pender (Nebraska) Republic, December 1916.
Pender (Nebraska) Times, March 1900, February-December 1902, January-October 1903, January-December 1904, April-November 1905, August 1906, June-October 1909, March-November 1910, December 1914.
Thurston Republic, May 1896, February-June 1897.
Walthill (Nebraska) Times, September 1916.
Walthill (Nebraska) Citizen, October 1916.
Winnebago (Nebraska) Chieftain, December 1909, January-September 1910.

BOOKS AND ARTICLES

Aitchison, Clyde B. "Mormon Settlements in the Missouri Valley." In *Proceedings and Collections of the Nebraska State Historical Society*, 15:7–25. Lincoln: Jacob North and Co., Printers, 1907.

American Indian Correspondence: The Presbyterian Historical Society Collection of Missionary Letters, 1833–1893. 35 reels. Westport, Conn.: Greenwood Press, 1978. Microfilm.

Athearn, Robert G. *William Tecumseh Sherman and the Settlement of the West*. Norman: University of Oklahoma Press, 1956.

Babbitt, Charles Henry. *Early Days at Council Bluffs*. Washington, D.C.: Press of Byron S. Adams, 1916.

Barnes, R. H. *Two Crows Denies It: A History of Controversy in Omaha Sociology*. Lincoln: University of Nebraska Press, 1984.

Beers, Henry Putney. *French and Spanish Records of Louisiana*. Baton Rouge: Louisiana State University Press, 1989.

Behrens, Jo Lea Wetherilt. "In Defense of `Poor Lo': *The Council Fire*'s Advocacy of Native American Civil Rights, 1878–1889." Master's thesis, University of Nebraska at Omaha, 1992.

Bennett, Richard E. *Mormons at the Missouri, 1846–1852: "And Should We Die. . . ."* Norman: University of Oklahoma Press, 1987.

Berthrong, Donald J. "Cattlemen on the Cheyenne-Arapaho Reservation, 1883–1885." *Arizona and the West* 13 (spring 1971): 5–32.

Bohlken, Robert L., and C. James Keck. "An Experience in Territorial Social Compensation: Half-Breed Tract, Nebraska Territory." *Northwest Missouri State University Studies*, February 1973, 3–12.

Brackenridge, Henry Marie. *Journal of a Voyage up the River Missouri; Performed in Eighteen Hundred and Eleven*. Baltimore: Coale and Maxwell, 1815.

Bradbury, John. *Travels in the Interior of America in the Years 1809, 1810, and 1811*. In *Early Western Travels, 1748–1846*, vol. 5, edited by Reuben Gold Thwaites. Cleveland: Arthur H. Clark Co., 1904.

Brooks, Juanita, ed. *On the Mormon Frontier: The Diary of Hosea Stout, 1844–1861.* 2 vols. Salt Lake City: University of Utah Press, 1964.

Chapman, Berlin B. "The Nemaha Half-Breed Reservation." *Nebraska History* 38 (March 1957): 1–24.

———. *The Otoes and Missourias*. Stillwater, Okla.: Times Journal Publishing Co., 1965.

Chaput, Donald. "Generals, Indians, Agents, Politicians: The Doolittle Survey of 1865." *Western Historical Quarterly* 3 (July 1972): 269–82.

Chittenden, Hiram Martin, and Alfred Talbot Richardson, eds. *Life, Letters, and Travels of Father Pierre-Jean de Smet, S.J., 1801–1873*, vol. 3. New York: Francis P. Harper, 1905. Reprint, New York: Kraus Reprint Co., 1969.

Clark, Jerry E., and Martha Ellen Webb. "Susette and Susan La Flesche: Reformer and Missionary." In *Being and Becoming Indian: Biographical Studies of North American Frontiers*, edited by James A. Clifton, 137–59. Chicago: Dorsey Press, 1989.

Clark, John G., ed. *The Frontier Challenge: Responses to the Trans-Mississippi West*. Lawrence: University Press of Kansas, 1971.

Clow, Richmond R. "Taxing the Omaha and Winnebago Trust Lands, 1910–1971: An Infringement of the Tax-Immune Status of Indian Country." *American Indian Culture and Research Journal* 9, no. 4 (1985): 1–22.

Cohen, Felix S. *Handbook of Federal Indian Law.* 1942. Reprint, Albuquerque: University of New Mexico Press, 1974.

Coleman, Michael C. *Presbyterian Missionary Attitudes toward American Indians, 1837–1893*. Jackson: University Press of Mississippi, 1985.

Council Fire 12 (June 1889): 70.

Dary, David A. *The Buffalo Book*. Athens: Swallow Press/Ohio University Press, 1989.

DeVoto, Bernard. *Across the Wide Missouri*. Boston: Houghton-Mifflin Co., 1947.

Dippie, Brian W. *The Vanishing American: White Attitudes and U.S. Indian Policy*. Lawrence: University Press of Kansas, 1982.

Dorsey, James Owen. "Migrations of Siouan Tribes." *American Naturalist* 20 (March 1886): 210–22.

———. "To A. B. Meacham, January 19, 1880." *Council Fire* 3 (March 1880): 43.

Dougherty, John. "A Description of the Fur Trade in 1831." Edited by Richard E. Jensen. *Nebraska History* 56 (spring 1975): 109–20.

Ewers, John C. "The Influence of the Fur Trade upon the Indians of the Northern Plains." In *People and Pelts: Selected Papers of the Second North American Fur Trade Conference*, edited by Malvina Bolus, 1–26. Winnipeg, Manitoba: Peguis Publishers, 1972.

Farb, Robert C. "Robert W. Furnas as Omaha Indian Agent, 1864–1866." *Nebraska History* 32 (September 1951): 186–203; 32 (December 1951): 268–83.

Farnham, Thomas Jefferson. *Farnham's Travels in the Great Western Prairies*. In *Early Western Travels, 1748–1846*, vol. 28, edited by Reuben Gold Thwaites. Cleveland: Arthur H. Clark Co., 1906.

Fletcher, Alice C. "The Allotted Indians' Difficulties." *Outlook*, April 11, 1896, 660–61.

———. *Historical Sketch of the Omaha Tribe of Indians in Nebraska*. Washington, D.C.: Judd and Detweiler, 1885.

———. "Hunting Customs of the Omahas." *Century Illustrated Monthly Magazine* 50 (May-October 1895): 691–702.

————. "Lands in Severalty to Indians: Illustrated by Experiences with the Omaha Tribe." *Proceedings of the American Association for the Advancement of Science* 33 (1885): 654–65.

————. "Personal Studies of Indian Life: Politics and 'Pipe-Dancing.'" *Century Illustrated Monthly Magazine* 45 (November 1892-April 1893): 441–55.

————. "The Problem of the Omahas." *Southern Workman* 15 (May 1886): 55.

————. "Tribal Life among the Omahas," *Century Illustrated Monthly Magazine* 51 (November 1895–April 1896): 450–61.

Flinn, John. "Firewater and the Indians." *Indian School Journal* 7 (April 1907): 25–27.

Fontenelle, Henry. "History of Omaha Indians." In *Transactions and Reports of the Nebraska State Historical Society* 1:76–83. Lincoln: State Journal Co., 1885.

Fortune, Reo F. *Omaha Secret Societies.* Columbia University Contributions to Anthropology, vol. 14. New York: Columbia University Press, 1932.

Frissell, H. B. "A Visit to the Omahas." *Southern Workman* 16 (November 1887): 117.

Fritz, Henry E. *The Movement for Indian Assimilation, 1869–1890.* Philadelphia: University of Pennsylvania Press, 1963.

Giffen, Fannie Reed. *Oo-Mah-Ha Ta-Wa-Tha (Omaha City).* Lincoln, Nebr.: N. p., 1898.

Gilmore, Melvin R. "First Prohibition Law in America." *Journal of American History* 4 (July-September 1910): 397–98.

————. "The True Logan Fontenelle." *Publications of the Nebraska State Historical Society*, 19:64–71. Lincoln: Nebraska State Historical Society, 1919.

Green, Norma Kidd. *Iron Eye's Family: The Children of Joseph La Flesche.* Lincoln, Nebr.: Johnsen Publishing Co., 1969.

————. "The Make-Believe White Man's Village." *Nebraska History* 56 (summer 1975): 242–47.

Hagan, William T. *The Indian Rights Association: The Herbert Welsh Years, 1882–1904.* Tucson: University of Arizona Press, 1985.

————. "Kiowas, Comanches, and Cattlemen, 1867–1906: A Case Study of the Failure of U.S. Reservation Policy." *Pacific Historical Review* 40 (August 1971): 333–55.

Hamilton, William. "Autobiography of Rev. William Hamilton." *Transactions and Reports of the Nebraska State Historical Society*, 1:60–73. Lincoln: State Journal Co., 1885.

Hertzberg, Hazel W. *The Search for an American Indian Identity: Modern Pan-Indian Movements.* Syracuse: Syracuse University Press, 1971.

Holford, David M. "The Subversion of the Indian Land Allotment System, 1887–1934." *Indian Historian* 8 (spring 1975): 11–21.

Hoopes, Alban W. *Indian Affairs and Their Administration, with Special Reference to the Far West, 1849–1860.* Philadelphia: University of Pennsylvania Press, 1932.

Houck, Louis. *The Spanish Regime in Missouri*. 2 vols. Chicago: R. R. Donnelly and Sons Co., 1909.

Hoxie, Frederick E. "Beyond Savagery: The Campaign to Assimilate the Indians, 1880–1920." Ph.D. diss., Brandeis University, 1977.

———. *A Final Promise: The Campaign to Assimilate the Indians, 1880–1920*. Lincoln: University of Nebraska Press, 1984.

Hu-pe-dha[n]. "To A. B. Meacham, December 20, 1878." *Council Fire* 2 (February 1879): 29.

Hyde, George E. *The Pawnee Indians*. Norman: University of Oklahoma Press, 1951.

———. *Red Cloud's Folk*. Norman: University of Oklahoma Press, 1957.

———. *Spotted Tail's Folk: A History of the Brulé Sioux*. Norman: University of Oklahoma Press, 1961.

Illick, Joseph E. "'Some of Our Best Indians Are Friends . . .': Quaker Attitudes and Actions Regarding the Western Indians during the Grant Administration." *Western Historical Quarterly* 2 (July 1971): 283–94.

Indian Claims Commission. *Omaha Tribe of Nebraska*. New York: Clearwater Publishing Co., 1973.

Indian Rights Association. *Indian Rights Association Papers*. 136 reels. Glen Rock, N.J.: Microfilming Corporation of America, 1975.

"The Indian Temperance Question." *Indian's Friend* 7 (February 1895): 5.

"In Self-Defence [*sic*]." *Council Fire* 3 (January 1880): 12–13.

Irving, Washington. *Astoria; or, Anecdotes of an Enterprise Beyond the Rocky Mountains*, vol. 1. Philadelphia: Carey, Lea, and Blanchard, 1836.

James, Edwin. *Account of an Expedition from Pittsburgh to the Rocky Mountains, Performed in the Years 1819, 1820 . . . under the Command of Maj. S. H. Long*. In *Early Western Travels, 1748–1846*, vol. 28, edited by Reuben Gold Thwaites. Cleveland: Arthur H. Clark Co., 1906.

Johannsen, Robert W., ed. *The Letters of Stephen A. Douglas*. Urbana: University of Illinois Press, 1961.

Johnson, Sally A. "The Sixth's Elysian Fields: Fort Atkinson on the Council Bluffs." *Nebraska History* 40 (March 1959): 1–38.

Judd, Neil M. *The Bureau of American Ethnology: A Partial History*. Norman: University of Oklahoma Press, 1967.

Keller, Robert H., Jr. *American Protestantism and United States Indian Policy, 1869–82*. Lincoln: University of Nebraska Press, 1983.

Kinney, J. P. *A Continent Lost, a Civilization Won: Indian Land Tenure in America*. Baltimore: Johns Hopkins University Press, 1937.

Kneale, Albert H. *Indian Agent*. Caldwell, Idaho: Caxton Printers, 1950.

Kvasnicka, Robert M., and Herman J. Viola, eds. *The Commissioners of Indian Affairs, 1824–1977*. Lincoln: University of Nebraska Press, 1979.

La Farge, Oliver, ed. *The Changing Indian*. Norman: University of Oklahoma Press, 1942.

La Flesche, Francis. "Alice C. Fletcher." *Science* 58 (August 1923): 115.

———. *The Middle Five: Indian Boys at School*. 1900. Reprint, Lincoln: University of Nebraska Press, 1978.

La Flesche, Susan. "The Omahas and Citizenship." *Southern Workman* 20 (April 1891): 177.

Lane, Franklin K. "From the War-Path to the Plow." *National Geographic* 27 (January 1915): 73–87.

Lee, Dorothy Sara, and Maria La Vigna, eds. *Omaha Indian Music: Historic Recordings from the Fletcher/La Flesche Collection.* Washington, D.C.: American Folklife Center of the Library of Congress, in Cooperation with the Omaha Tribal Council, 1985.

"Letter from Dr. La Flesche." *Indian's Friend* 3 (February 1891): 3.

"Letter from the Omahas, February 5, 1878." *Council Fire* 1 (March 1878): 42.

Leupp, Francis E. *The Indian and His Problem.* New York: Charles Scribner's Sons, 1910.

Lurie, Nancy Oestreich. "The Lady from Boston and the Omaha Indians." *American West* 3 (fall 1966): 31–33, 80–85.

McDermott, John Francis. *The Spanish in the Mississippi Valley, 1762–1804.* Urbana: University of Illinois Press, 1974.

McDonnell, Janet A. "Competency Commissions and Indian Land Policy, 1913–1920." *South Dakota History* 11 (winter 1980): 21–34.

———. *The Dispossession of the American Indian, 1887–1934.* Bloomington: Indiana University Press, 1991.

———. "Land Policy on the Omaha Reservation: Competency Commissions and Forced Fee Patents." *Nebraska History* 63 (fall 1982): 399–411.

McKee, Howard I. "The Platte Purchase." *Missouri Historical Review* 32 (January 1938): 129–47.

McLaughlin, James. *My Friend the Indian.* Seattle: Superior Publishing Co., 1970.

McNickle, D'Arcy. "Indian and European: Indian-White Relations from Discovery to 1887." *Annals of the American Academy of Political and Social Science* 311:1–11. Philadelphia: American Academy of Political and Social Science, 1957.

Malin, James C. "Indian Policy and Westward Expansion." *Bulletin of the University of Kansas*, vol. 22. Humanistic Studies, vol. 2. Lawrence: University of Kansas, 1921.

———. *The Nebraska Question, 1852–1854.* Ann Arbor, Mich.: Edwards Brothers, 1953.

———. "The Nebraska Question: A Ten-Year Record, 1844–1854." *Nebraska History* 35 (March 1954): 1–15.

———. "Thomas Jefferson Sutherland, Nebraska Boomer." *Nebraska History* 34 (September 1953): 181–214.

Manypenny, George W. *Our Indian Wards.* Cincinnati: Robert Clarke and Co., 1880.

———. "Shall We Persist in a Policy That Has Failed?" *Council Fire* 8 (November 1885): 153–56.

Mardock, Robert Winston. *Reformers and the American Indian.* Columbia: University of Missouri Press, 1971.

Mark, Joan. *A Stranger in Her Native Land: Alice Fletcher and the American Indians.* Lincoln: University of Nebraska Press, 1988.

Martin, Calvin. *Keepers of the Game: Indian-Animal Relations and the Fur Trade*. Berkeley: University of California Press, 1978.

Mattison, Roy H. "The Indian Frontier on the Upper Missouri to 1865." *Nebraska History* 39 (September 1958): 241–66.

Mead, Margaret. *The Changing Culture of an Indian Tribe*. New York: Columbia University Press, 1932. Reprint, New York: Capricorn Books, 1966.

"Men Fined in Indian Land Cases." *Indian School Journal* 13 (February 1913): 280.

Merrill, Moses. "Extracts from the Diary of Rev. Moses Merrill, a Missionary to the Otoe Indians from 1832 to 1840." *Transactions and Reports of the Nebraska State Historical Society*, 4: 160–91. Lincoln: State Journal Co., 1892.

Milner, Clyde A., III. *With Good Intentions: Quaker Work among the Pawnees, Otos, and Omahas*. Lincoln: University of Nebraska Press, 1982.

Milroy, R. H. "To A. B. Meacham, October 13, 1879." *Council Fire* 2 (December 1879): 191.

"Miss Fletcher Sadly Disappointed." *Council Fire* 10 (February 1887): 27.

Moulton, Gary E., ed. *The Journals of the Lewis and Clark Expedition*. 8 vols. Lincoln: University of Nebraska Press, 1983–93.

Mulder, William, and A. Russell Mortensen, eds. *Among the Mormons: Historic Accounts by Contemporary Observers*. New York: Alfred A. Knopf, 1958.

Nasatir, Abraham P., ed. *Before Lewis and Clark: Documents Illustrating the History of the Missouri, 1785–1804*. 2 vols. St. Louis: St. Louis Historical Documents Foundation, 1952.

Olson, James C. *History of Nebraska*. Lincoln: University of Nebraska Press, 1955.

"The Omaha and His Land." *Indian School Journal* 16 (January 1916): 261.

"The Omaha Experiment a Failure." *Council Fire* 10 (April-May 1887): 61–62.

"The Omahas: An Unhopeful Outlook." *Council Fire* 7 (November-December 1884): 180–82.

"An Omaha Speech in 1884." *Indian's Friend* 10 (November 1897): 11–12.

O'Shea, John M., and John Ludwickson. *Archaeology and Ethnohistory of the Omaha Indians: The Big Village Site*. Lincoln: University of Nebraska Press, 1992.

———. "Omaha Chieftainship in the Nineteenth Century." *Ethnohistory* 39 (summer 1992): 316–52.

Otis, D. S. *The Dawes Act and the Allotment of Indian Lands*. Edited by Francis Paul Prucha. Norman: University of Oklahoma Press, 1973.

Peters, Robert C., ed. *A Comprehensive Program for Historic Preservation in Omaha*. Omaha: Landmarks Heritage Preservation Commission, 1980.

Picotte, Susan La Flesche. "Another Appeal." *Indian's Friend* 12 (March 1900): 8–9.

"Plain Talk by the Omahas." *Council Fire* 2 (September 1879): 139.

Priest, Loring Benson. *Uncle Sam's Stepchildren: The Reformation of United States Indian Policy, 1865–1887*. New Brunswick, N.J.: Rutgers University Press, 1942.

Prucha, Francis Paul. *American Indian Policy in Crisis: Christian Reformers and the Indian, 1865–1900*. Norman: University of Oklahoma Press, 1976.

————. *American Indian Policy in the Formative Years: The Indian Trade and Intercourse Acts, 1790–1834*. Cambridge: Harvard University Press, 1962.

————. *Indian Peace Medals in American History*. Madison: State Historical Society of Wisconsin, 1971.

"Quaker Report on Indian Agencies in Nebraska, 1869." *Nebraska History* 54 (summer 1973): 151–219.

Ray, P. Orman. *The Repeal of the Missouri Compromise: Its Origin and Authorship*. Boston: J. S. Conner and Co., 1965.

Ridington, Robin. "Omaha Survival: A Vanishing Indian Tribe That Would Not Vanish." *American Indian Quarterly* 11 (winter 1987): 37–51.

————. "A Sacred Object as Text: Reclaiming the Sacred Pole of the Omaha Tribe." *American Indian Quarterly* 17 (winter 1993): 83–99.

Ronda, James P. *Lewis and Clark among the Indians*. Lincoln: University of Nebraska Press, 1984.

Schilz, Thomas F., and Joyce L. D. Schilz. "Beads, Bangles, and Buffalo Robes: The Rise and Fall of the Indian Fur Trade along the Missouri and Des Moines Rivers, 1700–1820." *Annals of Iowa* 49 (summer/fall 1987): 5–25.

Sheldon, Addison E. "Land Systems and Land Policies in Nebraska." *Publications of the Nebraska State Historical Society*, Vol. 22. Lincoln: Nebraska State Historical Society, 1936.

Smith, G. Hubert. *Omaha Indians: Ethnohistorical Report on the Omaha People*. New York: Garland Publishing, 1974.

Smith, Jane F., and Robert M. Kvasnicka. *Indian-White Relations: A Persistent Paradox*. Washington, D.C.: Howard University Press, 1976.

Springer, William F. "The Omaha Indians: What They Ask of the United States Government." *Indian Historian* 9 (winter 1976): 30–33.

Stearn, E. Wagner, and Allen E. Stearn. *The Effect of Smallpox on the Destiny of the Amerindian*. Boston: Bruce Humphries, 1945.

Sunder, John E. *Joshua Pilcher: Fur Trader and Indian Agent*. Norman: University of Oklahoma Press, 1968.

Tate, Michael L. *The Upstream People: An Annotated Research Bibliography of the Omaha Tribe*. Native American Bibliography Series, no. 14. Metuchen, N.J.: Scarecrow Press, 1991.

Thayer, James B. "The Dawes Bill and the Indians." *Atlantic Monthly* 61 (March 1888): 315–22.

Thorne, Tanis C. "Black Bird, 'King of the Mahars': Autocrat, Big Man, Chief." *Ethnohistory* 40 (summer 1993): 410–37.

Thwaites, Reuben Gold, ed. *Collections of the State Historical Society of Wisconsin*, vol. 17. Madison: Wisconsin State Historical Society, 1906.

————. *Original Journals of the Lewis and Clark Expedition, 1804–1806.* 7 vols. New York: Arno Press, 1969.

Tibbles, Susette La Flesche. "Perils and Promises of Indian Citizenship." *Our Day* 5 (June 1891): 460–71.

Tibbles, Thomas H. *Buckskin and Blanket Days: Memoirs of a Friend of the Indians.* Garden City, N.Y.: Doubleday and Co., 1957.

————. *Ploughed Under: The Story of an Indian Chief.* New York: Fords, Howard and Hulbert, 1881.

Trennert, Robert A., Jr. *Alternative to Extinction: Federal Indian Policy and the Beginnings of the Reservation System, 1846–51.* Philadelphia: Temple University Press, 1975.

————. "The Mormons and the Office of Indian Affairs: The Conflict over Winter Quarters, 1846–1848." *Nebraska History* 53 (fall 1972): 381–400.

Unrau, William E. *White Man's Wicked Water: The Alcohol Trade and Prohibition in Indian Country, 1802–1892.* Lawrence: University Press of Kansas, 1996.

Valentine, Robert G. "Making Good Indians." *Sunset* 24 (June 1910): 599–612.

Wanken, Helen M. "'Women's Sphere' and Indian Reform: The Women's National Indian Association, 1879–1901." Ph.D. diss., Marquette University, 1981.

Washburn, Wilcomb E. *The American Indians and the United States: A Documentary History.* 4 vols. New York: Random House, 1973.

————. *The Assault on Indian Tribalism: The General Allotment Law (Dawes Act) of 1887.* Edited by Harold M. Hyman. Philadelphia: J. B. Lippincott Co., 1975.

Wedel, Mildred M. "The Ioway, Oto, and Omaha Indians in 1700." *Journal of the Iowa Archaeological Society* 28 (January 1981): 1–13.

Welch, Rebecca Hancock. "Alice Cunningham Fletcher: Anthropologist and Indian Rights Reformer." Ph.D. diss., George Washington University, 1980.

"The Whiskey Decision a Bad Thing for the Allotted Indian." *Indian's Friend* 18 (September 1905): 6–7.

White, Richard. "The Winning of the West: The Expansion of the Western Sioux in the Eighteenth and Nineteenth Centuries." *Journal of American History* 65 (September 1978): 319–43.

Will, George F., and George E. Hyde. *Corn among the Indians of the Upper Missouri.* St. Louis: William Harvey Miner Co., 1917.

Wishart, David J. *An Unspeakable Sadness: The Dispossession of the Nebraska Indians.* Lincoln: University of Nebraska Press, 1994.

Index

Yankton, 189; attacks on Omahas by, 24, 73; heirship lands, proceeds from, 248n.41; Omahas defeated by, 11; war against, 25
Yankton agency, 188, 190
Yellow Smoke: and Gatewood Treaty, 62; and Sacred Pole, 206, 207

Young, Brigham: John Miller, conflict with, 52, 219n.85; and Mormon battalion, 49; and treaty with Omahas, 51–52. *See also* Mormons
Young, S. A. M., 188–89